WITHDRAWN

# Performing Arts Resources

#  Performing Arts Resources

Edited by Ted Perry
With the editorial assistance of Barbara Skluth

VOLUME THREE, 1976

**Drama Book Specialists (Publishers)
Theatre Library Association
New York**

Z
6935
P46
v. 3

© Copyright 1977 by Theatre Library Association

First Edition

All rights reserved

No part of this publication may be reproduced or transmitted in any form or by any means, electronic or mechanical, including photocopy, recording, or any information storage and retrieval system now known or to be invented, without permission in writing from the publishers, except by a reviewer who wishes to quote brief passages in connection with a review written for inclusion in a magazine, newspaper or broadcast.

All rights reserved under the International and Pan American Copyright Conventions. For information address Drama Book Specialists (Publishers), 150 West 52nd Street, New York, N.Y. 10019.

**Library of Congress Cataloging in Publication Data**

Perry, Ted
  Performing Arts Resources
    1. Performing arts—Library resources—United States—Periodicals.  I. Theatre Library Association.
Z6935.P46    016.7902'08    75-646287
ISBN 910482-84-5

Printed in the United States of America

# Table of Contents

Foreword..................................................... vi

Preface ...................................................... vii

By-Laws of the Theatre Library Association ... viii

Notes on Contributors............................. xv

**Mark Gladstone**
A Bibliography of U.S. Government Documents
Pertaining to Government Support
of the Arts, 1963-72................................... 1

**Gerald O'Grady**
Resources for the Oral History of the Independent
American Film at Media Study/Buffalo, New York .. 24

**Stephen Kovács**
Surrealist Cinema: A Selected Bibliography .......... 32

**Betty L. Corwin**
Theatre on Film and Tape ........................... 41

**Christopher Wheaton and
Richard B. Jewell**
The Cinema Library at the University of Southern
California ........................................... 61

**L. Terry Oggel**
A Short Title Guide to the Edwin Booth Literary
Materials at The Players ............................ 98

**Llewellyn H. Hedgbeth**
The Chuck Callahan Burlesque Collection ........... 143

Index to Volumes I & II .......................... 151

# Foreword

                              This third annual volume of *Performing Arts Resources* marks the end of a splendid beginning under the editorship of Ted Perry.

    As with all publications, changes will take place in the future under new editorship. It is hoped that this publication will continue to assist the scholar, librarian, collector and student in locating sources of performing arts materials whether in public or private collections.

    The Theatre Library Association is most grateful for Mr. Perry's pioneer work.

    If you are making your first acquaintance with TLA through this annual, you are invited to become a member and to become a contributor to future annuals.

                                      Robert M. Henderson
                                      President
                                      Theatre Library Association

# Preface

Attempting to provide documentation for theatre, film, television and popular entertainments, each annual volume of *Performing Arts Resources* includes articles on storage and use of non-print resources, studies of curatorship, indexes, bibliographies, subject matter guides to various archives and collections, analyses of individual collections and museums, descriptions of regional holdings in a particular field or subject matter, and thorough surveys of research materials, government holdings, and training programs in the performing arts. While the major portion of each annual volume of *Performing Arts Resources* is devoted to describing and indexing resources for research, some articles treat such issues as historiography, methodology and states of research in the performing arts.

Each annual volume of *Performing Arts Resources* is envisioned then as a collection of articles which will enable the performing arts student, scholar and archivist to locate, identify and classify information about theatre, film, broadcasting and popular entertainments.

# By-Laws of Theatre Library Association

### ARTICLE I
*Office*

The principal office of Theatre Library Association (the "Association") shall be at 111 Amsterdam Avenue, New York, New York 10023, or at such place in the State of New York as the Board of Directors may from time to time appoint.

### ARTICLE II
*Membership*

A. *Classes of Membership*
 1. There shall be the following classes of memberships:
 (a) *Institutional Memberships:* Open to any library, museum, university, college, club or theatre-related organization who shall pay required dues, as established by resolution of the Board of Directors. An institution may have an unlimited number of memberships, but no more than one vote.
 (b) *Individual Memberships:* Open to any librarian, curator, private collector, professor, teacher or member of the theatrical profession embracing stage, screen, radio, magic, television, circus or any other member of

the general public who shall pay required dues as established by resolution of the Board of Directors.

(c) *Ex-Officio Memberships:* All members of the Board of Directors shall be members of the Association.

B. *Voting*

Each member shall be entitled to vote in elections of the Board of Directors or to vote on other matters which may be before the membership of the Association. Directors shall be elected by a plurality of the votes cast at a meeting of the members entitled to vote in the election, and any other corporate action to be taken by vote of the members shall be authorized by a majority of the votes cast at a meeting of members by the members entitled to vote thereon, except as otherwise required by law.

C. *Membership Meetings*

1. Annual meetings of the membership of the Association for the election of directors and for any other matters which may be before the membership shall be held at times and places within the State of New York to be selected by the Board of Directors. Statutory notice of such meetings shall be provided.

2. Special meetings of the membership may be called, for any purpose or purposes, by the Board of Directors or upon the request of not less than 50 members of the Association. Statutory notice of all special meetings of the membership shall be provided.

3. At all meetings of the membership of the Association 50 members whether in person or by proxy shall constitute a quorum except where a greater number of members is required by statute.

4. Members of the Association may vote by proxy.

5. At the annual meetings of the membership, the Board of Directors shall present a report in accordance with the provisions of Section 519 of the New York Not-for-Profit Corporation Law. The report shall be filed with the records of the Association and either a copy or an abstract thereof entered in the minutes of the meeting.

D. *Qualifications*

Death, resignation as a member, non-payment of dues (except *ex officio* members) or removal of any director as provided in these By-Laws shall automatically terminate membership of such person in the Association.

E. *Liabilities and Property Rights Of Members*

No member of the Association or Board of Directors now or hereafter shall be personally liable to its creditors for any indebtedness or liability, and any and all creditors shall look only to the assets of the Association for payment.

## ARTICLE III

*The Board of Directors*

A. *Duties and Powers*

1. The Board of Directors shall sit as the trustees of the corporation and shall bear primary responsibility for carrying out the purposes of the Association and shall be empowered to do any and all things necessary for the fulfillment of these purposes.

2. The Board of Directors shall manage the affairs of the Association and control its property.

3. Duties

The Board of Directors shall be responsible for:

(a) the approval of the yearly budget;

(b) the election of the members of the Executive Committee of the Association; and

(c) the designation of committees other than the standing committees herein created.

4. Powers

The Board of Directors shall have the power to:

(a) remove any committee member or member of the Executive Committee for cause shown; and

(b) invalidate or ratify any actions taken by the Executive Committee or an Officer of the Association which it deems to be beyond the usual and ordinary purposes and business of the Association.

B. *Composition*
   1. *Number of Directors.* The number of directors constituting the entire board shall be 12. The number of directors may be increased or decreased by action of two-thirds of the members voting or two-thirds of the entire board subject to the limitation that no decrease shall shorten the term of any incumbent director.
   2. *Election and Term of Directors.* The directors of the corporation shall be divided into 3 classes, hereby designated class A, B and C. There shall be four directors in each class. The term of office of the initial class A directors shall expire at the next annual meeting of members following classification, the term of office of the initial class B directors at the second succeeding annual meeting and the term of office of the initial class C directors at the third succeeding annual meeting. At each annual meeting after the initial classification of directors, directors to replace those whose terms expire at such annual meeting shall be elected to hold office until the second succeeding annual meeting.
   3. *Newly Created Directorships and Vacancies.* Newly created directorships resulting from an increase in the number of directors and vacancies occurring in the board of directors for any reason may be filled by vote of a majority of the directors then in office regardless of their number. A director elected to fill a newly created directorship shall hold office until the next annual meeting at which the election of directors is in the regular order of business and until his successor is elected and qualified; a director elected to fill a vacancy shall hold office for the unexpired term.
   4. *Removal of Directors.* Any or all of the directors may be removed with or without cause by vote of the members, or for cause by a vote of the directors when there is a quorum of not less than a majority present at the meeting of directors at which such action is taken.

C. *Meetings*
   1. *Quorum of Directors.* A majority of the entire board shall constitute a quorum for the transaction of business or of any specified item of business and the vote of a majority of the board of directors present at the time of a vote, if a

quorum is present at such time, shall be the act of the board of directors.
2. *Place of meeting.* The Board of Directors may hold their meetings at such place or places within or without the State of New York as the Board may from time to time determine.
3. *Regular Meetings.* Regular meetings of the Board of Directors shall be held at such time and place as may be determined by the Board.
4. *Special Meetings: Notice.* Special meetings of the Board may be held at any time and place upon the call of the President or of any two Directors. Notice of the time, place and purpose of every regular and special meeting of the Board shall be given by the Secretary by mailing, telegraphing, cabling or delivering the same to each director, not less than five nor more than ten days before the meeting.

D. *Compensation*
No director or officer of the Association shall receive, directly or indirectly any salary, compensation or emolument therefrom either as such officer or director or in any other capacity, unless authorized by the concurring vote of two-thirds of all the directors or (notwithstanding any quorums requirement of these By-Laws) by the concurring vote of all the disinterested directors.

## ARTICLE IV

### Executive Committee

A. *Duties and Powers*
1. It shall be the responsibility of the Executive Committee to oversee the administration of the Association. It shall carry on the business of the Association in the interim between meetings of the Board of Directors. It shall have the specific powers which may from time to time be delegated to it by the Board of Directors.
2. The Executive Committee shall be responsible for
    (a) preparation of an agenda for meetings of the

Board of Directors, which shall be sent with the notification of such meetings;

(b) preparation of the proposed annual budget, which is to be presented to the Board of Directors for consideration by the end of January;

(c) supervision of the annual election; and

(d) supervision of the publications and mailings of the Association.

B. *Composition*

The Executive Committee of the Association shall be composed of:
1. The President of the Association
2. Vice-President
3. Secretary-Treasurer
4. Recording Secretary
5. One or more additional officers as the Board may deem necessary.

C. *Term of Office*

1. The officers of the Executive Committee shall take office immediately after their election and shall serve for two years or until their successors have been elected.

2. Vacancies on the Executive Committee shall be promptly filled by the Board of Directors. Persons elected to fill such vacancies shall serve until the selection of the next Executive Committee.

D. *Duties of the Officers*

1. President of the Association

(a) shall preside over all meetings of the Board of Directors, the Executive Committee, and the Association;

(b) shall be responsible for drawing up an agenda for meetings of the Executive Committee and the Board; and

(c) shall discharge the usual duties attendant to this office.

2. Secretary-Treasurer

(a) shall have charge of the finances of the Association and shall keep full and accurate accounts of receipts and disbursements in books belonging to the Association. The Treasurer shall deposit all moneys and other valuable effects in the name and to the credit of the Association in such depositary or depositaries as may be designated by the Board of Directors;

(b) shall be required to make a report in writing at the annual meeting of the Association and whenever called upon by the Executive Committee or the Board of Directors;

(c) shall be Chairman of the Budget Committee; and

(d) shall be responsible for sending out notices of meetings of the Executive Committee and of the Board of Directors.

3. Recording Secretary

(a) shall keep a record of the proceedings of the Executive Committee and of the Board of Directors; and

(b) shall be custodian of the records of the Association.

4. In case of the absence of an officer of the Association, or for any other reason which may seem sufficient to the Board of Directors, the Board may delegate the powers and duties of such officer for the time being to any other officer or to any Director.

## ARTICLE V

*Amendments*

These By-Laws may be amended by the affirmative vote of a majority of the directors in office at any meeting of the Board of Directors.

# Notes on Contributors

MARK GLADSTONE is a Media Librarian and Director of the Audio-Visual Department at Upsala College Library in East Orange, New Jersey.

GERALD O'GRADY is Director of the Center for Media Study and the Instructional Communication Center of the State University of New York at Buffalo, and Director of Media Study/Buffalo.

STEPHEN KOVÁCS is Assitant Professor, Department of Communication at Stanford University.

CHRISTOPHER WHEATON recently received his Ph.D. in Film History and Criticism from the University of Southern California. RICHARD B. JEWELL is a doctoral candidate in the same program.

BETTY L. CORWIN is the Project Director, Theatre on Film and Tape Collection at the Theatre Collection, The New York Public Library at Lincoln Center.

L. TERRY OGGEL teaches courses in American literature in the English Department of Northern Illinois University. He is regional associate editor of the forthcoming revised edition of *American Literary Manuscripts*.

LLEWELLYN H. HEDGBETH is a doctoral candidate in the Department of Drama at New York University.

The Theatre Library Association invites you to be a contributor to *Performing Arts Resources*. Manuscripts, questions or inquiries should be sent to:

>Dr. Mary C. Henderson, Editor
>859 Meadow Lane
>Franklin Lakes, New Jersey  07417

Mark Gladstone

# A Bibliography of U.S. Government Documents Pertaining to Government Support of the Arts, 1963-1972

## Scope and Coverage

This bibliography is comprised primarily of United States government documents which relate to state and federal support of the arts. It contains a list of documents of Congressional enabling legislation and executive departmental publications which pertain to the activities and work of the National Council on the Arts, the National Foundation on the Arts and the Humanities, the National Endowment for the Arts, the Federal Council on the Arts and Humanities and the work of the Office of Education in strengthening the arts. Selected documents which relate to state and local art commissions as well as studies of support for the arts conducted by state universities will also be found in this bibliography.

The publications contained in this bibliography cover the years 1963 through 1972. The year 1963 was selected as a starting point because it was in that year that President Kennedy appointed August Heckscher as special consultant on the arts to report on the financial state of the arts in this country, and to submit recommendations on how the federal government could enlarge its role in providing for its continued patronage and subsistence.

Previous to this time in American history, government support for the arts and the humanities had been expressed through spasmodic patronage rather than direct subsidy. Mr. Heckscher's report to Congress recommended establishment of a National Arts Foundation which would provide the focus for federal efforts to stimulate the arts.

It was not my intention to assemble a listing of documents that embodied every phase of government support of the arts since this nation was founded. There has indeed been funding for the arts prior to 1963 as exemplified by the existence and achievements of such long-standing institutions as the National Gallery of Art, the Smithsonian Institution and the Commission of Fine Arts. Nevertheless, contained herein are selected citations to government agencies as well as others that pre-date 1963. Reference to these citations appeared in indices published from 1963 through 1972.

When the federal government created the National Endowment for the Arts, they made provision to the states and territories for matching federal grants. This resulted in the establishment of individual state arts councils and agencies. It is for this reason that publications pertaining to these state arts councils and commissions are included.

Before any preliminary work was completed on the bibliography, the following guides to government documents were scrutinized:

Body, Alexander C. *Annotated Bibliography of Bibliographies on Selected Publications and Supplementary Guides to the*

*Superintendent of Documents Classification System.* Kalamazoo: Western Michigan University, 1967 and supplements 1-3.

Wynkoop, Sally. *Subject Guide to Government Reference Books.* Littleton: Libraries Unlimited, 1972.

The primary sources of information consulted in the preparation of this bibliography were the following:

*Monthly Catalog of U.S. Government Publications.* Washington, D.C.: Government Printing Office.

*Monthly Checklist of State Publications.* Washington, D.C.: Government Printing Office.

*United States Statutes at Large.* Washington, D.C.: Government Printing Office.

*Code of Federal Regulations.* Washington, D.C.: Government Printing Office. (See Title 45, Chapter XI).

*1972 and 1973 Catalogs of Federal Domestic Assistance.* Washington, D.C.: Government Printing Office.

*Library of Congress Catalog, a cumulative list of works represented by Library of Congress printed cards: Books, Subjects.* Washington, D.C.: Government Printing Office.

*Congressional Quarterly Almanac.* Washington, D.C.: Congressional Quarterly Inc., (Volumes: 1963-1972).

Public Affairs Information Service. *Bulletin.* New York: Public Affairs Information Service.

Quint, Barbara and Lois Newman. *Performing Arts Centers and Economic Aspects of the Performing Arts: a selective bibliography.* Santa Monica: The Rand Corporation, 1969.

# Arrangement of Bibliographic Citations and Subject Headings

The names of the agencies, departments, offices or branches of government that were charged with the authorship of the documents are used as main subject headings in this bibliography.

The only exceptions to the above statement are the entries listed with such headings as, "Art and State" and "Arts-(the name of the specific state or territory)." The latter are filed alphabetically as they all refer to state publications in support of the arts. A further exception is the use of the subject heading entitled, "U.S. laws, statutes etc."

The following is an illustration of the manner in which these subject headings are arranged:

1. "Art and State".
2. "Arts—(Arizona, etc., through Washington)".
3. U.S. Congress. (Congressional documents, reports and hearings are filed chronologically beginning with the 88th Congress, 1st session (1963) through the 92d Congress, 2d session (1972).
4. U.S. Education Office.
5. U.S. Department of Health, Education and Welfare.
6. U.S. Laws, statutes, etc., (Public laws are filed chronologically, by the number of the Congress and by the number of the law.)
7. Management and Budget Office.
8. National Council on the Arts.
9. National Endowment for the Arts.
10. National Foundation on the Arts and the Humanities.
11. U.S. President.
12. U.S. State Department.

Much of the bibliographic information contained in each entry duplicates citations as they appeared in the reference sources investigated.

It should be noted that this bibliography cannot be exhaustive and complete as there are many documents that are not included in the indices that were examined. For one reason or another, these publications escaped the attention of catalogers and indexers who were assigned the task of primary research.

## Availability and Location of Publications Cited

Most of the publications cited in this bibliography are available for perusal at the Library of Congress in Washington, D.C. Many of the federal documents printed by the Government Printing Office are also available for examination at designated depository libraries throughout the country. These libraries are listed in the September, 1973, issue of the *Monthly Catalog of United States Government Publications*. Many large academic and state libraries act as repositories for state art council publications.

A number of New York State Council on the Arts publications can be obtained by writing to the New York City offices of the New York State Council on the Arts at 250 West 57th Street, New York, N.Y. 10019. The most recent *New York State Council on the Arts Annual Report* specifically indicates that current and previous annual reports are available free of charge from its Arts Resources division. In addition, the New York State Council on the Arts' Information Center maintains a library of up-to-date information on the arts—especially as it relates to New York State. The Information Center's librarian is also available by appointment to assist in the search for data in the areas of the Council's purview. The Information Center is open to the public during the Council's regular office hours.

## Art and State

Flanagan, Hallie Ferguson. *Arena: The Story of the Federal Theatre Project of 1935-1939.* New York: Benjamin Blom, 1965.

Heckscher, August. "The City and the Arts." University of Pittsburgh, Institute of Local Government, Graduate School of Public and International Affairs, (Wherrett Lecture) 1964.

MacFayden, John H. "State Arts Councils: why they exist, how they fare." *State Government: The Journal of State Affairs,* Summer 1971, pp. 162-165.

Mangione, Jerre. *The Dream and the Deal: The Federal Writers' Project, 1935-1943.* Boston: Little Brown & Co., 1972.

O'Connor, Francis V. *Federal Support for the Visual Arts: The New Deal and Now; a report on the New Deal Art Projects in New York City and State with Recommendations for Present-Day Federal Support for the Visual Arts to the National Endowment for the Arts* ... 2d ed. Greenwich: New York Graphic Society, 1971.

———., comp. *The New Deal Art Projects: An Anthology of Memoirs.* Washington: Smithsonian Institution Press, 1972.

Phillips, Gifford, et al. "The Arts in a Democratic Society." Center for the Study of Democratic Institutions, Santa Barbara, 1966.

Rockefeller Brothers Fund, Inc., Arts Planning Committee: Special Studies Project, *The Performing Arts; Problems and Prospects; Rockefeller Panel Report on the Future of Theatre, Dance, Music in America.* New York: McGraw-Hill, 1965.

Scitovsky, Tibor, et al. "Arts in the Affluent Society: What's Wrong With the Arts is What's Wrong With Society." *American Economic Review*, May 1972, pp. 62-77.

Willard, Irma Sompayrac. *U.S. Government Sponsorship of Art, 1933-1943; survey and report on documents in national archives.* Washington?: Art Archives Report, 1945?

## State and Territorial Documents

### Arts—Alabama
State Council on the Arts and Humanities. *An Informative Summary of the Arts Activities in Alabama Occurring Between April 8, 1966, and September 30, 1970* (by M. J. Zakrzewski and Bonnye A. Ray. Montgomery, n.d.) 43 pp. illus.

### Arts—Arizona
Arizona Commission on the Arts and the Humanities. Report. 1966-67. (Scottsdale) 34 pp. illus. biennial. Has also a distinctive title: *Arts and Humanities in Arizona.* Commission created by Executive order of January 24, 1966.

### Arts—California
California Arts Commission. *Community Arts Councils.* (Sacramento, 1966) 15 pp.

Arts Commission. *The Arts in California; a report to the Governor and the Legislature by the California Arts Commission on the*

A Bibliography of U.S. Government Documents Pertaining
to Government Support of the Arts, 1963-72

*cultural and artistic resources of the State of California.* (Sacramento, 1966) 86 pp. illus.
University of California, Berkeley. Institute of Governmental Studies. *The States and the Arts, the California Arts Commission and the Emerging Federal-State Partnership.* (by Mel Scott. Berkeley, 1971) 129 pp.
University of California, Berkeley. Institute of Governmental Studies. *Partnership in the Arts: public and private support of cultural activities in the San Francisco Bay area.* (by Mel Scott. Berkeley, 1963. Franklin K. Lane Project Publication) v + 55 pp.
University of California, Berkeley. Institute of Governmental Studies. *Government and the Arts in the San Francisco Bay Area.* (by Mel Scott. Berkeley, Public Affairs Report 5: (1-4) October, 1964)

## Arts—Connecticut
Connecticut Commission on the Arts. *A Report to the Governor and the State Legislature.* (Hartford) 1965. 16 pp. illus.

## Arts—Georgia
University of Georgia, Athens. Institute of Government. *Organization of State Art Commissions; a report to the Georgia Art Commission.* (Athens) 1967. 381 pp. illus.

## Arts—Hawaii
Hawaii State Foundation on Culture and the Arts. *Report. 1969/70.* (Honolulu) 55 pp. illus. annual. Report year ends June 30.

## Arts—Illinois
Illinois Arts Council. *Report 1968/1970.* (Chicago) Report period ends June 30.
Advisory Commission on Financing the Arts in Illinois. *Report.* (Springfield) 1971. xvii + 127 pp.

## Arts—Indiana
Indiana Arts Commission. *Blueprint of the Arts in Indiana; report to Governor Branigin and the Legislature.* (Fort Wayne) 1967. 79 pp. illus.
Indiana Arts Commission. *Typical Programs Through the Indiana State Arts Commission, 1969-1970.* Indianapolis, 1970. 81 pp.

## Arts—Kansas
Kansas Cultural Arts Commission. (created in 1965 to develop,

support, preserve, and make available the artistic and cultural resources of Kansas). Myrta J. Anderson. *Your Government* (Kansas). 23: (3-4) Oct. 15, 1967. Bulletin of the Governmental Research Center, University of Kansas, Lawrence, Kansas 66045.

### Arts—Kentucky

Kentucky Arts Commission. *Report. 1966/67-1967/68.* (Frankfort) 2 v. illus. annual.

Kentucky Arts Commission. *Report. 1968/69.* (Frankfort) 27 pp. illus. annual.

Kentucky Arts Commission. *Report. 1969/70.* (Frankfort) 24 pp. illus. annual.

Kentucky Arts Commission. *Report. 1970/71.* (Frankfort) 43 pp. illus. annual.

### Arts—Maine

State Commission on the Arts and the Humanities. *Maine Cultural Heritage and Horizons.* 2d ed. 1967. (Augusta) 32 pp.

State Commission on the Arts and the Humanities. *Report. 1967-69.* (Augusta) biennial.

### Arts—Maryland

Maryland Arts Council. *The Arts and Your Community; a handbook on local arts council.* (Baltimore, n.d.) 14 pp.

Maryland Arts Council. *Report.* 1967/68. (Baltimore) 23 pp. illus.

Maryland Arts Council. *Report. 3d; 1968/69.* (Baltimore) 24 pp. illus. annual.

Maryland Arts Council. *Report. 1969/70.* (Baltimore) unpaged. illus. annual.

Maryland Arts Council. *Report. 1970/71.* (Baltimore) unpaged. illus. annual.

### Arts—Maryland. Laws, statutes, etc.

Laws, Statutes, etc. *An Act Creating the Maryland Arts Council,* Enacted by the General Assembly, March 31, 1967. (Baltimore, Arts Council, 1967) folder.

### Arts—Massachusetts

Massachusetts Council on the Arts and Humanities. *Report. 1st; 1966/67.* (Boston) 127 pp. illus. annual. Council created by Acts of 1966, Chp. 589.

Massachusetts Council on the Arts and the Humanities. *Report. 1967-71.* (Boston, 1971) 54 pp. illus.

A Bibliography of U.S. Government Documents Pertaining to Government Support of the Arts, 1963-72

### Arts—Michigan
State Council for the Arts. *Report. 1967.* (Detroit) 31 pp. illus. annual.

State Council for the Arts. *Report. 1968.* (Detroit) unpaged. illus. annual. Council created by Act 48, Public Acts of 1966.

State Council for the Arts. *Report. 1970.* (Detroit) 23 pp. illus. annual.

### Arts—Minnesota
Minnesota State Arts Council. *Report. 1968/70.* (Minneapolis) unpaged. illus. annual. Combined report.

### Arts—Mississippi
Mississippi Arts Commission. *The Arts Are Your Business, Participate.* (Jackson, n.d.) folder, illus.

### Arts—Missouri
State Council on the Arts. *Concepts for the Development of Local Arts Councils and other Art Groups; a handbook for basic orientation to matters dealing with the administration of arts programs and projects for the practical solution of routine problems and for reference in time of crisis or concern,* by Joseph O. Fischer. 2d ed. St. Louis, 1972. iv + 95 pp.

### Arts—New Hampshire
New Hampshire Commission on the Arts. (Manchester, 1965?) folder.

New Hampshire Commission on the Arts. *Report. 1967/68.* (Manchester) 20 pp. illus. annual. Report year ends June 30.

New Hampshire Commission on the Arts. *The Arts and New Hampshire.* (Manchester, 1968) folder, illus. Issued in cooperation with the Division of Economic Development.

### Arts—New Jersey
New Jersey Legislature. *Commission to Study the Arts in New Jersey.* Public hearings held September 14, (21, 29) 1965 (at) Newark (Camden and Trenton. Trenton, 1965) 3 v. Commission created under AJR no. 20 of 1962.

New Jersey Commission to Study the Arts. *The Arts and New Jersey; report.* Trenton, 1966. 188 pp. Commission created by joint resolution of the State Legislature on Feb. 5, 1962.

### Arts—New Mexico
New Mexico Arts Commission Report. 1st, 3d; 1965/66, 1967/68. (Santa Fe) 2 v. illus. annual. Report year ends June 30. 1965/66

10    PERFORMING ARTS RESOURCES

issue has also a distinctive title: *The Arts in New Mexico.* The commission established on March 19, 1965 by the 27th Legislature, Senate bill no. 32.

Arts Commission. *Report.* 4th-5th; (1968/69-1969/70) Santa Fe. 2 v. illus. annual.

### Arts—New York
New York State Council on the Arts. *Report to the Governor and the Legislature of the State of New York by the Council on the Arts* (New York, 1961).

New York State Council on the Arts. *Report. 1962.* (New York) 52 pp. illus.

———. *Report. 1965.* (New York) 64 pp. illus. annual.

———. *Report. 1966.* (Albany) 72 pp. illus. annual.

———. *Report. 1966/67.* (Albany) 88 pp. illus. annual.

———. *Report. 1967/68.* (New York) 96 pp. illus. annual.

———. *Report. 1968/69.* (New York) 112 pp. illus. annual.

———. *Report. 1969/70.* (New York) 136 pp. illus. annual.

———. *Report. 1970/71.* (New York) 133 pp. illus. annual.

———. *Report. 1971/72.* (New York) 137 pp. illus. annual.

### Arts—North Carolina
North Carolina Recreation Commission. Publication (Raleigh) 33. *Recreation and the Arts.* 1964. 24 pp. Has variant series title: *Bulletin.*

North Carolina Arts Council. *The Arts in North Carolina, 1967.* (Raleigh, 1967) 127 pp. illus. Council established by act of the General Assembly, effective April 7, 1967.

North Carolina Arts Council. (*Report*) 2d; 1969/71. (Raleigh) Report period ends in June.

### Arts—Ohio
Ohio Arts Council. *Report. 1971.* (Columbus) unpaged. illus. annual. Has also a distinctive title: *Arts in Austerity.*

### Arts—Oklahoma
Oklahoma Arts and Humanities Council. *Proceedings of the Governor's Conference on the Arts, University of Oklahoma, May 27-28, 1966.* (Oklahoma City, 1966) various pagings.

Oklahoma Arts and Humanities Council. *Report. 1967-69.* (Oklahoma City) 14 pp. illus. annual.

Oklahoma Arts and Humanities Council. *Council Programs. 1969-70.* (Oklahoma City) unpaged.

A Bibliography of U.S. Government Documents Pertaining to Government Support of the Arts, 1963-72   11

**Arts—Oregon**
Oregon Arts Commission. *Community Arts Councils.* Salem, 1967. 14 pp. Commission created by Oregon laws, 1967, Chp. 321, effective July 1, 1967.

**Arts—Pennsylvania**
Pennsylvania Council on the Arts. *Pennsylvania Culture; the arts, the artists, the audience.* Vol. 1. Editor-in-Chief: Vincent R. Artz. (Harrisburg, c. 1969) 73 pp. illus.

**Arts—South Carolina**
South Carolina Arts Commission. *Report. 2d; 1968/69.* (Columbia) unpaged. illus. annual.

**Arts—South Dakota**
South Dakota Fine Arts Council. *Report. 4th; 1970.* (By Charlotte Carver. Pierre) 28 pp. illus.

**Arts—Vermont**
Vermont Council on the Arts. *Report. 1969.* (Montpelier) unpaged. annual.
Vermont Council on the Arts. *Report. 1970.* (Montpelier) 27 pp. illus. annual.
Vermont Council on the Arts. *Report. 1971.* (Montpelier) unpaged. illus. annual.

**Arts—Virgin Islands**
Virgin Islands Council on the Arts. *Report. 1st; 1969/70.* (Charlotte Amalie) unpaged. illus. annual. Report year ends June 30.

**Arts—Virginia**
Virginia Cultural Development Study Commission. *The Forms of Culture; the old and the new.* Richmond, 1967. 123 pp. illus. (Senate document no. 9) Commission created by Acts of Assembly, 1966, SJR no. 67, approved March 11, 1966.

**Arts—Washington**
Washington State Arts Commission. *Report. 1966/67-1967/68.* (Olympia) 2 v. annual. Report year ends June 30.
Washington State Arts Commission. *What It Is, What It Does, How It Serves You.* Olympia, 1969. 71 pp.
Washington State Arts Commission. *A Congress of the Arts, Nov. 14-15, 1969.* Sponsored in cooperation with Allied Arts of Seattle, Inc., King County Arts Commission (and) Pacific Science Center (Olympia, 1969?) 45 pp.

Washington State Library, Olympia. *The Arts, A Selected Bibliography.* Prepared for the Mid-Columbia Region Focus on Arts and the Southwest Washington Congress of the Arts, 1970, by the library in cooperation with State Arts Commission. Olympia, 1970. 3 pp.

## Congressional Documents

House. Committee on Education and Labor. *Aid to Fine Arts. Hearing* before the Select Subcommittee on Education of the Committee on Education and Labor, House of Representatives, on H.R. 4172, H.R. 4174, and related bills to aid the fine arts in the United States, 87th Cong., 1st sess., 1961.

Senate. Committee on Labor and Public Welfare. *Government and the Arts. Hearings* before a special subcommittee of the Committee on Labor and Public Welfare, U.S. Senate, on S. 741, a bill to provide for the establishment of a federal advisory council on the arts to assist in the growth and development of fine arts in the United States; S. 785, a bill to establish a program of grants to states for the development of programs and projects in the arts, and for other purposes; and S. 1250, a bill to establish the United States arts foundation, 87th Cong., 2d sess., 1962.

Senate. Committee on Labor and Public Welfare. *To Establish a U.S. National Arts Foundation.* S. Rept. 2260 to Accompany S. 741 as amended, 87th Cong., 2d sess., 1962.

Senate. Committee on Labor and Public Welfare. *The Arts and the National Government: Report to the President,* submitted by August Heckscher, special consultant on the arts. S. Doc. 28, 88th Cong., 1st sess., 1963.

Senate. Committee on Labor and Public Welfare. *National Arts Legislation.* Hearings before special subcommittee on Arts, U.S. Senate, on S. 165 and S. 1316, 88th Cong., 1st sess., 1963.

Senate. Committee on Labor and Public Welfare. *Establishing National Council on the Arts and National Arts Foundation.* S. Rept. 780 To Accompany S. 2379, 88th Cong., 1st sess., 1963.

House. Committee on Public Works. *John F. Kennedy Center Act.* H. Rept. 1050, pt. 2 To Accompany H.R. Res. 871, 88th Cong., 2d sess., 1964.

A Bibliography of U.S. Government Documents Pertaining  13
to Government Support of the Arts, 1963-72

House. Committee on Education and Labor. *National Arts and Cultural Development Act of 1963.* Hearings before special subcommittee on Labor, House of Representatives, on H.R. 9587, 88th Cong., 2d sess., 1964.

House. Committee on Education and Labor. *National Arts and Cultural Development Act of 1964.* H. Rept. 1476 To Accompany H.R. 9586, 88th Cong., 2d sess., 1964.

Senate. Committee on Labor and Public Welfare. *National Arts and Humanities Foundations.* Joint Hearings before special subcommittee on Arts and Humanities of Committee on Labor and Public Welfare, U.S. Senate, and Special Subcommittee on Labor of Committee on Education and Labor, House of Representatives, on bills to establish National Foundation on Arts and Humanities, 89th Cong., 1st sess., 1965.

Senate. Committee on Labor and Public Welfare. *National Arts and Humanities Foundations.* Hearings before special subcommittee on Arts and Humanities, U.S. Senate, on bills to establish National Foundations on Arts and Humanities, 89th Cong., 1st sess., 1965.

House. Committee on Education and Labor. *National Arts and Humanities Foundations.* Hearings before Special Subcommittee on Labor, House of Representatives, on H.R. 334, H.R. 2043, and H.R. 3617, and similar bills, 89th Cong., 1st. sess., 1965.

House. Committee on Education and Labor. *National Foundation on Arts and Humanities Act of 1965.* H. Rept. 618, To Accompany H.R. 9460, 89th Cong., 1st sess., 1965.

House. Committee on Education and Labor. *National Foundation on Arts and Humanities, Questions and Answers,* compiled by Special Subcommittee on Labor, Committee Print. Washington, D.C.: Government Printing Office, 1965.

House. Committee on Appropriations. *Department of Interior and Related Agencies Appropriations for 1967.* Hearings before subcommittee, House of Representatives, on H.R. 14215, 89th Cong., 2d sess., 1966.

House. Committee on Appropriations. *Department of Interior and Related Agencies Appropriation Bill, 1967.* H. Rept. 1405 To Accompany H.R. 14215, 89th Cong., 1st sess., 1965.

House. Committee on Appropriations. *Supplemental Appropria-*

14    PERFORMING ARTS RESOURCES

tion Bill, 1966. Hearings before subcommittees, House of Representatives, on H.R. 11588, 89th Cong., 1st sess., 1965.

House. Conference Committee. *Department of Interior and Related Agencies Appropriations, 1967.* H. Rept. 1538 To Accompany H.R. 14215, 89th Cong., 1966.

Senate. Committee on Labor and Public Welfare. *Establishing National Foundation on Arts and Humanities.* S. Rept. 300 To Accompany S. 1483, 89th Cong., 1st sess., 1965.

Senate. Public Works Committee. *John F. Kennedy Center for Performing Arts, annual report of Board of Trustees.* Committee Print. Washington, D.C.: Government Printing Office, 1965.

Senate. Committee on Appropriations. *Department of Interior and Related Agencies Appropriations for Fiscal Year 1967.* Hearings before subcommittee, U.S. Senate, on H.R. 14215, 89th Cong., 2d sess., 1966.

Senate. Committee on Appropriations. *Interior Department and Related Agencies Appropriation Bill, 1967.* S. Rept. 1154 To Accompany H.R. 14215, 89th Cong., 2d sess., 1966.

House. Committee on Appropriations. *Department of Interior and Related Agencies Appropriations for 1968.* Hearings before subcommittee, House of Representatives, on H.R. 9029, 90th Cong., 1st sess., 1967.

House. Committee on Appropriations. *Department of Interior and Related Agencies Appropriation Bill, 1969.* H. Rept. 206 To Accompany H.R. 9029, 90th Cong., 1st sess., 1967.

Senate. Committee on Appropriations. *Department of Interior and Related Agencies Appropriations for Fiscal Year 1968.* Hearings before subcommittee, U.S. Senate, on H.R. 9020, 90th Cong., 1st sess., 1967.

Senate. Committee on Appropriations. *Interior Department and Related Agencies Appropriations Bill, 1968.* S. Rept. 233 To Accompany H.R. 9029, 90th Cong., 1st sess., 1967.

House. Conference Committee. *Department of Interior and Related Agencies Appropriations, 1968.* H. Rept. 343 To Accompany H.R. 9029, 90th Cong., 1st sess., 1967.

Senate. Committee on Labor and Public Welfare. *Arts and Humanities Amendments of 1967.* Joint Hearings before Special Sub-

A Bibliography of U.S. Government Documents Pertaining   15
to Government Support of the Arts, 1963-72

committee on Arts and Humanities of Committee on Labor and Public Welfare, U.S. Senate, and Special Subcommittee on Labor of Committee on Education and Labor, House of Representatives, on S. 2061 and H.R. 11308, 90th Cong., 1st sess., 1967.

House. Committee on Education and Labor. *Amendments to National Foundation on the Arts and the Humanities Act of 1965.* Hearings before Special Subcommittee on Labor, House of Representatives, on H.R. 11308, 90th Cong., 1st sess., 1967.

Senate. Committee on Labor and Public Welfare. *Arts and Humanities Amendments of 1967.* Hearings before Special Subcommittee on Arts and Humanities, U.S. Senate, on S. 2061, 90th Cong., 1st sess., 1967.

House. Committee on Education and Labor. *Amending National Foundation on the Arts and the Humanities Act of 1965.* H. Rept. 1066 To Accompany H.R. 11308, 90th Cong., 2nd sess., 1968.

House. Committee on Rules. *Consideration of H.R. 11308.* H. Rept. 1091 To Accompany H. Res. 1059, 90th Cong., 2d sess., 1968.

House. Committee on Appropriations. *Department of Interior and Related Agencies Appropriations for 1969.* Hearings before subcommittee, House of Representatives, 90th Cong., 2d sess., 1968.

Senate. Committee on Labor and Public Welfare. *Amending National Foundation on the Arts and the Humanities Act of 1965.* S. Rept. 1103 To Accompany H.R. 11308, 90th Cong., 2d sess., 1968.

House. Conference Committee. *Amending National Foundation on the Arts and the Humanities Act of 1965.* H. Rept. 1511 To Accompany H.R. 11308, 90th Cong., 2d sess., 1968.

Senate. Committee on Labor and Public Welfare. *Higher Education Amendments of 1968.* S. Rept. 1387 To Accompany S. 3769, 90th Cong., 2d sess., 1968.

House. Conference Committee. *Higher Education Amendments of 1968.* H. Rept. 1919 To Accompany S. 3769, 90th Cong., 2d sess., 1968.

House. Committee on Public Works. *John F. Kennedy Center Act Amendments, Limiting Use for Demonstration Purposes of any Federally owned Property in District of Columbia. Hearing* before Subcommittee on Public Buildings and Grounds, House of Representatives, on H.R. 11249, H.R. 9431, H.R. 1035 and related bills, 91st Cong., 1st sess., 1969.

House. Committee on Public Works. *John F. Kennedy Center.* H. Rept. 309 To Accompany H.R. 11249, 91st Cong., 1st sess., 1969.

Senate. Committee on Public Works. *John F. Kennedy Center. Hearing* before Subcommittee on Public Buildings and Grounds, U.S. Senate, on H.R. 11249, 91st Cong., 1st sess., 1969.

Senate. Committee on Public Works. *John F. Kennedy Center.* S. Rept. 327 To Accompany H.R. 11249, 91st Cong., 1st sess., 1969.

House. Committee on Appropriations. *Department of Interior and Related Appropriations for 1970.* Hearings before subcommittee, House of Representatives, 91st Cong., 1st sess., 1969.

House. Committee on Appropriations. *Department of Interior and Related Agencies Appropriations Bill.* H. Rept. 361 To Accompany H.R. 12781, 91st Cong., 1st sess., 1969.

Senate. Committee on Appropriations. *Interior Department and Related Agencies Appropriations Bill, 1970.* S. Rept. 420 To Accompany H.R. 12781, 91st Cong., 1st sess., 1969.

House. Committee on Rules. *Consideration on H.R. 11249.* H. Rept. 318 To Accompany H. Res. 447, 91st Cong., 1st sess., 1969.

Senate. Committee on Labor and Public Welfare. *Nomination of Nancy Hanks, of New York, to be Chairman of National Council on the Arts. Hearing,* U.S. Senate, 91st Cong., 1st sess., 1969.

House. Conference Committee. *Appropriations for Fiscal Year 1970.* H. Rept. 570 To Accompany H.R. 12781, 91st Cong., 1st sess., 1969.

House. Committee on Appropriations. *Department of Interior and Related Agencies Appropriations for 1971. Hearings* before subcommittee, House of Representatives, on H.R. 17619, 91st Cong., 2d sess., 1970.

House. Committee on Education and Labor. *Amendments to National Foundation on the Arts and the Humanities Act of 1965. Joint Hearings* before Select Subcommittee on Education, Committee on Education and Labor, House, and Special Subcommittee on Arts and Humanities of Committee on Labor and Public Welfare, on H.R. 15196 and S. 3238, 91st Cong., 2d sess., 1970.

A Bibliography of U.S. Government Documents Pertaining  17
to Government Support of the Arts, 1963-72

House. Committee on Education and Labor. *National Foundation on the Arts and the Humanities.* H. Rept. 936 To Accompany H.R. 16065, 91st Cong., 2d sess., 1970.

House. Committee on Education and Labor. *National Foundation on the Arts and the Humanities.* H. Rept. 936 To Accompany 16065, 91st Cong., 2d sess., 1970.

House. Committee on Appropriations. *Department of Interior and Related Agencies Appropriation Bill, 1971.* H. Rept. 1095 To Accompany H.R. 17619, 91st Cong., 2d sess., 1970.

Senate. Committee on Labor and Public Welfare. *National Foundation on the Arts and the Humanities Amendments of 1970.* S. Rept. 879 To Accompany S. 3215, 91st Cong., 2d sess., 1970.

House. Committee on Rules. *Consideration of H.R. 16065.* H. Rept. 1242 To Accompany H. Res. 1118, 91st Cong., 2d sess., 1970.

Senate. Committee on Appropriations. *Interior Department and Related Agencies Appropriations Bill, 1971.* S. Rept. 985 To Accompany H.R. 17619, 91st Cong., 2d sess., 1970.

House. Conference Committee. *National Foundation on the Arts and the Humanities Amendments of 1970.* H. Rept. 1292 To Accompany S. 3215, 91st Cong., 2d sess., 1970.

House. Conference Committee. *Department of Interior and Related Agencies Appropriations, 1971.* H. Rept. 1321 To Accompany H.R. 17619, 91st Cong., 2d sess., 1970.

House. Public Works Committee. *John F. Kennedy Center Act Amendments, 1971. Hearing* before Subcommittee on Public Buildings and Grounds, House of Representatives, on H.R. 9801, 92d Cong., 1st sess., 1971.

Senate. Public Works Committee. *Amending John F. Kennedy Center Act. Hearing* before Subcommittee on Buildings and Grounds, U.S. Senate, on S. 2900, 92d Cong., 1st sess., 1972.

Senate. Committee on Labor and Public Welfare. *Survey of United States and Foreign Government Support for Cultural Activities,* prepared for the Special Subcommittee on Arts and Humanities of the Committee on Labor and Public Welfare. Committee Print. Washington, D.C.: Government Printing Office, 1971.

House. Committee on Appropriations. *Department of Interior and Related Agencies Appropriations for 1972. Hearings* before Subcommittee on Department of Interior and Related Agencies,

House of Representatives, on H.R. 9417, 92d Cong., 1st sess., 1971.

House. Committee on Appropriations. *Department of Interior and Related Agencies Appropriation Bill, 1972.* H. Rept. 308 To Accompany H.R. 9417, 92d Cong., 1st sess., 1971.

House. Conference Committee. *Department of Interior and Related Agencies.* H. Rept. 386 To Accompany H.R. 9417, 92d Cong., 1st sess., 1971.

House. Committee on Appropriations. *Department of Interior and Related Agencies Appropriations for 1973. Hearings* before subcommittee, House of Representatives, 92d Cong., 2d sess., 1972.

Senate. Committee on Appropriations. *Department of Interior and Related Agencies Appropriations Bill, 1973.* S. Rept. 921 To Accompany H.R. 15418, 92d Cong., 2d sess., 1972.

House. Committee on Appropriations. *Department of Interior and Related Agencies Appropriation Bill, 1973.* H. Rept. 1119 To Accompany H.R. 15418, 92d Cong., 2d sess., 1972.

House. Committee on Education and Labor. *To Make Used Railroad Depots into Cultural Centers. Hearing* before Select Subcommittee on Education, House of Representatives, on H.R. 9719, 92d Cong., 2d sess., August 4, 1972.

# U.S. Laws, Statutes, etc., Pertaining to the Arts

Joint Resolution Providing for Renaming the National Cultural Center as the John F. Kennedy Center for the Performing Arts, Authorizing an Appropriation therefor, and for other Purposes. *Public law no. 260, 88th Congress.*

An Act Making Appropriations for the Department of the Interior and Related Agencies for the Fiscal Year Ending June 30, 1965, and for other purposes ... *Public law no. 356, 88th Congress.*

An Act to Provide for Establishment of National Council on the Arts to Assist in Growth and Development of the Arts in the United States. *Public law no. 579, 88th Congress.*

Supplemental Appropriation Act of 1965. An Act Making Supplemental Appropriations for the Fiscal Year Ending June 30, 1965, and for other Purposes ... *Public law no. 635, 88th Congress.*

An Act Making Appropriations for the Department of the Interior and Related Agencies for the Fiscal Year Ending June 30, 1966, and for other Purposes ... *Public law no. 52, 89th Congress.*

National Arts and Cultural Development Act of 1964, Amendments: An Act to Amend the National Arts and Cultural Development Act of 1964 with Respect to the Authorization of Appropriations Therein ... *Public law no. 125, 89th Congress.*

An Act to Provide for Establishment of National Foundation on Arts and Humanities to Promote Progress and Scholarship in Humanities and Arts in United States, and for other Purposes ... *Public law no. 209, 89th Congress.*

Supplemental Appropriations Act of 1966. An Act Making Supplemental Appropriations for the Fiscal Year Ending June 30, 1966, and for other Purposes ... *Public law no. 309, 89th Congress.*

An Act Making Appropriations for Department of Interior and Related Agencies for Fiscal Year 1967, and other Purposes ... *Public law no. 435, 89th Congress.*

National Endowment for the Arts American Revolution Bicentennial Commission, Cooperation in Planning ... *Public law no. 491, 89th Congress.*

Second Supplemental Appropriations Act of 1967. Making Supplemental Appropriations for the Fiscal Year Ending June 30, 1967, and for other Purposes ... *Public law no. 21, 90th Congress.*

An Act Making Appropriations for Department of Interior and Related Agencies for Fiscal Year 1968, and for other Purposes ... *Public law no. 28, 90th Congress.*

An Act to Amend the National Foundation on the Arts and the Humanities Act of 1965 ... *Public law no. 348, 90th Congress.*

An Act Making Appropriations for the Department of the Interior and Related Agencies for the Fiscal Year Ending June 30, 1969, and for other Purposes ... *Public law no. 425, 90th Congress.*

An Act to Amend the Higher Education Act of 1965, the National Defense Education Act of 1958, the National Vocational Student Loan Insurance Act of 1965, the Higher Education Facilities Act of 1963, and Related Acts. *Public law no. 575, 90th Congress.*

Second Supplemental Appropriations Act of 1969. An Act making Supplemental Appropriations for the Fiscal Year Ending June 30, 1969, and for other Purposes ... *Public law no. 47, 91st Congress.*

An Amendment to the John F. Kennedy Center Act to Authorize Additional Funds for such a Center. *Public law no. 90, 91st Congress.*

An Act Making Appropriations for Department of Interior and Related Agencies for Fiscal Year 1970, and for other Purposes ... *Public law no. 98, 91st Congress.*

Supplemental Appropriation Act, 1970. An Act Making Supplemental Appropriations for the Fiscal Year Ending June 30, 1970, and for other Purposes ... *Public law no. 166, 91st Congress.*

An Act to Extend Programs of Assistance for Elementary and Secondary Education, and for other Purposes ... *Public law no. 230, 91st Congress.*

Second Supplemental Appropriations Act, 1970. An Act Making Supplemental Appropriations for the Fiscal Year Ending June 30, 1970, and for other Purposes ... *Public law no. 305, 91st Congress.*

An Act to Amend the National Foundation on the Arts and the Humanities Act of 1965, and for other Purposes ... *Public law no. 346, 91st Congress.*

An Act Making Appropriations for Department of Interior and Related Agencies for Fiscal Year 1971, and other Purposes ... *Public law no. 361, 91st Congress.*

An Act Making Appropriations for Department of Interior and Related Agencies for Fiscal Year Ending June 30, 1972, and for other Purposes ... *Public law no. 76, 92d Congress.*

An Act Making Appropriations for Department of Interior and Related Agencies for Fiscal Year Ending June 30, 1973, and for other Purposes ... *Public law no. 369, 92d Congress.*

# U.S. Executive Departmental Documents

Office of Education. *Guidelines, Financial Assistance for Strengthening Instruction in Arts and Humanities in Public*

A Bibliography of U.S. Government Documents Pertaining to Government Support of the Arts, 1963-72

*Elementary and Secondary Schools, National Foundation on Arts and Humanities Act of 1965,* sec. 12. (with list of useful references.) Washington, D.C.: Government Printing Office, 1966.

Office of Education. *Federal Funds and Services for the Arts*; compiled by Judith G. Gault. (Prepared by Office of Research, National Endowment for the Arts.) Washington, D.C.: Government Printing Office, 1967.

Office of Education. *U.S. Office of Education Support for the Arts and the Humanities.* Washington, D.C.: Government Printing Office, 1969.

Office of Education. *U.S. Office of Education Support for Arts and Humanities, 1972*; (prepared by Diana Vogelsong.) Washington, D.C.: Government Printing Office, 1972.

Department of Health, Education and Welfare. *National Foundation on Arts and Humanities Act of 1965 (with list of selected references*; by Richard Grove.) Washington, D.C.: Government Printing Office, 1966.

Department of Health, Education and Welfare. *Arts and the Poor, New Challenge for Educators.* Report of the Conference on Role of Arts in Meeting the Social and Educational Needs of the Disadvantaged, Nov. 15-19, 1966, Gaithersburg, Md. Washington, D.C.: Government Printing Office, 1968.

Office of Management and Budget. *1972 Catalog of Federal Domestic Assistance.* Washington, D.C.: Government Printing Office, 1972.

National Endowment for the Arts.

*Purpose and Activities of National Foundation on the Arts and the Humanities as it Pertains to the Arts.* Washington, D.C.: Government Printing Office, 1966.

*Review of Scope and Exposure of Initial Programs of National Council on the Arts.* Washington, D.C.: Government Printing Office, 1966.

*Summary of State Arts Activities.* May 4, 1966. Washington, D.C.: Government Printing Office, 1966.

*Review of Programs and Planning of National Council on the Arts and National Endowment for the Arts, 1965-67.* Washington, D.C.: Government Printing Office, 1967.

*Review of Scope and Exposure of Initial Programs of National*

*Endowment for the Arts*, August 15, 1967. Washington, D.C.: Government Printing Office, 1967.

*National Endowment for the Arts and National Council on the Arts annual report, fiscal year 1967*. Washington, D.C.: Government Printing Office, 1968.

*Programs of the National Endowment for the Arts through August 30, 1968*. Washington, D.C.: Government Printing Office, 1968.

*Programs of National Endowment for the Arts, fiscal 1969*. Washington, D.C.: Government Printing Office, 1969.

*Programs of the National Endowment for the Arts through March 1969*. Washington, D.C.: Government Printing Office, 1969.

*National Endowment for the Arts and National Council on the Arts, annual report for fiscal year June 30, 1968*. Washington, D.C.: Government Printing Office, 1969.

*Programs of National Endowment for the Arts through Oct. 1969*. Washington, D.C.: Government Printing Office, 1969.

*Programs of National Council on the Arts and the National Endowment for the Arts, Oct. 1965-Apr. 1970*. Washington, D.C.: Government Printing Office, 1970.

*Annual Report, fiscal year 1969, the arts, National Endowment for the Arts and National Council on the Arts*. Washington, D.C.: Government Printing Office, 1970.

*1970 Annual Report, National Council on the Arts*. Washington, D.C.: Government Printing Office, 1971.

*Economic Aspects of the Performing Arts, Portrait in Figures*. Washington, D.C.: Government Printing Office, 1971.

*National Endowment for the Arts, National Council on the Arts, Our Programs*. Washington, D.C.: Government Printing Office, 1972.

*Annual Report, Fiscal Year 1972. National Council on the Arts*. Washington, D.C.: Government Printing Office, 1972.

*Visual Arts Program Guidelines, fiscal year 1973. National Council on the Arts*. Washington, D.C.: Government Printing Office, 1972.

National Foundation on the Arts and the Humanities. *National Foundation on the Arts and the Humanities*. Washington, D.C.: Government Printing Office, 1969.

A Bibliography of U.S. Government Documents Pertaining   23
to Government Support of the Arts, 1963-72

U.S. President. *Arts and Humanities, Message from President of United States.* (91st Cong., 1st Sess., *House Doc. No. 202*, Dec. 10, 1969.) 1969-. Richard M. Nixon. Washington, D.C.: Government Printing Office, 1969.

U.S. President. *Associated Councils of the Arts; the President's Remarks at the ACA's Annual Conference, May 26, 1971.* Speech: "The Arts, A Creative Partnership." 1969-. Richard M. Nixon. *Weekly Compilation of Presidential Documents.* 7:816-21. May 31, 1971. Washington, D.C.: Office of the Federal Register, National Archives and Records Service, 1971.

U.S. Department of State. Advisory Committee on the Arts.

*International Understanding through the Performing Arts: a Report on the Cultural Presentations Program of the Department of State, July 1, 1963-June 30, 1964.* International Information and Cultural Series 88, Pubn. 7819 (1965).

*Strengthening Cultural Bonds Between Nations through the Performing Arts: a Report on the Cultural Presentations Program of the Department of State, July 1, 1964-June 30, 1965.* International Information and Cultural Series 93, Pubn. 8038 (1966).

*Building Bridges Between Nations—through the Performing Arts: a Report on the Cultural Presentations Program of the Department of State, July 1, 1965-June 30, 1966.* International Information and Cultural Series 93, Pubn. 8254 (1967).

*Cultural Presentations USA, 1966-67, Report to Congress and the Public, by Advisory Committee on the Arts; with added section on athletic programs.* International Information and Cultural Series 95, Pubn. 8365 (1968).

*Cultural Presentations USA, 1967-68, Report to Congress and the Public, by Advisory Committee on the Arts; with added section on athletic programs.* International Information and Cultural Series 98, Pubn. 8438 (1969).

Gerald O'Grady

# Resources for the Oral History of the Independent American Film at Media Study/ Buffalo, New York

After almost weekly visits of independent filmmakers for screenings and discussions of their work and the teaching of a variety of courses organized around different aspects of it over a three-year period at the Center for Media Study, State University of New York at Buffalo, and after similar involvement of filmmakers in teaching workshops and screenings of their work at Media Study/Buffalo, a non-University foundation, Gerald O'Grady, Director of the Center for Media Study and of Media Study/Buffalo, activated the gathering of an Oral History of the Independent American Cinema in January, 1973.

Three filmmakers were invited to interview five fellow filmmakers each during an initial fifteen-week period.

Those invited to conduct the interviews were Stan Brakhage, who had engaged himself in a life-long study of the cinema and had been lecturing at the Art Institute in Chicago in recent years; Peter Kubelka, who had likewise deeply involved himself in cinema history for a quarter century and had founded the Oesterreichisches Filmmuseum in Vienna where he serves as Director; and Hollis Frampton, who was teaching film and art at Hunter College and Cooper Union, had been publishing a number of essays and interviews on film and photography in *Artforum* and *Film Culture*, and whose own films were being tended a retrospective showing at the Museum of Modern Art that spring, as Brakhage's had been two years earlier.

Brakhage interviewed Ian Hugo, Sidney Peterson, Larry Jordan, Kenneth Anger, James Broughton and Peter Kubelka. Kubelka interviewed Jack Smith, Jonas Mekas, Robert Breer and Stan Brakhage. Frampton, who had interviewed Brakhage separately for *Artforum*'s Eisenstein/Brakhage Special Issue (January, 1973), interviewed Michael Snow, Andrew Noren, Paul Sharits and Bruce Connor.

In the summer session of 1973, James Blue was invited to continue the series of interviews. A distinguished feature and documentary filmmaker in his own right (*The Olive Trees of Justice, The March*, etc.), Blue had taught at the University of Southern California at Los Angeles and the Advanced Study Center of the American Film Institute, and at the Media Center at Rice University. A few years earlier, he had been the recipient of a Ford Foundation grant to interview fifty international film directors who had used nonprofessional actors in their work. Some of these interviews appeared in *Film Comment* and all will be forthcoming in a major book. Blue interviewed Ralph Steiner, John Marshall, Robert Gardner, George Stoney and Willard Van Dyke. While all previous interviews were recorded on audiotape only, Blue also recorded his interviews on ½ inch videotape. This practice was also followed by Willard Van Dyke who, in the summer of 1974, interviewed Helen Van Dongen Durant, Richard Leacock, Irving Jacoby,

Henwar Rodakiewicz, William Jersey and Donn Alan Pennebaker.

A number of other interviews were done at different times as various filmmakers visited Buffalo. Hollis Frampton and Paul Sharits joined O'Grady as permanent members of the Center for Media Study (S.U.N.Y. at Buffalo) faculty in the fall of 1973. Sharits interviewed Gunvor Nelson, Brakhage visited to interview Ken Jacobs, Stan Vanderbeek and Ed Emshwiller interviewed each other and Emshwiller interviewed Hilary Harris. O'Grady continued to conduct a number of more casual (less extensive) interviews with film and videomakers, and the video activity will continue as Woody Vasulka joined the Center for Media Study staff in the fall of 1974. A complete list of audio and videotapes appears at the end of this report.

The Center for Media Study and Media Study/Buffalo plan to reinvite these and other interviewers such as Jonas Mekas, to conduct more than one hundred additional interviews over the next three years. The interviews are deposited in an archive of materials related to the Independent American Cinema; copies, at cost, are being deposited at Anthology Film Archives in New York City and other institutions which request them. The intent is that then the tapes will be transcribed and published in *Media Study*, a publication of Media Study/Buffalo. Access to the tapes and the right to publication will depend on the permission of the filmmaker or videomaker interviewed. These interviews will form the basic research materials for writing the history of the American Independent Cinema. For the Anthology Film Archives, which is supported for this purpose by the National Endowment for the Arts, each filmmaker is interviewed by Scott Nygren about the storage, current condition and plans for preservation of his original prints. This is one part of a project which is directed by P. Adams Sitney.

The interviews at Media Study are conducted as part of an ongoing graduate seminar and as part of a public screening and discussion program which is open to all students of S.U.N.Y. at Buffalo and to all citizens of Buffalo. The graduate students do research on the individual filmmakers, editing basic filmographies and bibliographies, and writing interpretative essays on their work in relation to various life records, letters, script designs, etc. Every attempt is made to have the seminar members screen as many of the filmmaker's works as possible before he appears for the interview. On the evening of the interview, the filmmaker appears at a one-man showing of his selected works. In the case of some filmmakers, there has been a two or three evening retrospective of their work.

The interviews are open-ended; some have gone on for as long as sixteen hours and the average has been four or five. They can be interrupted for coffee, food or a walk; they can resume the following day. They are recorded under high fidelity conditions at the studio of the Instructional Communication Center, S.U.N.Y. at Buffalo, of which O'Grady is also the Director. Some of the interviews have stressed childhood and early life experiences in relation to the growth of an artist; some have focused on the development of and experiment with style; others have provided information on the reception of the films and tapes, their distribution, the general political and cinematic climate; others have gotten into sometimes spirited discussion about aesthetics; all this and much more. Thus far, they comprise an extraordinarily valuable record, a magic carpet-like unreeling of political, social and psychological history; of the interaction of the consciousness of artists, after training in the more traditional media of painting and sculpture, with new and changing technologies; of the birth and growth of an independent film and video in the United States.

The attitude taken toward these interviews is this. Every effort is made to match the filmmaker with an interviewer who is knowledgeable about and sympathetic with his work. The visitor is encouraged to look on this occasion as an opportunity to "speak from the grave," to put on permanent record his or her views, ideas, life and vision. The hope is that he or she will be open, frank, direct. The intention is that filmmakers be made to feel at home, be treated as the esteemed guests they are; that they recognize that their Buffalo hosts are engaged in a common enterprise with them. Much as information about a personal life might be desired, this must be volunteered, given freely for the help of future filmmakers, historians and citizens. The filmmaker is encouraged to feel absolutely free to make the interviews suit his or her own needs, to take directions that best serve him or her. It is his or her tape. The Buffalo archive is the willing and grateful receiver of however much is revealed.

Those interviewed are asked to send ahead, bring with them or mail later any relevant materials, such as scripts, letters, scores, designs, for copying and deposit at the study center. All originals are returned immediately. Thus far materials include copies of Stan Brakhage's scrapbook, Bruce Baillie's notebooks compiled in the making of *Quick Billy*, Bruce Connor's talk taped at the Flaherty International Film Seminar, Jonas Mekas' poetry, and much else.

## Audio Tape Library

| Anger, Kenneth | interviewed by Stan Brakhage | 4/18/73 |
| | film show | 4/19/73 |
| Brakhage, Stan | interviewed by Peter Kubelka | 1/30/73 |
| | film show | 1/31/73 |
| Breer, Robert | interviewed by Peter Kubelka | 2/13/73 |
| | film show & preservation data | 2/13/73 |
| Broughton, James | interviewed by Stan Brakhage | 5/10/73 |
| | film show | 5/10/73 |
| | | 5/11/73 |
| Connor, Bruce | interviewed by Hollis Frampton | 4/12/73 |
| | film show & preservation data | 4/12/73 |
| Conrad, Tony | preservation data | 12/16/73 |
| Durant, Helen Van Dongen | interviewed by Willard Van Dyke | 8/1/74 |
| Frampton, Hollis | interviewed by Stan Brakhage | 12/73 |
| Gardner, Robert | interviewed by James Blue | 7/26/73 |
| Harris, Hilary | interviewed by Ed Emshwiller | 8/20/74 |
| Hill, Jerome | interviewed by Stan Brakhage | 4/21/71 |

Resources for the Oral History of the Independent **29**
American Film at Media Study/Buffalo, New York

| | | |
|---|---|---|
| Hugo, Ian | preservation data | 5/3/73 |
| Jacobs, Ken | interviewed by Stan Brakhage | 5/5/73 |
| Jacoby, Irving | interviewed by Willard Van Dyke | 8/22/74 |
| Jersey, William | interviewed by Willard Van Dyke | 8/30/74 |
| Jordan, Larry | interviewed by Stan Brakhage<br>film show<br>preservation data | 5/5/73<br>5/4/73<br>5/6/73 |
| Kubelka, Peter | interviewed by Stan Brakhage<br>film show<br>interviewed by Stan Brakhage<br>(part II) | 5/12/73<br>5/11/73<br>12/13/73 |
| Leacock, Richard | interviewed by Willard Van Dyke | 8/15/74 |
| Marshall, John | interviewed by James Blue<br>film show | 7/5/73<br>7/5/73 |
| Mekas, Jonas | interviewed by Peter Kubelka | 1/25/73 |
| Nelson, Gunvor | interviewed by Paul Sharits | 12/15/73 |
| Noren, Andrew | interviewed by Hollis Frampton<br>film show | 3/29/73<br>3/29/73 |
| Pennebaker, Donn Alan | interviewed by Willard Van Dyke | 7/25/74 |
| Peterson, Sidney | interviewed by Stan Brakhage<br>film show & preservation data | 5/17/73<br>5/17/73 |
| Rodakiewicz, Henwar | interviewed by Willard Van Dyke | 8/8/74 |
| Sharits, Paul | interviewed by Hollis Frampton<br>film show & preservation data | 3/1/73<br>3/1/73 |
| Smith, Jack | interviewed by Peter Kubelka | 1/18/73 |
| Snow, Michael | interviewed by Hollis Frampton<br>film show & preservation data | 3/18/73<br>3/18/73 |
| Steiner, Ralph | interviewed by James Blue<br>film show | 7/12/73<br>7/12/73 |
| Stoney, George | interviewed by James Blue<br>film show | 6/28/73<br>6/28/73 |

| | | |
|---|---|---|
| Vanderbeek, Stan | interviewed by Ed Emshwiller | 12/15/73 |
| | interviewed by Ed Emshwiller (part II) | 8/19/74 |
| Van Dyke, Willard | interviewed by James Blue | 8/2/73 |

## Video Tape Library

| | | |
|---|---|---|
| Durant, Helen Van Dongen | interviewed by Willard Van Dyke | 8/1/74 |
| Gardner, Robert | interviewed by James Blue | 7/26/73 |
| Jacoby, Irving | interviewed by Willard Van Dyke | 8/22/74 |
| Jersey, William | interviewed by Willard Van Dyke | 8/29/74 |
| Leacock, Richard | interviewed by Willard Van Dyke | 8/29/74 |
| Marshall, John | interviewed by James Blue | 7/5/73 |
| Pennebaker, Donn Alan | interviewed by Willard Van Dyke | 7/25/74 |
| Rodakiewicz, Henwar | interviewed by Willard Van Dyke | 8/8/74 |
| Steiner, Ralph | interviewed by James Blue | 7/12/73 |
| Stoney, George | interviewed by James Blue | 6/28/73 |
| Van Dyke, Willard | interviewed by James Blue | 8/2/73 |

## Other Related Materials

| | | |
|---|---|---|
| Bartlett, Scott | interviewed by Gerald O'Grady | |
| Brakhage, Stan | "Three Film Aesthetics" Lecture | Spring 1973 |
| | lectures at Hampshire College | Summer 1972 |
| Clarke, Shirley | interviewed by Gerald O'Grady | 5/18/73 |
| Dewitt, Tom | interviewed by Gerald O'Grady | 4/28/73 |
| Emshwiller, Ed | on "Dance Chromatic" on "Film with Three Dancers" | 4/2/73 |

Resources for the Oral History of the Independent American Film at Media Study/Buffalo, New York

|  |  |  |
|---|---|---|
|  | on "Relativity" interviewed by Gerald O'Grady |  |
| Frampton, Hollis | "Three Film Aesthetics" Lecture | Spring 1973 |
| Gerson, Barry | film show<br>film show | 4/30/73<br>8/23/73 |
| Jost, Jon | class discussion and film show | 5/7/73 |
| Kubelka, Peter | "Three Film Aesthetics" Lecture<br>interviewed on WADV and<br>WBFO radio | Spring 1973<br>2/25/73<br>3/11/73 |
| Landow, George | film show | 4/8/74 |
| Paik, Nam June | interviewed by Gerald O'Grady |  |
| Schneemann, Carolee | class discussion and film show | 4/23/73 |
| Smith, Jack | interviewed by Ira Sandler | 1/18/73 |
| Vanderbeek, Stan | interviewed by John Minkowsky<br>interviewed by Gerald O'Grady | 7/5/73 |
| Vasulka, Steina and Woody | interviewed by Gerald O'Grady |  |

In addition to these tapes, the archive contains materials presented at, and related to, several conferences held in Buffalo on topics related to the independent film and video, particularly the March, 1973 conference on Autobiography in the Independent Cinema and the December, 1973 conference, "Seminar in Teaching Making."

Steven Kovács

# Surrealist Cinema:
# A Selected Bibliography

*À Nous La Liberté* and *Entr'acte*, films by René Clair. Classic Film Scripts. New York, 1970.

Acerete, Julio C., et al. *Pour Buñuel.* Paris, 1962.

Achard, Paul. "Picabia m'a dit," *L'Action*, January 1, 1925, p. 4.

Adhémar, Jean and Julien Cain. *Man Ray, L'Exposition de l'oeuvre photographique à la Bibliothèque Nationale.* Paris, 1962.

*L'Âge D'or* and *Un Chien Andalou*, films by Luis Buñuel. Classic Film Scripts. New York, 1968.

Albert-Birot, Pierre. *Cinéma, poèmes et drames dans l'espace.* Paris, 1920.

———. "Du cinéma," *SIC*, Nos. 49-50 (October 15-30, 1919).

———. "Interview Albert-Birot—Apollinaire," *SIC*, Nos. 8-9-10 (August-October 1915).

Alquié, Ferdinand, ed. *Entretiens sur le surréalisme.* Paris, 1968.

———. *Philosophie du surréalisme.* Paris, 1955.

Amberg, George. "The Rationale of the Irrational," *The Minnesota Review*, III, No. 3 (Spring 1963), pp. 323-347.

Apollinaire, Guillaume. "L'amphion faux-messie ou histoires et aventures du baron d'Ormesan," *L'Hérésiarque et cie*. Paris, 1910.

———. "Avant le cinéma," *Nord-Sud*, No. 2 (April 15, 1917).

———. *L'Esprit nouveau et les poètes*. Paris, 1946.

———. *Les Mamelles de Tirésias*. Paris, 1918.

———. in *Paris-Journal*, July 15, 1914.

——— and André Billy. "La Bréhatine, cinéma-drame," *Archives des lettres modernes*, No. 126 (1971).

"Appel à la curiosité," *Le Théâtre et Comoedia Illustré*, March 1923.

Aragon, Louis. *Anicet ou le panorama*. Paris, 1964.

———. "Beautés de la guerre et leurs reflets dans la littérature," *Europe*, December 1935, p. 474.

———. "Charlot mystique," *Nord-Sud*, No. 15 (May 1918).

———. "Charlot sentimental," *Le Film*, March 18, 1918.

———. "Le croiseur *Potemkine*," *Clarté*, V, No. 4 (October-December 1926).

———. "Du décor," *Le Film*, September 16, 1918.

———. *Vampires*. Unpublished MS. 7206-10 of the Bibliothèque Littéraire Jacques Doucet, Paris. Partially quoted by Roger Garaudy, *L'Itinéraire d'Aragon*, Paris, 1961.

——— and André Breton. "Le Trésor des Jésuites," *Variétés* (June 1929), pp. 47-61.

Aranda, J. Francisco. *Luis Buñuel, biografía crítica*. Barcelona, 1969.

———. "Surrealist and Spanish Giant," *Films and Filming*, October-November 1961.

Artaud, Antonin. *Oeuvres complètes d'Antonin Artaud*. 7 vols. Paris: Gallimard, 1956-1967. Volume III contains Artaud's writing on the cinema.

*L'Avant-scène du cinéma*, Nos. 27-28 (June 15-July 15, 1963).

*L'Avant-scène du cinéma*, No. 86 (November 1968).

Bataille, Georges. "Le 'Jeu Lugubre,'" *Documents*, No. 7. p. 372.

Belz, Carl. "The Film Poetry of Man Ray," *Criticism* (Spring 1965), pp. 117-130.

Berger, Pierre. *Robert Desnos*. Paris, 1970.

Bosquet, Alain. *Entretiens avec Salvador Dalí*. Paris, 1966.

Bourgeade, Pierre. *Bonsoir Man Ray*. Paris, 1972.

Breton, André. *L'Amour fou*. Paris, 1937.

——. *Arcane 17*. Paris, 1947.

——. "Comme dans un bois," *L'Age du cinéma*, Nos. 4-5 (August-November 1951).

——. *Entretiens*. Paris, 1952.

——. *Manifestes du surréalisme*. Paris, 1971.

——. *Nadja*. Paris, 1949.

——. *Les Pas perdus*. Paris, 1924.

——. *Position politique du surréalisme*. Paris, 1971.

——. *Les Vases communicants*. Paris, 1955.

Buache, Freddy. *Luis Buñuel*. Lausanne, 1970.

Buñuel, Luis. "Metropolis," *Gaceta Literaria*. Madrid, 1927. Reprinted in "Luis Buñuel: Textes 1927-1928," *Cahiers du cinéma*, No. 223 (August-September 1970).

——. "Poésie et cinéma," trans. Michèle Firk and Manuel Michel, *Cinéma 59*, No. 37 (June 1959).

——. "*Un chien andalou*," *La Révolution surréaliste*, No. 12 (December 15, 1929).

——. "Une girafe," *Le Surréalisme au service de la révolution*, No. 6 (May 15, 1933).

——. Unpublished notes of the Columbia University Extension Film Study course, Museum of Modern Art, New York, April 10, 1940.

## Surrealist Cinema: A Selected Bibliography

Buñuel-Garcia, Conchita. "Mon frère Luis," trans. Marcel Oms, *Positif*, No. 42 (November 1961), pp. 19-25.

*Les Cahiers du mois*, "Cinéma," Nos. 16-17 (1925).

Camfield, William A. *Francis Picabia*. New York, 1970. (Catalog of the Solomon R. Guggenheim Museum.)

Canudo, Ricciotto. "Manifeste des sept arts," *L'Usine aux images*. Paris, 1927.

Clair, René. *Adams*. Paris, 1926.

——. *Cinéma d'hier, cinéma d'aujourd'hui*. Paris, 1970.

Crevel, René. "*Drame de cinéma*, par Louis Delluc," *La Revue Européenne*, No. 3 (May 1, 1923), pp. 109-110.

—— and Paul Éluard. "Un film commercial," *Le Surréalisme au service de la révolution*, No. 4 (December 1931), p. 29.

Dalí, Ana Maria. *Salvador Dalí vu par sa soeur*, trans. Jean Martin. Paris, 1960.

Dalí, Salvador. *L'Amour et la mémoire*. Paris, 1931.

——. "L'Ane pourri," *Le Surréalisme au service de la révolution*, No. 1 (July 1930), pp. 9-12.

——. *Babaouo*. Paris, 1932.

——. *Journal d'un génie*. Paris, 1964.

——. "Mes secrets cinématographiques," *La Parisienne*, February 1954, pp. 165-168.

——. *Le mythe tragique de l'Angélus de Millet*. Paris, 1963.

——. *Les passions selons Dalí*. Paris, 1968.

——. *The Secret Life of Salvador Dalí*, trans. Haakon M. Chevalier. London, 1948.

Daven, André-L. "*Entr'acte*," *Comoedia*, October 31, 1924.

De Maré, Rolf. "A propos de *Relâche*," *Comoedia*, November 27, 1924.

Delluc, Louis. *Charlot*. Paris, 1921.

——. *Cinéma et cie*. Paris, 1919.

——. *Photogénie*. Paris, 1920.

Demaitre, Ann. "The Theatre of Cruelty and Alchemy," *Journal of the History of Ideas*, XXXIII, No. 2 (April-June 1972), pp. 237-250.

Dermée, Paul. *Films*. Paris, 1919.

Desnos, Robert. *Cinéma*, ed. André Tchernia. Paris, 1966.

———. "Confession d'un enfant du siècle, I," *La Révolution surréaliste*, No. 6 (March 1926), pp. 18-20.

———. "Confession d'un enfant du siècle, II," *La Révolution surréaliste*, No. 8 (December 1, 1926), pp. 21-22.

———. *De l'erotisme, considéré dans ses manifestations écrites et du point de vue de l'esprit moderne*. Paris, 1953.

———. "Description d'une révolte prochaine," *La Révolution surréaliste*, No. 3 (April 1925), pp. 25-27.

———. "Imagerie moderne," *Documents*, No. 7 (1929), pp. 377-378.

———. "Journal d'une apparition," *La Révolution surréaliste*, Nos. 9-10 (October 1, 1927), pp. 9-11.

———. "Le Mystère d'Abraham juif," *Documents*, No. 5 (1929), p. 237.

———. "Pygmalion et le sphinx," *Documents*, II, No. 1 (1930), pp. 33-38.

———. "La Rédaction publicitaire radiophonique," *Publicité 1939*, 1939, pp. 43-44.

Desnos, Youki. *Les Confidences de Youki*. Paris, 1957.

Doniol-Valcroze, Jacques and André Bazin. "Entretien avec Luis Buñuel," *Cahiers du cinéma*, No. 36 (June 1954), p. 6.

Durgnat, Raymond. *Luis Buñuel*. Berkeley, 1970.

Éluard, Paul and Benjamin Péret. *152 proverbes mis au goût du jour*. Paris, 1925.

*Études cinématographiques*, Nos. 20-21 (1962). Issue "Luis Buñuel."

———, Nos. 22-23 (1963). Issue "Luis Buñuel."

———, Nos. 38-39 (Spring 1965). Issue "Surréalisme au cinéma."

*Europe*, "Desnos," Nos. 517-518 (May-June 1972).

Faure-Favier, Lucie. "Ceux que mes yeux ont vu ...," *Le Film*, November 19, 1918.

*Le Film*, ed. Louis Delluc, 1917-1918, especially his columns "Notes pour moi."

Freud, Sigmund. *The Basic Writings of Sigmund Freud*, ed. and trans. Dr. A. A. Brill. New York, 1938.

Fuentes, Carlos. "The Discreet Charm of Luis Buñuel," *The New York Times Magazine*, March 11, 1973.

Gauthier, Guy. "Le petit Buñuel illustré," *Image et son*, No. 157 (December 1962).

Gauthier, Xavière. *Surréalisme et sexualité*. Paris, 1971.

Goudal, Jean. "Surréalisme et cinéma," *La Revue hébdomadaire*, XXXIV, No. 8 (February 21, 1925).

"Hands off Love!," *La Révolution surréaliste*, Nos. 9-10 (October 1, 1927), pp. 34-37.

Jacob, Max. *Cinématoma*. Paris, 1920.

———. "Printemps et cinématographe mêlés," *Les Soirées de Paris*, No. 23 (April 15, 1914).

———. "Théâtre et cinéma," *Nord-Súd*, No. 12 (February 1918).

Kanesaka, Kenji. "A visit to Luis Buñuel." *Film Culture*, No. 41 (Summer 1966), pp. 60-67.

Knapp, Bettina L. *Antonin Artaud, Man of Vision*. New York, 1969.

Kovács, Steven. "Man Ray as Filmmaker," *Artforum*, November-December 1972.

Kyrou, Ado. *Luis Buñuel*. Paris, 1962.

———. *Le surréalisme au cinéma*. Paris, 1965.

Léger, Fernand. In *Chroniques du jour*, "Spécial Charlot" Nos. 7-8 (December 1926).

*Littérature*, 1919-1924 (Old and new series).

Man Ray. *Self-Portrait*. Boston/London, 1963.

*Man Ray à la Librairie Six*. Paris, 1921.

Man Ray Retrospective of the Los Angeles County Museum of Art. Los Angeles, 1966.

Matthews, J. H. *Surrealism and Film*. Ann Arbor, 1971.

Mitry, Jean. *René Clair*. Paris, 1960.

Mondragon. "Comment j'ai compris *Un Chien Andalou*," *Ciné-Club*, Nos. 8-9 (May-June 1959).

Moussinac, Léon. "Guerre," *L'Humanité*, December 14, 1930.

Nadeau, Maurice. *Histoire du surréalisme*. 2 vols. Paris, 1964.

Péret, Benjamin. *Anthologie de l'amour sublime*. Paris, 1956.

———. "L'escalier aux cent marches," *De derrière les fagots*. Paris, 1934.

———. "Pulchérie veut une auto (film)," *Littérature*, New series No. 10 (May 1, 1923).

Peyre, Henri. "The Significance of Surrealism," *Yale French Studies*, I, No. 2 (Fall-Winter 1948), pp. 34-49. Reprinted in *Yale French Studies*, XXXI (May 1964), pp. 23-36.

Piazza, Francois. "Considérations sur le *Chien Andalou* de Luis Buñuel et Salvador Dalí," *Psyché*, Nos. 27-28 (January-February 1949), pp. 147-156.

*Picabia Dossiers*. Bibliothèque Littéraire Jacques Doucet, Paris.

Picabia, Francis. "*Entr'acte*," *Orbes*, No. 3 (Spring 1932), pp. 131-132.

———. "*Entr'acte*," *This Quarter* (Monaco), I, No. 3 (1927), pp. 301-302.

———. "Instantanéisme," *Comoedia*, November 21, 1924, p. 4.

———. *Jésus-Christ rastaquouère*. Paris, 1920.

———. *La Loi d'accommodation chez les borgnes*. Paris, 1928.

———. *Poèmes et dessins de la fille née sans mère*. Lausanne, 1918.

———. "Première heure," *Mouvement accélérée*. November 1924.

———. "Relâche," *La Revue hébdomadaire*, December 27, 1924.

———. *Réveil-Matin*. Paris, 1954.

Pierre-Bodin, Richard. "Lettre ouverte à M. Paul Ginisty, Président de la Censure," *Le Figaro*, December 7, 1930.

Rebolledo, Carlos. *Luis Buñuel.* Paris, 1964.

Reverdy, Pierre. "Cinématographe," *Nord-Sud,* No. 16 (October 1918).

*La Révolution surréaliste.* 1924-1929.

Riera, Emilio Garcia. "The Eternal Rebellion of Luis Buñuel," trans. Jack Bolanos, *Film Culture,* No. 21 (Summer 1960).

Sadoul, Georges. *Le cinéma français.* Paris, 1962.

Sanouillet, Michel. *Dada à Paris.* Paris, 1965.

———. *Francis Picabia et "391."* 2 vols. Paris, 1960.

———. *Picabia.* Paris, 1964.

Sanvoisin, Gaëtan. "Pour la fin d'un scandale," *Le Figaro,* December 10, 1930.

*SIC,* special memorial edition honoring Apollinaire, Nos. 37-39 (January and February 15, 1919).

*Simoun,* "Robert Desnos," Nos. 22-25 (1956).

Soby, James Thrall, ed. *Man Ray/Photographies/1920-1934.* Paris/New York, 1934.

*Les Soirées de Paris,* 1913-1914, especially Maurice Raynal's column "Chronique cinématographique."

Soupault, Philippe. *Charlot.* Paris, 1957.

———. "Le Coeur volé" in Freddy Buache, ed., *Hommage à Jean Vigo,* Lausanne, 1962, pp. 29-38.

———. Film reviews in *L'Europe nouvelle,* a weekly column from the end of 1929 through 1932; in *Littérature,* 1919-1922; in *La Revue des vivants,* October 1931; in *Revue du cinéma,* February and December 1928, March, April and November 1931.

———. *Guillaume Apollinaire.* Marseille, 1957.

———. "Guillaume Apollinaire," *La Revue Européenne,* January 1, 1926, pp. 1-10.

———. Introduction to Guillaume Apollinaire, *Les Épingles,* Paris, 1928.

———. "Note 1 sur le cinéma," *SIC,* No. 25 (January 1918).

———. "Photographies animées," *SIC,* October-November 1918.

———. "Le vogue des films policiers—*La Maison de la flèche*," *L'Europe nouvelle*, January 31, 1931.

Stauffacher, Frank, ed. *Art in Cinema*. San Francisco, 1947.

*Surréalisme*, ed. Ivan Goll, October 1924, especially "Manifeste du surréalisme" and "Exemple du surréalisme: le cinéma." *Le Surréalisme au service de la révolution*. 1930-1933.

Tariol, Marcel. *Louis Delluc*. Paris, 1965.

Trébouta, Jacques. *Luis Buñuel, sa vie, son oeuvre en Espagne et en France*. Unpublished dissertation, Institut des Hautes Études Cinématographiques. Paris, 1958-1959.

Truffaut, François. "Rencontre avec Luis Buñuel," *Arts*, July 25, 1955, p. 5.

Tyler, Parker. *Classics of the Foreign Film*. London, 1962.

Tzara, Tristan. *Cinéma calendrier du coeur abstrait*. Paris, 1920.

Vaché, Jacque. *Les Lettres de guerre*. Paris, 1949.

Vigo, Jean. "Vers un cinéma social," *Positif*, No. 7 (May 1953).

Virmaux, Alain. "Artaud and Film," trans. Simone Sanzenbach, *Tulane Drama Review*, II, No. 1 (Fall 1966), pp. 154-165.

———. "La Bréhatine et le cinéma: Apollinaire en quête d'un langage neuf," *Archives des lettres modernes*, No. 126 (1971).

Vitrac, Roger. "Photographies animées," *Aventure*, No. 2 (December 1921).

Vovelle, José. "Magritte et le cinéma," *Cahiers de l'association pour l'étude de dada et surréalisme*, No. 4 (1970), pp. 103-113.

Betty L. Corwin

# Theatre on Film and Tape[1]

The final birth pang for the Theatre on Film and Tape Collection came at two a.m. on February 26, 1974 when Liza Minnelli took her final bow after a benefit midnight performance at the Winter Garden Theatre. The curtain was raised once more. Liza, after being presented with a special award by Clive Barnes, gave him a great bear hug and announced: "I'm about to make a little piece of history. This is probably the first time that a performer has ever kissed a critic!"

That gesture was captured for posterity on videotape. For theatre researchers, history was made in a much more significant way that night. It was the first time in America's theatre history that a Broadway production had been visually recorded during performance, not for television, not for motion pictures, not, in fact, for entertainment or for any commercial use whatsoever, but solely and specifically for theatre research purposes. A breakthrough had been made, and a new page in theatre documentation had been opened.

It happened at last because, like all historical developments, the time was ripe. The advent of videotape as well as low-light-level motion picture film had made it possible. In addition to the archival material already held in the Theatre Collection of The New York Public Library at Lincoln Center another dimension could now be added to theatre documentation: visually preserving the live production itself.

Lillian Gish, on the day of the dedication of the Katherine Cornell-Guthrie McClintic Reading Room at the Library in April, 1974 commented that it was "tragic" that Miss Cornell had never had a performance preserved on film. No one knows better than researchers how filmed records of great stars breathe life into the archives of the theatre. Excerpts from films by Duse and Bernhardt give testimony to that. Miss Bernhardt herself is reported to have said: "I rely on these films to make me immortal."

Motion pictures in which legendary figures of the theatre have performed are now precious and vital records: a performance by the Abbey Theatre Players in O'Casey's *Juno and the Paycock* directed by Alfred Hitchcock in 1930, transferred bodily from stage to screen; John Barrymore's *Hamlet*, partially preserved in the form of a screen test for a planned but unrealized production.

Today we see scenes from plays and musicals recreated for television; frequently whole productions are transferred, albeit transformed, for the television medium. Eli Landau has made an effort to bring great plays to the silver screen through the American Film Theatre. But, as drama critic John Simon said in reviewing the Landau series, "A screen adaptation, even by the playwright himself, is always a compromise, and in art, as in love, no compromise is possible. One thing we can do," he says, "is to film a renowned production exactly as it happened on stage, preserving a record of some great performances, staging, and design. This ... provides present and future students of theatre with an invaluable document."

Through the years there has been much talk and some action, but little success in establishing an American archive of filmed theatre. As early as 1911 when Charles Frohman made phonographic and motion picture records of

Ethel Barrymore in *Trelawney of the Wells*, he said: "We've no idea how the old tragedies and comedies of Shakespeare and Molière were presented and we would give thousands to know.... My idea is to keep phonograph and moving picture records of my plays for my own use, just the way I keep the bound manuscripts. Then when I have done with them and they have become historically valuable, to turn them over to libraries and museums."

No known records indicate what happened to Frohman's idea, but now, sixty years later, how much richer our theatrical heritage would be had his plan been carried out.

The ultimate record of the actual production, in full performance, has never been systematically preserved in the United States until now. As far as is known, the only other system in existence is the Theatre Klank in Beeld, (Sound and Image) in Amsterdam, an archive of films and videotapes solely concerning the theatre. Every worthwhile theatrical production is filmed and is available for rent for educational purposes.[2]

Previous attempts at recording live productions in this country faced two large stumbling blocks: resistance from theatrical guilds and unions and lack of funds. We perceived the solution to these two problems as intertwined. Our solution was to get the unions to permit us to film or videotape during performance, and to pay no one unless extra work was done for our benefit.

One by one, The New York Public Library won union confidence and approval. We calmed their fears of private gain from commercial interests without benefit to union members. We assured them that their creative efforts would be protected against piracy. We convinced them that historical preservation of today's theatre is beneficial to their interests and that a non-profit, publicly-available and prestigious institution such as The New York Public Library is the appropriate place for such preservation. Finally, an agreement was signed and the groundwork laid.

Our next step was to secure financial assistance. With the Library struggling to continue existing services, a new project could not be added to its budget. Money was raised from individuals and some small foundations and, as of October, 1974, Theatre on Film and Tape received a grant from the National Endowment for the Arts. This guaranteed the preservation of more than a dozen productions for that theatrical year. Eventually we plan to record enough Broadway, off-Broadway and off-off Broadway, as well as out-of-town shows to have a rich representation of each theatrical season.

Numerous benefits are reaped from filmed performances, which are capable of disclosing qualities not found in other sources of research. Just a brief segment of Ben Vereen's dancing in *Pippin* demonstrates the performer's distinctive style; one can study Long Wharf director Arvin Brown's approach to O'Neill's classic *Long Day's Journey Into Night*. Perhaps a comparative interpretation by another director will be available in the future. The development of John-Michael Tebelak and Stephen Schwartz, the writer-director and composer of *Godspell*, can be followed as their careers progress. The imaginative sets by Boris Aronson in the musical *Company* can be viewed in use.

Nuance and style, notoriously difficult to document, have been captured in the catlike movements of Elizabeth Ashley's Maggie in *Cat on a Hot Tin Roof*, and in the ingenuity of Al Carmines in his production of *The Journey of Snow White*. We experience the powerful impact of the performances of former convicts in *Short Eyes* as well as the emotional pitch of that drama. The pace, rhythm and magnetism of a performer like Liza Minnelli come to life before our eyes. No other method of documentation catches the joyousness, vitality and exuberant audience reaction of *Godspell*, the spontaneity of Street Theatre, the silent effectiveness of Claude Kipnis' pantomime, or the virtuosity of Bil Baird's Marionettes—all of which the Collection has preserved.

Our professional staff sees virtually everything in the New York area. We keep well informed of developments and have wide-ranging catholic tastes. Our feeling is that almost every production has something to recommend it. Even the "flops" tell something of the state of the theatre or reflect society at a given time.

In making our choices, the important factors we weigh include the following:
1. outstanding quality of whatever kind: writing, acting, directing, scenic and costume design. We must even eventually consider the length of the run,
2. qualities of uniqueness which may lead to eventual historical importance,
3. a balance among types and styles of theatre,
4. special production features such as unusual staging, cast changes, revivals,
5. mime and choreography, which lend themselves poorly to other means of documentation,
6. special attractions representing theatrical traditions of other countries,
7. efforts of major figures even when less than successful,
8. further documenting the careers of artists who have already deposited their archives in the New York Public Library Theatre Collection, such as Helen Hayes, Maurice Evans and Edward Albee.

Theatre on Film and Tape, even at this early stage, is growing into a significant archive. At present the collection contains 129 reels of 67 hours of films and videotapes for theatrical productions, dialogues and special events. The tapes and films are not meant to be entertaining or aesthetically satisfying. We shoot without dissolves, fades or other sophisticated techniques. The result is a simple study print of all that transpires on the stage.

Requests to see films and tapes are increasing as word of their existence gets around. Although the unions place a two to five year restriction on playback, much of the collection is currently available for viewing. It is limited, however, to the Library and Museum of the Performing Arts at Lincoln Center and no copies can be made for other libraries or institutions. Our present facilities accommodate a single viewer or a small group at one showing.

Viewing samples of our videotapes one sees that our tapes *do* have flaws. Faced with the unpredictable hazards of filming during performance, we cope with dim stage lighting, sound and visual distractions, and cameras placed so as not to distract the audience. We are also prey to unforseen mechanical difficulties. The subway shook beneath us while taping *Golden Bat*, the theatre's air-conditioning hummed during *Long Day's Journey Into Night*. *Liza* had to be taped twice because of a blown fuse.

At the beginning, Actors' Equity required that we use only one camera and that everyone on stage be on camera at all times. This resulted in jerky camera work and inadequate coverage of important scenes that cried out for close-ups. Our plea to Equity was strengthened by an appeal from Harold Prince. He called the one-camera technique "self-defeating" when we taped *Company*. This led the union to permit the use of two cameras and selected close-ups.

Aware of our problems, we continue to work on improving our techniques. Despite an occasional compromise in quality we feel that the films will be redeemed in the future by the wonder of seeing a legendary figure or a past theatre period come alive.

Quite by chance the project has become an important resource for any study of Samuel Beckett. In addition to *Waiting for Godot* and *MacGowran in the Works of Beckett*, we videotaped two significant dialogues; one, between Alan Schneider, noted for his direction of Beckett's plays, and critic John Lahr, whose father was hailed for his performance in *Waiting for Godot*; the other between actor Jack MacGowran, considered the foremost interpreter of Beckett's work, and Edward Albee, who claims Beckett as an inspiration. They both knew him and they just talked personally, intimately, revealingly about Samuel Beckett, the man, rather than the playwright. They agreed with Beckett that his work speaks for itself.

I remember the evening we taped *MacGowran in the Works of Beckett*. He asked whether our equipment was quiet, explaining that Beckett's silences were as eloquent as his words. The record of MacGowran's performance reflects those silences.

Two years later Jack MacGowran was dead. In a moving eulogy, Joseph Papp said: "We'll never forget the small, frail figure of the man, skull shaven, standing in a long, frayed coat on a stage surrounded by a cosmic set—shuffling, scratching, mumbling—then in a rich beautiful voice, resonant and unlikely in that tiny source, his words penetrated our lives—the words of his friend, Sam Beckett." It is heartening to have preserved that treasured performance for posterity.

In addition to those concerning Beckett, other lively and provocative dialogues between renowned figures in the American theatre have been videotaped. Geraldine Fitzgerald and Arvin Brown talked of the revival of *Long Day's Journey Into Night*; Claude Kipnis, the pantomimist, and Dore Schary discussed the art of mime; two of America's most outstanding puppeteers, Bil Baird and Jim Henson, spoke of their art.

The Stanley Prager Memorial Collection centers on similar conversations related to comedy and musicals—dialogues with Richard Rodgers, Neil Simon, Liza Minnelli, George Abbott, Garson Kanin and other outstanding personalities.

Many of these creative people, talented, productive, thoughtful, often have not had the time nor been disposed to write. The dialogues capture their thought, voices, speech patterns, face and body movements, personalities and style—plus other qualities never conveyed by the printed word or still photographs. Exposure to Liza Minnelli's glow, Lotte Lenya's charm, Garson Kanin's articulateness or Neil Simon's impromptu wit cannot help but broaden the dimension of a researcher's understanding.

In a further attempt to recapture a little of the past we would like to film readings by major performers in roles for which they are famous.

Our plans include preserving examples of regional theatre, street theatre, social, protest and labor drama which has never received much documentation.

Intrigued with the idea of documenting the genesis of a production, we recently videotaped the growing pains of the pre-production phases of the musical version of *Tobacco Road* in a pre-New York tryout.

Another task involves locating lost filmed treasures of the

past. Recently Paul Myers, the curator of the Theatre Collection at the Lincoln Center Library, and I had an extraordinary experience of *déjà vu*, looking at a half-hour of nostalgic film snippets of Rodgers and Hart musicals. Neither of us dreamed we would ever again see George M. Cohan bound across the stage in that inimitable style of his in *I'd Rather Be Right*, or Vivienne Segal seducing Harold Lang in *Pal Joey*, or Ray Bolger dancing in *By Jupiter*. These treasures were given as a gift to the Theatre Collection. Seeing these films, limited and fragmentary as they are, confirmed our conviction that even technically imperfect documentation is of enormous value.

The future may bring a revolution in home entertainment which will find us sitting in our living rooms watching a favorite theatrical production on our own videotape recorders just as we listen to a sound recording today. Henry Fonda's stage performance of *Clarence Darrow*, presented in condensed form on television last September, is an example of a taped play as it might be packaged and distributed for personal, school or library use—a lesson in history as well as drama. In the event of such documentation under commercial aegis, the Library's project would convert to one of acquisition of these tapes or films and to filling in whatever gaps will exist in the coverage. Even now, the Time-Life Video Library and the Learning Corporation of America list a number of theatre-related films and tapes for rent or sale. Our goal will continue to be that of providing the most extensive documentation possible for our users, through whatever sources are available.

The essence of theatre is that it is alive—that it is a shared experience between actor and audience for which there is no substitute. Even the Theatre on Film and Tape Collection cannot recreate the magical ambience of a live performance. It can, however, bring us a significant step closer to that experience, and it can provide a valuable new tool for theatre researchers of tomorrow. As Frohman said more than a half century ago: "Think of the inestimable service filmed archives will be to managers and lovers of the drama a thousand or two thousand years hence. Certainly we owe it not only to the great artists of this profession, but also to those who come after us."

In the following list of holdings the designations "P" indicates a purchase, "G" indicates a gift.

# The Theatre on Film and Tape Collection List of Holdings

### Stage Productions and Special Events

*Golden Bat* by Yutaka Higashi, Japanese rock-musical, videotaped at Sheridan Square Playhouse on October 27 and November 12, 1970. Our first videotaping and a real challenge because of the unusual staging, low light levels, and sound considerations.

*Spoon River Anthology* by Edgar Lee Masters, adapted and arranged by Charles Aidman. Produced and donated by the Snarks, Ltd., an amateur acting group. Taped on December 13, 1970. Not a professional presentation, but a welcome record of a respected work.

*MacGowran in the Works of Beckett,* adapted by Jack MacGowran with the advice of Samuel Beckett, was taped at the New York Shakespeare Festival Public Theatre on January 19, 1971. A fine record with minor technical problems (ghosting) but a valuable document of an extraordinary interpreter in selections from one of the foremost playwrights of today.

*The Rivals* by Richard Brinsley Sheridan, this version by Harry O. Uher. Produced and donated by the Amateur Comedy Club on February 15, 1971 at the Club House. The Collection's first tape of a classic work.

*Waiting for Godot* by Samuel Beckett was taped on February 23, 1971 at the Sheridan Square Playhouse. This new version of the play, directed by Alan Schneider, provides a good record of this modern classic and enlarges our documentation of Samuel Beckett's work.

*The Trial of the Catonsville Nine* by Daniel Berrigan, S.J., was taped on March 4, 1971 at the Good Shepherd-Faith Church. It represents the Collection's first production by the Phoenix Theatre and is a drama of special historical as well as theatrical importance.

*The Journey of Snow White*, a new work written and composed by Al Carmines, also produced and donated by Mr. Carmines. It was taped at the Judson Memorial Church on March 18, 1971, and unlike the productions taped by the Library which are restricted by union agreement, was done with 3 cameras. Despite its deviation from our required standards for the Collection, it is a welcome contribution as an example of the work of this contemporary talent. (G)

*Now is the Time for All Good Men*, book and lyrics by Gretchen Cryer and music by Nancy Ford, was taped at the Equity Library Theatre on March 14, 1971. Our first tape of an Equity Library Theatre production and an opportunity to capture a revival of the first work of a pair of talented collaborators who have since gone on to write another successful musical.

*The House of Blue Leaves* by John Guare, was taped at the Truck and Warehouse Theatre on June 15, 1971. The author, considered to be one of our most promising playwrights, won the New York Drama Critics Circle Award for 1970-71 for *The House of Blue Leaves* as the best American play and the Obie Award for an earlier play in 1968.

*Long Day's Journey into Night*, a revival of the Eugene O'Neill classic starring Geraldine Fitzgerald and Robert Ryan, was taped at the Promenade Theatre on July 8, 1971. Considered by many to be the greatest of American plays, this production was unanimously hailed by the drama critics and referred to by Clive Barnes of *The New York Times* as "one of the glorious highlights of many a season."

*Claude Kipnis Mime Theatre* presenting "Imaginings" was videotaped on December 16, 1971 at the Provincetown Playhouse in New York. As our first record of mime, which lends itself so poorly to other forms of documentation, the tape of this fine company of pantomimists, in twelve separate scenes created by Claude Kipnis, becomes a valuable addition to the collection.

*Company*, a musical produced and directed by Harold Prince, was videotaped at the National Theatre in Washington, D.C. on May 20, 1972. A polished, sophisticated production, the show ran for 88 weeks in New York, was awarded the New York Drama

Critics Circle Award, the Tony Award as best musical and won Tonys for Harold Prince as director of a musical, for Stephen Sondheim for music and lyrics, for George Furth for the book, and for Boris Aronson for best scenery in a musical. This is a milestone addition to the collection, being the first Broadway show to be preserved, albeit taped from a touring company.

*The Obie Awards 1971-72.* Hosted by Groucho Marx, the 17th Annual Awards for the season's best Off-Broadway productions were presented by *The Village Voice* at the Village Gate on May 8, 1972. Included on the tape are excerpts from the production of *Don't Bother Me, I Can't Cope.* (P)

*Three productions from the Lincoln Center Street Festival 1972, presented on the Plaza at Lincoln Center:*

*Choices*, with book and lyrics by Peter Copani and music by Robert Tuthill and Peter Copani, was presented on August 23, 1972. Produced by the Inwood People's Performing Company Street Theatre Workshop, the rock musical is a campaign against drugs. (P)

*Everyman and Roach*, a play written by Geraldine Fitzgerald and Brother Jonathan, OFS, produced by the Mt. Morris Everyman Theatre Company, New York City, was given on August 27, 1972. This show dealt with the struggle for Everyman to live, achieve success and face death. (G)

*Blind Junky*, a rock musical with book and lyrics by Peter Copani and music by Peter Copani and Robert Tuthill, was presented on August 31, 1972 by the Everyman Company of Brooklyn. With a strong anti-drug point of view, the author presents a cross-section of slum streets, junkies, prostitutes and pushers, and shows their dehumanizing effect on their community. (P)

*Circle in the Square*, an evening of highlights from past productions was videotaped at the Circle in the Square-Joseph E. Levine Theatre on October 26, 1972. With Dustin Hoffman narrating, the program included brief scenes from the following:

*Our Town* by Thornton Wilder (Moses Gunn)
*Grass Harp* by Truman Capote (Patricia Brooks)
*Io Son L'Umile* by Cilea (Patricia Brooks)
*Under Milk Wood* by Dylan Thomas (Donald Davis)
*Desire Under the Elms* by Eugene O'Neill (Colleen Dewhurst and Alan Mixon)
*Othello* by William Shakespeare (James Earl Jones)
*A Moon for the Misbegotten* by Eugene O'Neill (Salome Jens)

*F. Jasmine Adams* by Carson McCullers and G. Wood (Theresa Merritt)
*Ah, Wilderness!* by Eugene O'Neill (Geraldine Fitzgerald and Donald Davis)
*Little Murders* by Jules Feiffer (Vincent Gardenia)

*Play It Again, Sam* by Woody Allen and starring Jack Gilford was taped at the Coachlight Dinner Theatre in East Windsor, Connecticut, on November 17, 1972. With dinner theatre mushrooming all over the country, representation of this popular entertainment form is important to the collection. This particular production was chosen because of its fine performances and high professional quality.

*Much Ado About Nothing.* Joseph Papp's New York Shakespeare Festival production of the Shakespeare comedy was videotaped for television where it was presented on February 2, 1973. The televised version includes the original cast as it appeared on Broadway. (G)

The opening night of the Lincoln Square Community Council Coffee House, "The Pokey" was videotaped on March 22, 1972.

*Liza* at the Winter Garden Theatre was videotaped on January 25, 1974 during a special midnight performance for the Actors' Fund of America. This was the first solo performance taped for the Collection. Liza Minnelli sings old and new songs plus special material written for her by John Kander and Fred Ebb and joins four dancers in dances choreographed by Bob Fosse. The tape also records the presentation by Clive Barnes of an award to Miss Minnelli from the Actors' Fund of America.

*The Yale Repertory Theatre Company.* A documentary production of *The Tempest* was televised on WTNH in Connecticut on December 3, 1973. Alvin Epstein, Associate Artistic Director of the Yale Repertory Theatre, and Jeremy Geidt, who acts in the company and is a professor of acting at the Yale School of Drama, discuss and demonstrate the development of the production. (G)

*Case of Libel* by Henry Denker (20-minute filmed scene as reproduced on the Ed Sullivan TV Show, CBS). This play, which opened in New York on October 13, 1963, was suggested by Louis Nizer's story, "My Life in Court" in which Nizer wrote of representing war correspondent Quentin Reynolds in a libel case against columnist Westbrook Pegler. Members of the cast in this filmed sequence include Van Heflin, Sidney Blackmer and Larry Gates. (G)

*Bil Baird's Marionettes in "Pinocchio"* were taped at the Bil Baird Theater on April 11, 1974. This production demonstrates the work of this outstanding puppeteer and his company in a charming original production. The tape also includes *Bil Baird's Variety*, a selection of puppet virtuosity embodying many styles and types of puppetry.

*Short Eyes* by Miguel Pinero was videotaped on April 12 and 13, 1974. An example of the use of theatre for rehabilitation, the play was started by Mr. Pinero, a former convict, in a drama workshop at Sing Sing. It was produced, after he was paroled, by The Family, a theatre group of former convicts and addicts directed by Marvin Felix Camillo at the Theater of the Riverside Church. Moved by Joseph Papp to the New York Shakespeare Festival Public Theater, the play was presented at the Anspacher Theater with its original cast, made up almost entirely of formers convicts and members of The Family.

*Pippin*—a segment, 1 minute, 45 seconds. Ben Vereen in a dance sequence used as a television commercial. (G)

*Ken Rubenstein Ritualistic Experimental Theatre* was videotaped in rehearsal at the White Barn Theatre in Westport, Conn. on August 10, 1974.

*Godspell,* a rock-folk-vaudeville musical based upon the Gospel According to St. Matthew, was videotaped on August 23, 1974 at the Promenade Theatre. Conceived and directed by John-Michael Tebelak with music and lyrics by Stephen Schwartz, *Godspell* imaginatively portrays Jesus as a clown and brings the Bible to life through mime, magic, song, dance and charade. Recognized for its vitality and joyousness, the production has won several awards and has been playing to capacity audiences for the past three years.

*Stars of the Yiddish Rialto*, an exhibition (Vincent Astor Gallery, The New York Public Library, 1973).

*WPA One-Act Play: Something About Yesterday* by Susan H. Schulman (1972). (G)

*Rodgers and Hart Musicals*—a 16mm film of excerpts from live performances of Rodgers and Hart productions, including

*Jumbo, I Married an Angel, Too Many Girls, By Jupiter, No Strings, I'd Rather Be Right, Pal Joey* and *A Connecticut Yankee*; second reel includes *Allegro* and *Oklahoma*. (G)

*Cat on a Hot Tin Roof*—The American Shakespeare Theatre production of the Tennessee Williams play, directed by Michael Kahn, was filmed on October 23, 1974 at the ANTA Theatre. Hailed by the critics, this production starred Elizabeth Ashley and Keir Dullea.

*Tobacco Road, a Musical Play*—Pre-production conference, backers' audition, some dance auditions, and production conference videotaped in New York and at the Westport Country Playhouse, 1974.

*The Wager*—Videotaped at the Eastside Playhouse on December 14, 1974. A comedy by Mark Medoff, directed by Anthony Perkins, starring Kristoffer Tabori.

*LaMama Experimental Theatre*—Three one-act plays written and directed by Julie Bovasso were videotaped on January 22, 1975. Miss Bovasso acts in two of them. *Schubert's Last Serenade, The Final Analysis, The Super Lover*.

*In Gay Company*—A musical review, a parody of both the homosexual scene and society's attitude toward it, was videotaped at the Little Hippodrome, a dinner theatre, on February 7, 1975.

*Blasts and Bravos: An Evening with H. L. Mencken* was videotaped on February 22, 1975 at the Cherry Lane Theatre. The one-man performance was performed and directed by Paul Shyre.

*Ontological-Hysterical Theater—Pandering to the Masses: A Misrepresentation* was videotaped on April 13, 1975. The play was written, directed and designed by Richard Foreman, considered one of the most inventive of contemporary American playwrights.

*Juno and the Paycock*—The Mark Taper Forum production starring Maureen Stapleton, Jack Lemmon and Walter Matthau and directed by George Seaton was videotaped in December 1974 in a special studio performance. (P)

*Manhattan Theatre Project—Alice in Wonderland*, an experimental "classic" directed by Andre Gregory was videotaped at the New York Shakespeare Festival Public Theatre on April 23, 1975.

Theatre on Film and Tape 55

*Roundabout Theatre Company—James Joyce's Dubliners* by J. W. Riordan, was videotaped at the company's Stage One Theatre on April 30, 1975. Directed by Gene Feist with music and lyrics by Philip Campanella, the play is based on the biography "My Brother's Keeper" by Stanislaus Joyce, the novelist's brother.

*Philemon*—a musical with words by Tom Jones and music by Harvey Schmidt, collaborators of the long-running "The Fantasticks" was videotaped at the Portfolio Theatre on May 17, 1975.

*Equus*—by Peter Shaffer was filmed at the Plymouth Theatre on June 4, 1975. Winner of Tony awards for best play and for John Dexter's direction, the play starred Anthony Hopkins and Peter Firth of the original British production.

*A Chorus Line*—Conceived, choreographed and directed by Michael Bennett with a book by James Kirkwood and Nicholas Dante, music by Marvin Hamlisch and lyrics by Edward Kleban. This production was unanimously acclaimed as an innovative, exciting memorable musical. It was videotaped at the New York Shakespeare Festival Public Theatre on July 12, 1975.

*Candide*—Hugh Wheeler's musical adaptation of Voltaire's novel, produced by the Chelsea Theatre Center of Brooklyn, was filmed at the Broadway Theatre on September 17, 1975. Directed by Harold Prince with a score by Leonard Bernstein, lyrics by Richard Wilbur, Stephen Sondheim and John Latouche, settings by Eugene and Franne Lee and choreography by Patricia Birch. Filmed in color with three cameras (by special permission of Actors' Equity Association) we were able to capture the imaginative environmental concept of the musical as it was played on several stages all around the theatre.

*Pictures in the Hallway*, by Sean O'Casey, adapted by Paul Shyre, was recreated at the Library and videotaped for the Collection as a Memorial to Margaret Webster on October 31, 1975. The dramatic reading, which featured three members of the original 1956 New York production, marked the first time the Library produced and recorded its own production.

*All Over* by Edward Albee was videotaped in a production of the Hartford Stage Company on November 12, 1975. Directed by Paul Weidner, the tape enriches the Collection with the playwright's perceptive but scathing drama about death as performed by a fine resident theatre company.

*Ah, Wilderness!* by Eugene O'Neill was videotaped at the Circle in the Square Theatre on November 20, 1975. This Long Wharf Theatre production of O'Neill's only comedy was brought to New York after a successful run in New Haven. Directed by Arvin Brown, the cast includes Geraldine Fitzgerald, Theresa Wright and members of the Long Wharf resident theatre.

*Charley Chestnut Rides the I.R.T.* by Arthur Sainer was presented at the Theatre for the New City in April, 1975. Directed by Crystal Field, the musical interweaves the use of puppets and actors. (G)

*Two productions at the Mark Taper Forum* in Los Angeles, marking the beginning of repertory theatre for the Center Theatre Group, were videotaped for the collection. Directed by Gordon Davidson, the productions differed widely, demonstrating the stretch of talents of the members of the new ensemble company.

*Two Much Johnson*, written by William Gillette in 1894 and adapted by Burt Shevelove, is a classic American farce complete with chases, duals and pratfalls. It was videotaped on December 13, 1975.

*The Shadow Box*, a new and serious drama by Michael Cristofer, deals with life in the face of death. The play concerns three families facing the terminal illness of one of its members. Three tales, thematically the same, are separated or threaded together on a single set by Robert Zentis with skillful lighting by H. R. Poindexter. Videotaped December 14, 1975.

*The Royal Family* by George S. Kaufman and Edna Ferber, revived at the Helen Hayes Theatre, was filmed on February 18, 1976. A classic comedy of the 1920s satirizing the Barrymore family, the production earned a Tony Award for the director, Ellis Rabb. Featuring highly-praised performances by Mr. Rabb and Rosemary Harris, it also provided us with a rare and treasured opportunity to add a record of a fine performance by Eva LeGallienne to the archives.

*Fragments of a Trilogy. The Trojan Women,* based on the ancient Greek of Euripides and *Electra*, based on the ancient Greek of Sophocles, were presented by the Great Jones Repertory Project and videotaped at LaMama E.T.C. on February 19, 1976. Conceived and directed by Andrei Serban, with music by Elizabeth Swados, these experimental productions are staged in an environmental setting which converts a theatrical space into a public festival; action explodes all around; sounds are of music and a combination of Latin, Greek and an invented theatrical language. The use of a newly-developed low-light-level camera for these often darkly-lit works marked a breakthrough in theatre documentation.

*The Lost Ones* by Samuel Beckett, presented by Mabou Mines and directed by Lee Breuer, was videotaped in the Little Theatre at the New York Shakespeare Festival Public Theatre on March 16, 1976. An unusual experimental production, it is performed in an environment recreating a cylinder: a small, tiered, foam-wall, carpeted room. The audience, provided with binoculars, watches actor David Warrilow move miniature figures about a small model of a set as he describes the cylinder and its population.

*27 Wagons Full of Cotton* by Tennessee Williams and *A Memory of Two Mondays* by Arthur Miller were filmed at the Playhouse on March 20, 1976. As revived by the Phoenix Theatre, these short plays represent early works by the two now-famous playwrights. The films capture the mood and fine ensemble work in both plays as directed by Arvin Brown as well as the emergence of actress Meryl Streep, singled out by critics for her striking performance in *27 Wagons Full of Cotton*. The double-bill presents an interesting contrast of the styles of the two writers.

**Videotaped Dialogues**

1. **Jack MacGowran** and **Edward Albee** talk of Samuel Beckett, whom they both knew. (1971)

2. **John Lahr** and **Alan Schneider** converse about Samuel Beckett and various aspects of the theatre. (1971)

3. **Geraldine Fitzgerald** and **Arvin Brown** discuss the directorial approach to *Long Day's Journey Into Night* and the interpretations of the role of Mary Tyrone. (1971)

4. **Claude Kipnis**, pantomime artist, and **Dore Schary** reflect on mime as a unique art form as well as a vital component of all the performing arts. (1972)

5. **Lotte Lenya** and **George Voskovec** reminisce about the European theatre in the early thirties, Kurt Weill, Berthold Brecht and their own careers. (1972) S.P.*

*The Stanley Prager Memorial Collection

6. **Richard Rodgers** and **Stanley Green** discuss Mr. Rodgers' early years, the influences on his career and his relationships with his collaborators, touching on many of the Broadway musicals and films for which he composed the scores. (1973) S.P.*

7. Street Theatre producers, **Geraldine Fitzgerald, Hazel Bryant, Mical Whitaker** and **Brother Jonathan** talk about the origins of the Street Theatre Festival at Lincoln Center and other aspects of this special form of theatre. (1973)

8. **Joseph Papp**, at Town Hall, discusses his attitudes toward various aspects of contemporary theatre and answers questions from the audience. (1973)

9. **E. Y. Harburg** and **Fred Saidy** converse about Mr. Harburg's early career as a lyricist and musical shows on which the two collaborated. Focus on *Finian's Rainbow* and the difficulties of producing a controversial musical in the 1950s. (1973) S.P.*

10. **Alan Arkin** and **Mel Gussow** discuss various phases of Arkin's career as well as his thoughts on preparing for an acting role, directing for theatre and film, and play doctoring. (1973) S.P.*

11. **Joseph Stein** and **Morton Gottlieb** talk of the role of the book writer, reactions to the musical form, the technique of creating a musical, the development of *Fiddler on the Roof* from idea to reality, and the conversion of the straight play *Enter Laughing* into a musical. (1973) S.P.*

12. **Liza Minnelli, Fred Ebb** and **John Kander.** The dialogue reveals the participants' enormous admiration for each other's talents which, they explain, led to the development of an unusual and successful three-way collaboration. (1974) S.P.*

13. **Neil Simon** interviewed by **Gene Shalit.** They talk of the relationship between playwright and director, how Simon gets ideas for and then develops his plays, the need for good translations of foreign productions, and other thoughts on Simon's past, present and future. (1974) S.P.*

14. **Bil Baird** and **Jim Henson** (creator of the Muppets which appear on the television show "Sesame Street") discuss

people who influenced their careers, various aspects of creating and manipulating puppets, and the appeal of puppetry for children. (1974)

15. **George Abbott** interviewed by **Garson Kanin.** Discussion covers various phases of Mr. Abbott's career and his attitudes toward his work in the American Theatre. (1974) S.P.*

16. **Martin Esslin,** Director of Drama at BBC and an authority on the Theatre of the Absurd, talks with playwright **Israel Horovitz.** (1974) S.P.*

17. **Boris Aronson** and **Garson Kanin** discuss various aspects of Mr. Aronson's fifty years as a stage designer, painter and theatre consultant. (1975) S.P.*

18. **Jerry Bock** and **Sheldon Harnick.** Conversation deals with the origin of their collaboration, how they work together and the several musicals for which they have written the music and lyrics. (1974) S.P.*

19. **Harold Prince** and **Stephen Sondheim** with critic, **Brendan Gill.** Mr. Gill probes their individual careers, their collaborative efforts and their development of an idea into a finished music production. (1975) S.P.*

20. **Lehman Engel** and **Wesley Addy** were associated with Margaret Webster on several productions. They reflect on Miss Webster's wide range of talents as actress, director and lecturer on the theatre, adding insight into her personality as well as her career. (1975) M.W.**

21. **Joe Smith** of the famed vaudeville team of **Smith and Dale,** interviewed by actor **Ted Erwin.** They reminisce about the many years that the comedy pair worked together and re-enact two of the team's most popular sketches, "The Tax Inspector" and "Dr. Kronkhite." In the latter skit Madeline Lee plays the part of the nurse and Jack Gilford is the offstage voice. (1975) S.P.*

22. **Eva LeGallienne,** one of the great actresses of the American Theatre, reminisces with **Josephine Hutchinson** and **Staats Cotsworth** about her outstanding theatrical career

\*\*In memory of Margaret Webster

and her struggle to establish a permanent repertory theatre in the U.S. (1975) M.W.**

23. **Mrs. Sean O'Casey** converses with **Brendan Gill** about her life with the famous Irish author-playwright, as well as about her own careers as actress and writer. (1976)

# Notes

1. Adapted from remarks made in November, 1974 before the American Society for Theatre Research.

2. L. S. Hoefnagels, Director, Theater Klank en Beeld, Herengracht 168, Amsterdam, Holland.

Christopher D. Wheaton and
Richard B. Jewell

# The Cinema Library at the University of Southern California[1]

The Cinema Library of the University of Southern California is housed within Doheny Library on the USC campus. Items of special interest and of value may be found in the Cinema Library under the following general headings: 1) tape-recorded interviews with members of the film fraternity—technicians, producers, writers, agents, actors, directors and publicists; 2) items donated by individuals and organized within more than one hundred special collections, such as the Robert Wise Collection; 3) items donated by motion picture studios and organized as the MGM Collection, the Paramount Research Department Collection, the Twentieth Century-Fox Set Still Collection, and so forth; 4) unpublished screenplays, scenarios and drafts of screenplays for more than 3,000 feature-length motion pictures; 5) a large collection of foreign-language publications relating to motion pictures which were originally deposited in the Farmington Collection; and 6) additional items, such as clipping files, pressbooks, still photographs (filed alphabetically by film title in the Neal Graham Collection), and other such memorabilia. This report will focus only upon the first two of these headings, as descriptions of the holdings under the remaining four would be altogether too lengthy.

A larger and more detailed description of the materials contained in this article, as well as a listing of the library's script materials (cross-referenced by author), may be found in our *Primary Cinema Sources: Index to Screenplays, Interviews, and Special Collections at the University of Southern California* to be published by G. K. Hall & Co., 70 Lincoln St., Boston, Massachusetts 02111.

## Tape-Recorded Interviews

There have been three main sources for the taped interviews which are listed below: Arthur Knight's classes, Sol Lesser's classes and the American Society of Cinematographers.

Arthur Knight, noted critic and author of *The Liveliest Art*, has been recording interviews of producers, writers, directors, performers and executives in his weekly classes at USC since 1961. The format for these interviews occasionally varies, but generally Knight introduces his guest and begins a short discussion with him concerning the movie to be shown that evening. The interview is continued after the screening, many times using the particular film only as a jumping-off point for larger issues. The discussion is soon turned over to the class and the students ask questions of the guest. As is usual in such sessions, the students' questions range from banality to the limits pf perceptivity.

Sol Lesser, the successful film producer of Tarzan epics, among other features, has been teaching a class at USC in Motion Picture Business since 1967. His guests tend to be specialists in the problems of studio operation, production, distribution, exhibition and legal procedures relating to motion pictures. His interview format remains the same as

The Cinema Library at the University of Southern California

Knight's, although no films are shown. Both the Lesser and Knight interviews are at times difficult to interpret, as student questions are often unheard.

The ASC tapes featuring interviews with cameramen were collected by the American Society of Cinematographers and the tapes on file at USC were dubbed from the Society's collection.

Abbreviations used to identify those interviewed:

a—actor, actress
ag—agent
c—cameraman, cinematographer
co—composer
cr—critic
d—director

e—editor
ex—executive
law—lawyer
nov—novelist
p—producer
w—writer, screenwriter

| Catalog number | Name | Date | Interviewer/ Format | Film Shown/ Subject discussed |
|---|---|---|---|---|
| T169 | Aberbach, Hy | 2-25-65 | Knight | *Ensign O'Toole* (TV) |
| T433 | Abrahams, Mort (p) | 2-10-72 | Knight | |
| T386 | Aherne, Brian (a) | 3-17-68 | — | Vivian Leigh Dinner |
| T119 | Aldrich, Robert (d) | 2-21-63 | Knight | *Whatever Happened to Baby Jane* |
| C-2 | Alonzo, John (c) | 4-6-72 | Panel | The Technology of Survival |
| T463 | Alonzo, John (c) | 9-28-72 | Knight | *Sounder* |
| T467 | Alonzo, John (c) | Fall, 72 | Knight | *Lady Sings the Blues* |
| T124 | Altman, Robert (d) | 4-4-63 | Knight | *Combat* (TV) |
| T386 | Anderson, Judith (a) | 4-17-68 | — | Vivian Leigh Dinner |
| T169 | Anderson, Walt | 2-25-65 | Knight | *Ensign O'Toole* (TV) |
| T445-1 | Arkoff, Sam (p) | 3-18-71 | Panel | Film and Finance |
| T407 | Arnold, John | n.d. | ASC | |
| T275 | Astaire, Fred (a) | 2-12-67 | — | Cole Porter Dinner |
| T114 | Axelrod, George (w) | 1963 | Knight | *Manchurian Candidate* |
| C-6 | Axelrod, Jonathan (d) | 4-8-72 | Panel | The Young Film Maker and the Future |
| T162 | Ayers, Jerry (p) | 10-22-64 | Knight | |
| T216 | Ayers, Jerry (p) | 10-20-66 | Knight | |
| T170 | Bach, Richard (nov) | 3-11-65 | Knight | *Avalanche* |
| T425 | Badaracco, Jacob A. | n.d. | ASC | |
| T168 | Baily, John | 2-18-65 | Knight | |
| T408 | Balshofer, Fred J. | n.d. | ASC | |
| T148 | Baron, Allen (d) | 4-2-64 | Knight | *Pie in the Sky* |
| T85 | Barrett, Allan | 9-28-61 | Knight | *Blast of Silence* |
| T41 | Barrett, Rona (columnist) | 1-16-61 | Panel | Hollywood Trade Papers |
| | Barrymore, Ethel (see Colt, Ethel Barrymore) | | | |

# 64  PERFORMING ARTS RESOURCES

| Catalog number | Name | Date | Interviewer/ Format | Film Shown/ Subject discussed |
|---|---|---|---|---|
| T108 | Barsha, Leon (e) | 10-19-62 | Knight | |
| T157 | Barsha, Leon (e) | 5-21-64 | Knight | *Lady in a Cage* |
| T128 | Bartlett, Hall (p) | 5-16-63 | Knight | *The Caretakers* |
| T290 | Bartlett, Hall (p) | 4-10-69 | Knight | *Changes* |
| T388 | Baxter, Frank (a) | 3-23-69 | —— | Helen Keller Dinner |
| T123 | Begley, Ed (a) | 3-28-63 | Knight | *Sweet Bird of Youth* |
| T203 | Benedek, Lazlo (d) | 5-24-66 | Knight | |
| T403 | Bennet, Spencer (d) | n.d. | ASC | |
| T38 | Bergen, Edgar (a) | 10-24-60 | Panel | Comedy |
| T128 | Bergen, Polly (a) | 5-16-63 | Knight | *The Caretakers* |
| T116 | Bernstein, Elmer (co) | 1-63 | Knight | *To Kill A Mockingbird* |
| T468 | Bill, Tony (a) | Fall, 72 | Knight | *Deadhead Miles* |
| T124 | Black, John | 4-4-63 | Knight | *Combat* (TV) |
| T140 | Blaugh, Louis (law) | 1-23-64 | Knight | *Dr. Strangelove* ... |
| T143 | Blaugh, Louis (law) | 2-27-64 | Knight | *Dr. Strangelove* ... |
| T386 | Bloom, Claire (a) | 3-17-68 | —— | Vivian Leigh Dinner |
| T213 | Blumofe, Robert F. (p) | 9-29-66 | Knight | |
| T72 | Bock, Jerry (co) | 5-5-61 | Panel | Musical Comedy |
| T279 | Boetticher, Budd (d) | 1-9-69 | Knight | |
| C-1 | Bogdanovich, Peter (d) | 4-6-68 | Panel | The Art of Survival |
| T263 | Bogdanovich, Peter (d) | 5-3-68 | Knight | *Targets* |
| T297 | Bogdanovich, Peter (d) | 2-28-68 | Panel | Jean-Luc Godard |
| T320 | Bollinger, Henri | 10-22-70 | Knight | *Fools* |
| T318 | Boolootian, R. A., M.D. | 10-12-70 | Lesser | The Medical Film |
| T158 | Bourguignon, Serge (d) | 6-4-64 | Knight | *Sundays and Cybele* |
| T179 | Bourguignon, Serge (d) | 5-6-65 | Knight | |
| T362 | Bowers, William (w-p) | 5-17-71 | Lesser | |
| T88 | Bradbury, Ray (w) | 10-26-61 | Knight | *Moby Dick* |
| T89 | Bradbury, Ray (w) | 11-2-62 | Knight | |
| T90 | Bradbury, Ray (w) | 11-21-63 | Knight | *Moby Dick* |
| T164 | Bradbury, Ray (w) | 11-12-64 | Knight | How Not to be a Snob |
| T182 | Bradbury, Ray (w) | 5-26-65 | Knight | |
| T194 | Bradbury, Ray (w) | 1-20-66 | Knight | *Our Man Flint* |
| T254 | Bradbury, Ray (w) | 12-66 | Knight | |
| T454 | Bradbury, Ray (w) | 5-10-70 | Knight | |
| T337 | Bradbury, Ray (w) | 3-4-71 | Knight | *The Andromeda Strain* |
| T445-3 | Bradbury, Ray (w) | 3-19-71 | Panel | Film Technology and the Audience |
| T313 | Bridges, James (w-d) | 10-1-70 | Knight | *The Baby Maker* |
| T258 | Brodax, Al (p) | 10-19-68 | Knight | *The Yellow Submarine* |
| T85 | Brodie, Mal (w) | 9-28-61 | Knight | *Blast of Silence* |
| T261 | Brooks, Richard (d) | 1-4-67 | Knight | *In Cold Blood* |
| T441 | Brown, Roscoe Lee (a) | Fall, 72 | Knight | *The Cowboys* |
| T360 | Bryant, Baird | 4-1-71 | Knight | *Celebration at Big Sur* |
| T273 | Bryant, Baird | 5-5-67 | Knight | *Vipers* |
| T335 | Buchanan, Larry | 2-25-71 | Knight | *Strawberries Need Rain* |
| T190 | Buchholz, Horst (a) | 11-18-65 | Knight | *That Man From Istanbul* |
| T230 | Burch, Ruth | 12-4-67 | Lesser | |
| T115 | Cacoyannis, Michael (d) | 1-63 | Knight | |

The Cinema Library at the 65
University of Southern California

| Catalog number | Name | Date | Inter-viewer/ Format | Film Shown/ Subject discussed |
|---|---|---|---|---|
| T167 | Cacoyannis, Michael (d) | 1-14-65 | Knight | |
| T458 | Capra, Frank (d) | 10-31-72 | Knight | |
| T479 | Capra, Frank (d) | 4-17-72 | Lecture | |
| T312 | Carr, Alan | 9-24-70 | Knight | *C.C. and Co.* |
| T188 | Case, James (Man. KCET-TV) | 11-4-65 | Knight | |
| T223 | Chamie, Al | 10-9-67 | Lesser | |
| C-5 | Champlin, Charles (cr) | 4-8-72 | Panel | Critics and the Symbiosis of Survival |
| T343 | Champlin, Charles (cr) | 12-14-70 | Lesser | |
| T445-2 | Champlin, Charles (cr) | 3-18-71 | Panel | Film Criticism and the Audience |
| T338 | Champlin, Charles (cr) | 3-4-71 | Mayer | |
| T386 | Champlin, Charles (cr) | 3-17-68 | ——— | Vivian Leigh Dinner |
| T415 | Clarke, Charles G. | n.d. | ASC | |
| T96 | Clayton, Jack (p-d) | 12-14-61 | Knight | *The Innocents* |
| T37 | Colt, Ethel Barrymore (a) | 10-20-60 | Tusher | The Professional Life of Show Girls |
| T41 | Connally, Mike | 1-16-61 | Panel | Hollywood Trade Papers |
| T178 | Cook, Fiedler (d) | 6-65 | Knight | |
| T386 | Cooper, Gladys (a) | 3-17-68 | ——— | Vivian Leigh Dinner |
| T228 | Copeland, Jack | 11-20-67 | Lesser | |
| T257 | Copeland, Jack | 3-4-68 | Lesser | |
| T253 | Copeland, Jack | 1971 | Lesser | |
| T297 | Corman, Roger (d) | 2-28-68 | Panel | Jean-Luc Godard |
| T398 | Cornell, Katherine (a) | n.d. | Francis | *The Miracle Worker*, the stage play |
| T91 | Cortez, Stanley (c) | 11-9-61 | Knight | |
| T177 | Cortez, Stanley (c) | 4-1-65 | Knight | *Naked Kiss* |
| T386 | Cotten, Joseph (a) | 3-17-68 | ——— | Vivian Leigh Dinner |
| T388 | Cotton, Joseph (a) | 3-23-69 | ——— | Helen Keller Dinner |
| T351 | Cox, Judd | 3-29-71 | Lesser | |
| T174 | Cukor, George (d) | 3-18-65 | ——— | Aldous Huxley Dinner |
| T386 | Cukor, George (d) | 3-17-68 | ——— | Vivian Leigh Dinner |
| T154 | Cukor, George (d) | 8-13-61 | Harvey | Ethel Barrymore |
| T69 | Cukor, George (d) | 1-9-59 | | *Adam's Rib* |
| T70 | Cukor, George (d) | 5-25-61 | Knight | *Little Women* |
| T253 | Cukor, George (d) | 11-66 | Knight | |
| T304 | Cukor, George (d) | 2-17-70 | Knight | |
| T83 | Curtis, Tony (a) | 9-20-61 | Knight | |
| T284 | Curtis, Tony (a) | 3-3-68 | Knight | *The Boston Strangler* |
| T364 | Daley, Robert | 9-22-71 | Knight | *Play Misty for Me* |
| T41 | Damon, Mark | 1-16-61 | Panel | Hollywood Trade Papers |
| T401 | Daniels, William H. (c) | n.d. | ASC | |
| T276 | D'Antoni, Phil (p) | 11-14-68 | Knight | *Bullitt* |
| T369 | D'Antoni, Phil (p) | 11-4-71 | Knight | *The French Connection* |
| T165 | Daves, Delmer (w-p-d) | 11-15-64 | Knight | *3:10 to Yuma* |
| T299 | Daves, Delmer (w-p-d) | 9-20-69 | | History of the Western |
| T157 | Davis, Luther (w) | 5-21-64 | Knight | *Lady in a Cage* |

**66** PERFORMING ARTS RESOURCES

| Catalog number | Name | Date | Inter-viewer/ Format | Film Shown/ Subject discussed |
|---|---|---|---|---|
| T136 | Davis, Wray | 10-30-63 | Knight | *The Year of the Tiger* |
| T372 | Del Conte, Ken (a) | 12-4-71 | Knight | *Love: Vampire Style* |
| T360 | Demetrakas, Johanna (a) | 4-1-71 | Knight | *Celebration at Big Sur* |
| T456/7 | Demy, Jacques (d) | 12-5-67 | Knight | |
| T280 | Demy, Jacques (d) | 1-14-69 | Knight | |
| C-1 | Dern, Bruce (a) | 4-6-72 | Panel | The Art of Survival |
| T441 | Dern, Bruce (a) | Fall, 72 | Knight | *The Cowboys* |
| T460 | Didion, Joan (nov) | 10-19-72 | Knight | *Play It As It Lays* |
| T240 | Dmytryk, Edward (d) | 11-16-67 | Knight | |
| T278 | Dmytryk, Edward (d) | 1-2-69 | Knight | |
| T102 | Donner, Richard (d) | 3-23-62 | Knight | |
| T87 | Duning, George (co) | 10-12-61 | Knight | |
| T388 | Dunne, Irene (a) | 3-23-69 | —— | Helen Keller Dinner |
| T460 | Dunne, John Gregory (w) | 10-19-72 | Knight | *Play It As It Lays* |
| C-5 | Ebert, Roger (cr) | 4-8-72 | Panel | Critics and the Symbiosis of Survival |
| T417 | Edeson, Arthur (c) | n.d. | ASC | |
| C-3 | Edwards, Blake (w-p-d) | 4-7-72 | Lecture | The Economics of Survival |
| T236 | Edwards, George (p) | 10-12-67 | Knight | *Games* |
| T198 | Eisner, Lotte (cr) | 3-29-69 | Knight | |
| T445-3 | Elder, Lonnie (w) | 3-20-71 | Panel | Now Movies and the Audience |
| T315 | Ellis, Syd (w) | 9-28-70 | Lesser | |
| T329 | Enders, Robert (p) | 12-3-70 | Knight | *How Do I Love Thee* |
| T221 | Fadiman, William (story editor) | 2-12-68 | Lesser | |
| T222 | Fadiman, William (story editor) | 9-25-67 | Lesser | |
| T199 | Faire, Rudy (e) | 4-14-66 | Knight | |
| C-5 | Farber, Manny (cr) | 4-8-72 | Panel | Critics and the Symbiosis of Survival |
| T445-2 | Farber, Stephen | 3-18-71 | Panel | Film Criticism and the Audience |
| T200 | Fleischman, Stanley (law) | 4-28-66 | Knight | Censorship |
| T409 | Folsey, George J. (c) | n.d. | ASC | |
| T305 | Folsey, George J. (c) | 2-24-70 | Knight | |
| T453 | Fonda, Henry (a) | 4-4-71 | —— | Oscar Hammerstein Dinner |
| T175 | Forbes, Bryan (d) | 11-19-64 | Knight | *Seance on a Wet Afternoon* |
| T241 | Ford, Glenn (a) | 11-30-67 | Knight | *The Rage* |
| T142 | Foreman, Carl (w-p-d) | 1-2-64 | Knight | *Key* |
| T319 | Foreman, Jack (studio manager) | 10-19-70 | Lesser | |
| T348 | Foreman, Jack (studio manager) | 3-15-71 | Lesser | |
| T109 | Fowler, Gene (e) | 10-26-62 | Knight | *Angel's Flight* |
| T133 | Fowler, Gene (e) | 10-10-63 | Knight | *A Child is Waiting* |
| T163 | Fowler, Gene (e) | 10-29-64 | Knight | *Choice* |
| T97 | Fowler, Marjorie (w) | 1962 | Knight | |
| T154 | Fowler, Marjorie & Gene | 4-30-64 | Knight | |

## The Cinema Library at the University of Southern California 67

| Catalog number | Name | Date | Interviewer/ Format | Film Shown/ Subject discussed |
|---|---|---|---|---|
| T327 | Fraker, William (c-d) | 11-19-70 | Knight | *Monte Walsh* |
| T95 | Frankenheimer, John (d) | 11-30-61 | Panel | Cinema Symposium |
| T114 | Frankenheimer, John (d) | 1963 | Knight | *Manchurian Candidate* |
| T143 | Frankovich, Michael (p) | 2-27-64 | Knight | *Dr. Strangelove* ... |
| T322 | Frederickson, Gray | 10-24-70 | Knight | *Little Fauss and Big Halsey* |
| T375 | Freed, Arthur (p) | 1-11-72 | Knight | |
| T367 | Freed, Bert (a) | 10-21-71 | Knight | The Actor as Worker and Artist |
| T277 | Friedkin, William (d) | 12-18-68 | Knight | *The Birthday Party* |
| T323 | Friedman, Tully (law) | 11-2-70 | Lesser | Legal end of documentary films |
| C-6 | Froug, William (w) | 4-8-72 | Lecture | The Young Film Maker and the Future |
| T297 | Fuller, Sam (d) | 2-28-68 | Panel | Jean-Luc Godard |
| T193 | Gardner, Herb (dramatist) | 1-13-66 | Knight | *A Thousand Clowns* |
| T281 | Garfein, Jack (d) | 2-13-69 | Lecture | Film directing |
| T285 | Garfein, Jack (d) | 3-6-69 | Lecture | Film directing |
| T289 | Garfein, Jack (d) | 3-20-69 | Lecture | Film directing |
| T291 | Garfein, Jack (d) | 4-10-69 | Lecture | Film directing |
| T446 | Garfein, Jack (d) | 11-70 | Lecture | Film directing |
| T386 | Garson, Greer (a) | 3-17-68 | ——— | Vivian Leigh Dinner |
| T122 | Gidding, Nelson (w) | 3-21-63 | Knight | *Nine Hours to Rama* |
| T145 | Giesler, Abner | 3-12-64 | Knight | |
| T324 | Glass, George | 11-5-70 | Knight | *So This is New York* |
| T41 | Glazer, Barney | 1-16-61 | Panel | Hollywood Trade Papers |
| T259 | Godard, Jean-Luc (d) | 2-26-68 | Lippincott | |
| T296 | Godard, Jean-Luc (d) | 2-27-68 | Lippincott | |
| T297 | Godard, Jean-Luc (d) | 2-28-68 | Panel | Jean-Luc Godard |
| T298 | Godard, Jean-Luc (d) | 2-29-68 | Youngblood | Young film makers |
| T125 | Gold, Ernest (co) | 4-18-63 | Knight | |
| T22 | Gold, Herbert | 12-16-62 | | Lecture |
| T359 | Gold, Leon | 4-10-71 | Lesser | |
| T189 | Golding, David (publicist) | 11-11-65 | Knight | *Guys and Dolls* |
| T192 | Goldman, Les | 1-6-66 | Knight | Animation |
| T368 | Goldstein, Emanuel | 11-2-71 | Knight | |
| T468 | Goldstone, Dina (a) | Fall, 72 | Knight | *Deadhead Miles* |
| T295 | Goldstone, James (d) | 5-1-69 | Knight | *Winning* |
| T352 | Goldstone, James (d) | 4-22-71 | Knight | *Red Sky at Morning* |
| T356 | Gomberg, Sy (w) | 5-10-71 | Knight | The blacklist |
| T311 | Gomberg, Sy (w) | 4-28-70 | Knight | The blacklist |
| T95 | Gordon, Michael (d) | 11-30-61 | Panel | Cinema symposium |
| T197 | Gordon, Ruth (a) | 3-17-66 | Knight | |
| T388 | Gordon, Ruth (a) | 3-23-69 | ——— | Helen Keller Dinner |
| T360 | Gottlieb, Carl | 4-1-71 | Knight | Celebration at Big Sur |
| T237 | Grassoff, Alex | 10-19-67 | Knight | *The Young American* |
| T157 | Grauman, Walter (d) | 5-21-64 | Knight | *Lady in a Cage* |
| T86 | Greenberg, Henry | 10-5-61 | Knight | *Al Capone* |

**68**  PERFORMING ARTS RESOURCES

| Catalog number | Name | Date | Interviewer/Format | Film Shown/Subject discussed |
|---|---|---|---|---|
| T134 | Greenspan, Lon | 10-17-63 | Knight | *Tom Jones* |
| T320 | Gries, Thomas S. (d) | 10-22-70 | Knight | *Fools* |
| T202 | Hagen, Earle (co) | 5-24-66 | Knight | |
| T354 | Hamilburg, Michael (ag) | 4-29-71 | Knight | *Derby* |
| T459 | Handler, Ken | 10-5-72 | Knight | *Bad Blood* |
| T341 | Hansard, William | 11-3-70 | Lesser | Front projection |
| T162 | Hansert, Burt | 10-22-64 | Knight | |
| T358 | Hansford, Bill | 4-3-71 | Lesser | |
| T79 | Harrington, Curtis (d) | 4-20-61 | Knight | *Night Tide* |
| T236 | Harrington, Curtis (d) | 10-12-67 | Knight | *Games* |
| T243 | Harrington, Pat (a) | 2-1-68 | Knight | *The President's Analyst* |
| T121 | Harris, James B. (p) | 3-13-63 | Knight | *Lolita* |
| T287 | Harvey, Anthony (d-e) | 3-18-69 | Knight | *Lion in Winter* |
| T300 | Hawks, Howard (d) | 9-7-69 | | History of the Western |
| T388 | Hayes, Helen (a) | 3-23-69 | —— | Helen Keller Dinner |
| T438 | Head, Edith (dress design) | 2-72 | —— | Banquet honoring her |
| T480 | Head, Edith (dress design) | 5-7-72 | —— | |
| T71 | Heston, Charlton (a) | 1-4-61 | Knight | |
| T388 | Heston, Charlton (a) | 3-23-69 | —— | Helen Keller Dinner |
| T106 | Hill, George Roy (d) | 10-5-62 | Knight | *Period of Adjustment* |
| T150 | Hiller, Arthur (d) | 4-9-64 | Knight | *Americanization of Emily* |
| T333 | Hiller, Arthur (d) | 1-21-71 | Knight | *Love Story* |
| T227 | Hilton, Arthur | 11-13-67 | Lesser | |
| T117 | Hirschman, Herbert | 1-4-63 | Knight | *In His Image* |
| T438 | Hitchcock, Alfred (d) | 2-72 | —— | Banquet honoring him |
| T230 | Holsopple, Ted | 12-4-67 | Lesser | |
| T200 | Hopkins, Henry | 4-28-66 | Knight | Censorship |
| T79 | Hopper, Dennis (a) | 4-20-61 | Knight | *Night Tide* |
| T400 | Howe, James Wong (c) | n.d. | ASC | |
| T271 | Howe, James Wong (c) | 3-30-67 | Knight | |
| T314 | Huffaker, Clair (w) | 10-8-70 | Knight | *Flap* |
| T386 | Hyde-White, Wilfred (a) | 3-17-68 | —— | Vivian Leigh Dinner |
| T141 | Jackson, Horace (w) | 1-9-64 | Knight | *Living Between Two Worlds* |
| T469 | Jacobs, Arthur P. (p) | 5-17-72 | Knight | *Play It Again, Sam* |
| T112 | Jewison, Norman (d) | 12-7-62 | Knight | *Forty Pounds of Trouble* |
| T301 | Jewison, Norman (d) | 9-24-69 | Knight | *Gaily, Gaily* |
| T141 | Johnson, Bobby (p) | 1-9-64 | Knight | *Living Between Two Worlds* |
| T363 | Johnson, Lamont (d) | 5-20-71 | Knight | *A Gunfight* |
| T192 | Jones, Charles M. (animator) | 1-6-66 | Knight | His cartoons |
| T333 | Jones, Robert (e) | 1-21-71 | Knight | *Love Story* |
| T342 | Kamins, Bernie (publicist) | 12-7-70 | Lesser | |
| T107 | Kamp, Irene and Louis (w) | 10-12-62 | Knight | *Paris Blues* |
| T275 | Kanin, Garson (w) | 2-12-67 | —— | Cole Porter Dinner |

The Cinema Library at the 69
University of Southern California

| Catalog number | Name | Date | Interviewer/ Format | Film Shown/ Subject discussed |
|---|---|---|---|---|
| T79 | Kartarium, Aram | 4-20-61 | Knight | *Night Tide* |
| T101 | Kauffman, Millard (w) | 3-16-62 | Knight | *Reprieve* |
| T160 | Kershner, Irvin (d) | 10-1-64 | Knight | *Luck of Ginger Coffey* |
| T275 | Kelly, Gene (a) | 2-12-67 | —— | Cole Porter Dinner |
| T453 | Kelly, Gene (a) | 4-4-71 | —— | Oscar Hammerstein Dinner |
| T137 | Kin, Mu (a) | 11-14-63 | Knight | |
| T445-4 | Knight, Arthur (cr) | 3-21-71 | Panel | Film and its Audience |
| T371 | Knight, Arthur (cr) | 11-18-72 | Panel | Motion Picture Advertising and Publicity |
| T434 | Knight, Arthur (cr) | 1-6-72 | Lecture | The Apostrophe: Whose Film is it? |
| T462 | Knight, Arthur (cr) | 11-16-72 | Lecture | The Extreme Close-up |
| T118 | Knight, Arthur (cr) | 2-14-63 | Lecture | Film criticism |
| T138 | Knight, Arthur (cr) | 12-5-63 | Lecture | Film criticism |
| T161 | Knight, Arthur (cr) | 10-8-64 | Lecture | Film criticism |
| T445-5 | Koch, Howard (w) | 3-21-71 | —— | *A New Leaf* |
| T365 | Kostal, Irwin (co) | 10-71 | Lecture | *West Side Story* |
| T308 | Kramer, Larry (p) | 4-3-70 | Knight | *Women in Love* |
| T366 | Kramer, Stanley (p-d) | 10-8-71 | Knight | *Bless the Beasts and Children* |
| T66 | Kramer, Stanley (p-d) | 1-7-60 | MacCann | |
| T83 | Kramer, Stanley (p-d) | 9-61 | Knight | |
| T95 | Kramer, Stanley (p-d) | 11-30-61 | Panel | Cinema Symposium |
| T180 | Kramer, Stanley (p-d) | 5-13-65 | Knight | |
| T219 | Kramer, Stanley (p-d) | 12-14-66 | Knight | |
| T386 | Kramer, Stanley (p-d) | 3-17-68 | —— | Vivian Leigh Dinner |
| C-8 | Krantz, Steve (p) | 8-8-72 | Knight | *Fritz the Cat* |
| T357 | Kranze, Ben (d) | 6-7-71 | Lesser | |
| T317 | Kranze, Ben (d) | 10-7-70 | Lesser | |
| T201 | Krisman, Serge (art dir.) | 5-12-66 | Knight | |
| T100 | Kubrick, Stanley (p-d) | 1-23-64 | Knight | by phone |
| T386 | Lanchester, Elsa (a) | 3-17-68 | —— | Vivian Leigh Dinner |
| T465 | Lang, Charles (c) | 3-4-72 | Knight | *Butterflies are Free* |
| T480 | Lang, Fritz (d) | 4-23-72 | none | |
| T77 | Lasky, Jesse, Jr. (p) | 4-6-61 | Knight | |
| T73 | Laughlin, Tom (a) | 2-23-61 | Knight | *We Are All Christ* |
| T262 | Laven, Arnold (d) | 10-16-67 | Lesser | |
| T129 | Lear, Norman (w-p) | 5-23-63 | Knight | *Come Blow Your Horn* |
| T264 | Lear, Norman (w-p) | 12-12-63 | Knight | *The Night They Raided Minsky's* |
| T386 | Leigh, Vivian | 3-17-68 | | Vivian Leigh Memorial Dinner |
| T374 | Lemmon, Jack (a) | 12-9-71 | Knight | *Kotch* |
| T110 | Lemmon, Jack (a) | 11-9-62 | Knight | *Days of Wine and Roses* |
| T233 | Lennart, Isobel (w) | 9-26-68 | Knight | |
| T275 | Lerner, Alan Jay (co) | 2-12-67 | —— | Cole Porter Dinner |
| T113 | Lerner, Irving (p-d) | 12-7-62 | Knight | *To Be A Man* |
| T115 | Lerner, Irving (p-d) | 1-63 | Knight | |

# 70 PERFORMING ARTS RESOURCES

| Catalog number | Name | Date | Interviewer/ Format | Film Shown/ Subject discussed |
|---|---|---|---|---|
| T302 | Lerner, Irving (p-d) | 10-3-69 | | The Royal Hunt of the Sun |
| T309 | Lerner, Irving (p-d) | 4-7-70 | Knight | American documentary |
| T386 | LeRoy, Mervyn (d) | 3-17-68 | ——— | Vivian Leigh Dinner |
| T65 | Lesser, Sol (p) | 12-10-59 | MacCann | |
| T268 | Lesser, Sol (p) | 9-18-67 | Lecture | Film production |
| T266 | Lesser, Sol (p) | 2-5-68 | Lecture | Film production |
| T316 | Lesser, Sol (p) | 9-29-70 | Lecture | Film production |
| T346 | Lesser, Sol (p) | 2-8-71 | Lecture | Film production |
| T337 | Levin, Boris (art dir.) | 3-4-71 | Knight | The Andromeda Strain |
| T262 | Levy, Jules (p) | 10-16-67 | Lesser | |
| T232 | Levy, Jules (p) | 2-19-68 | Lesser | |
| T342 | Levy, Jules (p) | 12-7-70 | Lesser | |
| T126 | Lewis, Jerry (a-d-p) | 5-2-63 | Knight | The Nutty Professor |
| T293 | Linder, Carl (c) | 10-22-68 | ——— | The Devil is Dead |
| T336 | Lipton, David (ex) | 3-1-71 | Lesser | |
| T355 | Livingston, David | 5-7-71 | Knight | Willie Wonka and the Chocolate Factory |
| T350 | Loden, Barbara (d-w-a) | 3-25-71 | Knight | Wanda |
| T78 | Lombard, Henry (ex) | 4-13-61 | Knight | |
| T120 | Loy, Nonnie (d) | 3-7-63 | Knight | Four Days of Naples |
| T105 | Lubin A. Ronald (d) | 9-29-62 | Knight | Billy Budd |
| T445-4 | Lucas, George (d) | 3-20-71 | Panel | Now Movies and the Audience |
| T445-5 | Lucas, George (d) | 3-20-71 | ——— | THX1138 |
| T418 | Lyons, Reggie (c) | n.d. | ASC | |
| T137 | MacCann, Richard (cr-hist) | 11-14-63 | Knight | |
| T68 | Maddow, Ben (w-d) | n.d. | MacCann | |
| T480 | Maibaum, Richard (w-p) | 7-29-72 | ——— | |
| T81 | Malden, Karl (a) | 5-61 | Knight | One-Eyed Jacks |
| T435 | Mamoulian, Rouben (d) | 2-29-72 | Knight | |
| C-1 | Mamoulian, Rouben (d) | 4-6-72 | Lecture | The Art of Survival |
| T449 | Mamoulian, Rouben (d) | 12-9-69 | ——— | |
| T135 | Mann, Abby (w) | 10-24-63 | Knight | Judgement at Nurenberg |
| T445-4 | Mann, Abby (w) | 3-20-71 | Panel | Now Movies and the Audience |
| T163 | Mann, Graham (e) | 10-29-64 | Knight | Choice |
| T111 | Manulis, Martin (p-d) | 11-16-62 | Knight | |
| T355 | Margulies, Stan (p) | 5-7-71 | Knight | Willie Wonka and the Chocolate Factory |
| T112 | Margulies, Stan (p) | 12-7-62 | Knight | Forty Pounds of Trouble |
| T215 | Marion, Frances (w) | 10-6-66 | Knight | |
| T333 | Marley, John (a) | 1-21-71 | Knight | Love Story |
| T80 | Marquette, Desmond | 4-27-61 | Sloan | Storm Over Eden |
| T251 | Mascot, Lawrence | 12-66 | Knight | |
| T438 | Matthau, Walter (a) | 2-72 | ——— | Banquet honoring him |
| T445-5 | Matthau, Walter (a) | 3-21-71 | ——— | A New Leaf |
| T386 | Matthau, Walter (a) | 3-17-68 | ——— | Vivian Leigh Dinner |
| T93 | Mayer, Arthur (dist) | 11-16-61 | Knight | Connection |

| Catalog number | Name | Date | Interviewer/ Format | Film Shown/ Subject discussed |
|---|---|---|---|---|
| T445-3 | Mayer, Arthur (dist) | 3-19-71 | Panel | Film Education and the Audience |
| T470/ T478 | Mayer, Arthur (dist) | Fall, 72 | Lectures | Motion Picture Business |
| T444-1 thru 9 | Mayer, Arthur (dist) | Spring, 72 | Lectures | Motion Picture Business |
| T248 | Mayer, Gerald (p-d) | 5-9-68 | Knight | |
| T283 | McClay, Booker (p) | 2-27-69 | Knight | *77 South* |
| T286 | McClay, Booker (p) | 3-13-69 | Knight | *Hell in the Pacific* |
| T274 | McGann, William (c-d) | n.d. | | |
| T207 | McGann, William (c-d) | Spring, 66 | Knight | |
| T275 | Merman, Ethel (a) | 2-12-67 | —— | Cole Porter Dinner |
| T453 | Mercer, Johnny | 4-4-71 | —— | Oscar Hammerstein Dinner |
| T60 | Milestone, Lewis (d) | n.d. | MacCann | |
| T63 | Milestone, Lewis (d) | 2-59 | Mackey | |
| C-6 | Milius, John (w-d) | 4-8-72 | Panel | The Young Film Maker and the Future |
| T402 | Miller, Arthur C. (c) | n.d. | ASC | |
| T415 | Miller, Arthur C. (c) | n.d. | ASC | |
| T409 | Miller, Arthur C. (c) | n.d. | ASC | |
| T436 | Miller, Jonathan | 2-17-72 | Knight | |
| T402 | Miller, Virgil (c) | n.d. | ASC | |
| T414 | Mitchel, George (c) | n.d. | ASC | |
| T419 | Mohr, Hal (c) | n.d. | ASC | |
| T358 | Mohr, Hal (c) | 4-3-71 | Lesser | |
| T345 | Mohr, Hal (c) | 1-11-71 | Lesser | |
| T324 | Morgan, Henry (a) | 11-5-70 | Knight | *So This is New York* |
| T466 | Morrissey, Paul (d) | 10-16-72 | Knight | *Heat* |
| T124 | Morrow, Vic (a-w-d) | 4-4-63 | Knight | *Combat* (TV) |
| T186 | Morrow, Vic (a-w-d) | 10-7-65 | Knight | *Genet's Death Watch* |
| T116 | Mulligan, Robert (d) | 1-63 | Knight | *To Kill a Mockingbird* |
| T445-2 | Murphy, Art (cr) | 3-18-71 | Panel | Film criticism and the Audience |
| C-3 | Murphy, Art (cr) | 4-7-72 | Panel | The Economics of Survival |
| C-5 | Murphy, Art (cr) | 4-8-72 | Panel | Critics and the Symbiosis of Survival |
| T104 | Nelson, Peter (p) | 5-11-62 | Knight | |
| T249 | Nelson, Ralph (d-p) | 3-23-68 | Knight | *Charly* |
| T38 | Newhart, Bob (a) | 10-24-60 | Panel | Comedy |
| T162 | Olsen, Dale (publicist) | 10-22-64 | Knight | |
| T410 | Overbaugh, Ray (c) | n.d. | ASC | |
| T225 | Palmer, Charles "Cap" (p) | 10-3-67 | Lesser | |
| T344 | Palmer, Charles "Cap" (p) | 1-4-71 | Lesser | Non-theatrical films |
| T13 | Parker, Dorothy (w) | 4-25-62 | Knutson/ Durbin | |
| PAC 1 | Parsons, Louella (columnist) | —— | —— | "Hollywood Hotel" 21 tapes of radio programs |
| T416 | Peck, Gregory (a) | n.d. | ASC | |
| T116 | Peck, Gregory (a) | 1-63 | Knight | *To Kill A Mockingbird* |
| T166 | Peerce, Larry (d) | 1-7-65 | Knight | *One Potato, Two Potato* |

## 72 PERFORMING ARTS RESOURCES

| Catalog number | Name | Date | Interviewer/ Format | Film Shown/ Subject discussed |
|---|---|---|---|---|
| T328 | Perkins, Harry | 11-23-70 | Lesser | |
| T405 | Physioc, Lewis | n.d. | ASC | |
| T294 | Pogostin, S. Lee (w-d) | 4-24-69 | Knight | Hard Contract |
| T282 | Polanski, Roman (d) | 3-13-69 | Knight | Rosemary's Baby |
| T265 | Poll, Martin (p) | 12-5-68 | Knight | Sylvia |
| T287 | Poll, Martin (p) | 3-18-69 | Knight | Lion in Winter |
| T196 | Pollack, Sydney (d) | 2-17-66 | Knight | |
| T303 | Pollack, Sydney (d) | 12-18-69 | —— | They Shoot Horses, Don't They |
| C-1 | Pollack, Sydney (d) | 4-6-72 | Panel | The Art of Survival |
| T67 | Post, Ted (p-d) | 2-17-62 | MacCann | |
| T340 | Pouliot, Steve | 4-12-71 | Lesser | |
| T231 | Powers, James | 1-15-68 | Lesser | |
| T224 | Pratt, James | 10-23-67 | Lesser | |
| T95 | Preminger, Otto (d) | 11-30-61 | Panel | Cinema Symposium |
| T72 | Prince, Harold (co) | 5-5-61 | Panel | Musical Comedy |
| T204 | Rackin, Marty (w) | 5-26-66 | Knight | |
| T463 | Radnitz, Robert (p) | 9-28-72 | Knight | Sounder |
| T76 | Radnitz, Robert (p) | 3-23-61 | Knight | A Dog of Flanders |
| T155 | Radnitz, Robert (p) | 5-7-64 | Knight | |
| C-3 | Radnitz, Robert (p) | 4-7-72 | Panel | Who Goes to the Movies and Why? |
| T272 | Radnitz, Robert (p) | 4-17-69 | Knight | My Side of the Mountain |
| T445-1 | Radnitz, Robert (p) | 3-18-71 | Panel | Film and Finance |
| T443 | Radnitz, Robert (p) | 3-23-72 | Knight | Film marketing |
| T453 | Raitt, John (a) | 4-4-71 | —— | Oscar Hammerstein Dinner |
| T195 | Rajanan, Indo (w) | 2-15-66 | Knight | |
| T72 | Raksin, David (co) | 9-22-61 | Knight | |
| T152 | Randall, Tony (a) | 2-20-64 | Knight | Pillow Talk |
| T176 | Ransohoff, Martin (ex) | 9-30-65 | Knight | Cincinnati Kid |
| T445-1 | Ransohoff, Martin (ex) | 3-18-71 | Panel | Film and Finance (Film conference) |
| T307 | Rapper, Irving (d) | 3-19-70 | Knight | |
| T82 | Reinhardt, Gottfried (p-w) | 5-4-61 | Knight | Town Without Pity |
| T428 | Rennahan, Ray (c) | n.d. | ASC | |
| T172 | Reynolds, William (e) | 3-25-65 | Knight | Compulsion |
| T247 | Reynolds, William (e) | 4-18-68 | Knight | |
| T463 | Ritt, Martin (d) | 9-28-72 | Knight | Sounder |
| T480 | Ritt, Martin (d) | 3-5-72 | ? | |
| T131 | Ritt, Martin (d) | 10-63 | Knight | Edge of the City |
| T269 | Rivkin, Allen (w) | 10-2-67 | Lesser | |
| T445 | Rivkin, Allen (w) | 3-18-71 | Panel | Film criticism and the Audience |
| T63 | Robson, Mark (d-p) | 2-59 | Mackey | MA thesis interview |
| T81 | Rosenberg, Frank P. (p) | 5-61 | Knight | One-Eyed Jacks |
| T310 | Rosenman, Leonard (co) | 4-30-70 | Knight | Film music |
| T447 | Rosensweig, Barney | 4-20-72 | Knight | Who Fears the Devil? |
| T363 | Rosenthal, Laurence (co) | 5-20-71 | Knight | A Gunfight |

The Cinema Library at the          73
University of Southern California

| Catalog number | Name | Date | Interviewer/ Format | Film Shown/ Subject discussed |
|---|---|---|---|---|
| T421 | Rosher, Charles (c) | n.d. | ASC | |
| T469 | Ross, Herbert (d) | 5-17-72 | Knight | *Play It Again, Sam* |
| T94 | Rossen, Robert (d) | 10-19-61 | Knight | |
| T412/3 | Rosson, Harold (d-p) | n.d. | ASC | |
| T139 | Rosten, Leo (journalist) | 12-12-63 | Knight | |
| T229 | Rubin, Edward | 11-27-67 | Lesser | |
| T256 | Rubin, Edward | 2-26-68 | Lesser | |
| T325 | Rubin, Edward | 11-9-70 | Lesser | |
| T349 | Rubin, Edward | 3-21-71 | Lesser | |
| T306 | Rubin, Ronald (p) | 2-26-70 | Knight | |
| T243 | Rubin, Stanley (p) | 2-1-68 | Knight | *The President's Analyst* |
| T322 | Ruddy, Albert S. (p) | 10-24-70 | Knight | *Little Fauss and Big Halsey* |
| T388 | Russell, Rosalind (a) | 3-23-69 | ———— | Helen Keller Dinner |
| T422 | Ruttenberg, Joseph (c) | n.d. | ASC | |
| T441 | Rydell, Mark (d) | Fall, 72 | Knight | *The Cowboys* |
| C-2 | Said, Fouad (c-p) | 4-6-72 | Panel | The Technology of Survival |
| T95 | Sanders, Denis | 11-30-61 | Panel | Cinema Symposium |
| T288 | Scharf, Walter (co) | 3-20-69 | Knight | *Funny Girl* |
| T456 | Schlesinger, John (ex) | 10-27-67 | | |
| T191 | Schulberg, Budd (w-p) | 12-9-65 | Knight | *On the Waterfront* |
| T331 | Scodinak, Curt (w) | 1-5-71 | Knight | Writing in the 30's |
| T59 | Seaton, George (w-d) | n.d. | MacCann | |
| T411 | Seitz, John (c) | n.d. | ASC | |
| T156 | Shagan, Steve (w) | 5-14-64 | Knight | *From Russia With Love* |
| T423 | Sharp, Henry (c) | n.d. | ASC | |
| T424 | Sharp, Henry (c) | n.d. | ASC | |
| T267 | Shartin, Arnold | 3-11-68 | Lesser | |
| T144 | Shavelson, Melville (w-d) | 3-5-64 | Knight | |
| T464 | Shavelson, Melville (w-d) | 5-20-72 | Knight | *War Between Men & Women* |
| T245 | Shavelson, Melville (w-d) | 1967 | Knight | *Cast a Giant Shadow* |
| C-2 | Shavelson, Melville (w-d) | 4-6-72 | Lecture | The Technology of Survival |
| T246 | Shavelson, Melville (w-d) | 3-28-68 | Knight | *Yours, Mine, and Ours* |
| T445-1 | Shavelson, Melville (w-d) | 3-18-71 | Panel | Film and Finance |
| T272 | Shedlo, Ronald (p) | 10-26-68 | Knight | *Whisperers* |
| T226 | Sholem, Lee (d) | 11-6-67 | Lesser | |
| T326 | Sholem, Lee (d) | 11-16-70 | Lesser | |
| T339 | Sholem, Lee (d) | 3-8-71 | Lesser | |
| T64 | Shurlock, Geoffrey | 5-11-59 | MacCann | Censorship |
| T200 | Shurlock, Geoffrey | 5-28-66 | Knight | Censorship |
| T332 | Siegel, Don (d) | 1-7-71 | Knight | *The Beguiled* |
| T249 | Silliphant, Sterling (w-p) | 3-23-68 | Knight | *Charly* |
| T270 | Silverstein, Elliot (d) | 2-16-67 | Knight | *The Happening* |
| T321 | Simes, John (publicist) | 10-26-70 | Lesser | |

## 74   PERFORMING ARTS RESOURCES

| Catalog number | Name | Date | Interviewer/ Format | Film Shown/ Subject discussed |
|---|---|---|---|---|
| T275 | Sinatra, Frank (a) | 2-12-67 | —— | Cole Porter Dinner |
| T218 | Singer, Alexander (p) | 11-4-66 | Knight | |
| T312 | Smith, Roger (p) | 9-24-70 | Knight | C.C. and Co. |
| T438 | Solow, Syd (p) | 2-72 | —— | Banquet honoring him |
| C-2 | Solow, Syd (p) | 4-6-72 | Panel | The Technology of Survival |
| T330 | Spigelgass, Leonard (w) | 12-1-70 | —— | |
| T386 | Steiger, Rod (a) | 3-17-68 | —— | Vivian Leigh Dinner |
| T267 | Stern, Ezra E. (law) | 3-11-68 | Lesser | |
| T132 | Stern, Stewart (w) | 10-3-63 | Knight | Teresa |
| T84 | Stevens, George (p-d) | 9-21-61 | Knight | Giant |
| T310 | Stevens, Leith (co) | 4-3-70 | Knight | Film music |
| T103 | Stevens, Leslie (w-ex) | 4-13-62 | Knight | |
| T404 | Struss, Karl (c) | n.d. | ASC | |
| T370 | Stuart, Malcolm (p) | 11-9-71 | Knight | Mastermind |
| T355 | Stuart, Mel (d) | 5-7-71 | Knight | Willie Wonka and the Chocolate Factory |
| T442 | Stuart, Mel (d) | 4-13-72 | Knight | One is a Lonely Number |
| T260 | Stulberg, Gordon (ex) | 10-31-68 | Knight | |
| C-3 | Stulberg, Gordon (ex) | 4-7-72 | Panel | The Economics of Survival |
| T127 | Sturges, John (d) | 5-9-63 | Knight | The Great Escape |
| T359 | Swerdloff, Art | 4-10-71 | Lesser | |
| T406 | Tannura, Phillip (c) | n.d. | ASC | |
| C-5 | Thomas, Kevin (cr) | 4-8-72 | Panel | Critics and the Symbiosis of Survival |
| T100 | Thompson, J. Lee (d) | 3-9-62 | Knight | Flame Over India |
| T136 | Thompson, Marshall (a) | 10-30-63 | Knight | The Year of the Tiger |
| T109 | Thoroby, William | 10-26-62 | Knight | Angel's Flight |
| T439 | Tidyman, Ernest (w) | 3-16-72 | Knight | French Connection |
| C-1 | Tidyman, Ernest (w) | 4-6-72 | Knight | The Art of Survival |
| T72 | Tiomkin, Dimitri (co) | 2-14-61 | Panel | Musical Comedy |
| T171 | Tiomkin, Dimitri (co) | 3-18-65 | Knight | |
| T214 | Togawa, Naoki (cr) | 10-4-66 | Knight | |
| T200 | Trotter, Thomas | 4-28-66 | Knight | Censorship |
| T437 | Trumbell, Douglas (d) | 2-24-72 | Knight | Silent Running |
| T146 | Turman, Lawrence (p) | 3-19-64 | Knight | The Best Man |
| T43 | Tusher, William | 2-1-61 | Panel | Agents and Publicity |
| T420 | Van Trees, James (c) | n.d. | ASC | |
| T456 | Varda, Agnes (w-d) | 12-5-67 | Knight | |
| T296 | Varda, Agnes (w-d) | 2-27-68 | Lippincott | |
| T61 | Vidor, King (d) | 5-5-57 | MacCann | |
| T297 | Vidor, King (d) | 2-28-68 | Panel | Jean-Luc Godard |
| T99 | Vidor, King (d) | 2-9-62 | Knight | The Big Parade |
| T250 | Vogel, Joseph (w-p-d) | 9-24-68 | Knight | The Numbers Man |
| T429 | Vogel, Paul C. (c) | n.d. | ASC | |
| T445-3 | Vorkapich, Slavko (e) | 3-19-71 | Panel | Film Education and the Audience |
| T83 | Wald, Jerry (w-p) | 9-13-61 | Knight | |
| T426 | Walker, Joe (c) | n.d. | ASC | |

| Catalog number | Name | Date | Inter-viewer/ Format | Film Shown/ Subject discussed |
|---|---|---|---|---|
| T239 | Wallach, Eli (a) | 11-10-67 | ? | The Tiger Makes Out |
| T363 | Walsh, David (c) | 5-20-71 | Knight | A Gunfight |
| T364 | Walter, Jessica (a) | 9-22-71 | Knight | Play Misty for Me |
| T427 | Warrenton, Gilbert (c) | n.d. | ASC | |
| T373 | Weingarten, Lawrence (p) | 1-4-72 | Knight | |
| T217 | Weisbart, David (p) | 10-27-66 | Knight | |
| T332 | Weissman, Murray | 1-7-71 | Knight | The Beguiled |
| T361 | Welles, Orson (a-p-d) | 5-12-71 | ? | |
| T153 | Wendkos, Paul (d) | 4-23-64 | Knight | Angel Baby |
| T244 | West, Mae (a) | 3-3-68 | Knight | |
| T467 | Weston, Jay (p) | Fall, 72 | Knight | Lady Sings the Blues |
| T166 | Weston, Sam (p) | 1-7-65 | Knight | One Potato, Two Potato |
| T151 | Wexler, Haskell (c) | 4-16-64 | Knight | A Face in the Rain |
| T187 | Wexler, Haskell (c) | 10-16-65 | Knight | The Loved One |
| T158 | Wicki, Bernhard (d-a) | 6-4-64 | Knight | |
| T252 | Wilde, Cornell (a-d) | 3-10-67 | Knight | The Naked Prey |
| T19 | Willingham, Calder (w) | 5-19-63 | ? | |
| T334 | Wilson, John (p-w-d) | 2-18-71 | Knight | Shinbone Alley |
| T74 | Wilson, Richard (p-d) | 3-9-61 | Knight | Citizen Kane |
| T41 | Winchell, Joan | 1-16-61 | Panel | Hollywood Trade Papers |
| T242 | Winkler, Irwin (p) | 12-1-67 | ? | Point Blank |
| T181 | Winters, Shelley (a) | 4-29-65 | Knight | A Place in the Sun |
| T445-5 | Wise, Robert (p-d) | April, 71 | ? | The Andromeda Strain |
| T62 | Wise, Robert (p-d) | Feb., 59 | Mackey | |
| PAC 3 | Wise, Robert (p-d) | — | — | Music samples from Rio Conchos Sound of Music The Sand Pebbles |
| T130 | Wise, Robert (p-d) | 9-26-63 | Knight | The Haunting |
| T159 | Wise, Robert (p-d) | 9-24-64 | Knight | |
| T337 | Wise, Robert (p-d) | 3-4-71 | Knight | The Andromeda Strain |
| T93 | Wyler, William (p-d) | 1-25-62 | Knight | The Children's Hour |
| T235 | Yates, Peter (p-d) | 10-3-68 | Knight | Bullitt |
| T129 | Yorkin, Bud (p-d) | 5-23-63 | Knight | Come Blow Your Horn |
| T461 | Youngstein, Max E. (ex) | 11-28-72 | Knight | |
| T445 | Youngstein, Max E. (ex) | 3-18-72 | Panel | Film and Finances |
| T137 | Yu, Kim (d) | 11-14-63 | Knight | |
| T95 | Zinneman, Fred (d) | 11-30-61 | Panel | Cinema Symposium |

# The University of Southern California Film Conference Tapes

The annual University of Southern California Film Conference began as the Aspen Film Conference in Aspen, Colorado. Economic factors and the relative convenience of holding the conference in Los Angeles prompted its move to USC, where it has been held for the past three years.

The purpose of the Conference is to encourage leading members of the film industry to share their expertise or points of view on matters of general interest, with their fellow panelists and with the students, teachers and industry members who attend the event each year.

Distinguished panelists have included Rouben Mamoulian, Jean Renoir, King Vidor, Ray Bradbury, Arthur Mayer and Charles Champlin, among many others. The general format for the panels features a keynote speaker, followed by input on the subject from each member of the panel, and a general discussion which later includes questions from the audience.

**1972 Film conference, April 6-8**

    C-1   "The Art of Survival"
           Keynote address: Rouben Mamoulian
           Panel: Peter Bogdanovich, Bruce Dern, Sydney Pollack, Ernest Tidyman, Bennett Tramor

    C-2   "The Technology of Survival"
           Keynote address: Melville Shavelson
           Panel: John Alonzo, Wilton Holm, Monroe Price, Fouad Said, Sid Solow, Charles Woodward, Mort Zarkoff

    C-3   "The Economics of Survival"
           Keynote address: Blake Edwards
           Panel: William O. Brown, Al Dorskind, Zane Lubin, Art Murphy, Gordon Stulberg, Aubrey Solomon

    C-4   "Who Goes to the Movies and Why?"
           Keynote address: Robert Radnitz
           Panel: Peter Bart, Dr. Allan Casebier, Bruce Corwin, Peter Gruber, Doe Mayer

    C-5   "Critics and the Symbiosis of Survival"
           Keynote address: Beverly Walker
           Panel: Charles Champlin, Roger Ebert, Manny

The Cinema Library at the 77
University of Southern California

      Farber, Art Murphy, Kevin Thomas, Steve Greenberg

C-6 "The Young Film Maker and the Future"
Keynote address: William Froug
Panel: Tamara Assayev, Jonathan Axelrod, David Giler, John Milius, Rick Vaughnes

C-7 "The Techniques of Survival"
Keynote address: Wilton Holm
Arthur Knight moderates discussion with previous panelists.

## 1971 Film Conference, March 18-21

T445 #1 "Film and Finance"
Panel: Sam Arkoff, Art Murphy, Robert Radnitz, Martin Ransohoff, Mel Shavelson, Max Youngstein
"Film and Audience Research"
Keynote address: Gordon Stulberg
Panel: William Chesney, Dr. Bernard Kantor, Roger Seltzer

T445 #2 "Film Criticism and the Audience"
Keynote address: Dr. Henry Breitrose
Panel: Dr. Allan Casebier, Charles Champlin, Art Murphy, Allen Rivkin, Stephen Farber

T445 #3 "Film Education and the Audience"
Keynote address: Marsha Kinder
Panel: Dr. James Loper, Arthur Mayer, Lenore Navarro, Robert Radnitz, Slavko Vorkapich, Steve Pouliot
"Film Technology and the Audience"
Keynote address: Ray Bradbury

T445 #4 "Now Movies and the Audience"
Keynote address: George Lucas
Panel: Dr. Allan Casebier, Lonnie Elder, Abby Mann, George McQuilkin, Craig Fisher
"Film and its Audiences"
Synthesis by Arthur Knight

T445 #5  Evening screenings with discussion featuring Robert Wise (*Andromeda Strain*), George Lucas (*THX 1138*), Walter Matthau and Howard Koch (*A New Leaf*).

## Individual Collections

The individual collections collected by and housed within the USC Cinema Library are the result of donations from the persons or organizations for which each collection is named. They contain materials which pertain not only to films, but also to all the performing arts, especially radio and television. The collections themselves may be divided into three categories of organization: those which have been formally itemized and cataloged by the library staff (22), those which have been informally itemized by the authors of this work (10), and those collections which have not as yet been organized or assessed (62) so that no description is possible at this time. The Library is, at one and the same time, both blessed and cursed with a wealth of materials.

These collections contain a multiplicity of materials, but personal papers, memorabilia, scripts and still photographs are the most common elements. The collections vary greatly in size; some contain fewer than ten items, others have literally thousands. Due to space limitation, the contents of the individual collections which have been itemized can only be briefly described. An attempt has been made to provide enough information to enable the potential user to decide whether or not the collection would be valuable for his purposes.

### The Edward Anhalt Collection

Edward Anhalt (1914-    ) began writing in Hollywood in the late 1940s. He received Academy Awards for *Panic in the Streets* (1950) and *Becket* (1964).

The Edward Anhalt Collection is large and would be of particular value to a student of screenwriting. Naturally, scripts and script drafts are its major strength. The collection contains:

  1. Scripts and other items relating to thirty films and

television programs (several unproduced). Many of the scripts have personal comments written by Anhalt.
2. Miscellaneous materials pertaining to the 1960 Writer's Guild of America strike.
3. Miscellaneous publicity clippings, 1952-1965.
4. Biographical memoir written in 1965.
5. Numerous items are available about each of the following films:

  *Becket* (1964)
  *The Boston Strangler* (1968)
  *Bugsy Siegel* (unproduced)
  *Hour of the Gun* (1967)
  *The Madwoman of Chaillot* (1968)
  *The Passion of Mary Magdalene* (unproduced)
  *Peter the Great* (unproduced)
  *The Salzburg Connection* (1972)
  *The Sniper* (unproduced)
  *The Young Savages* (1961)

## The Jim and Henny Backus Collection

Jim Backus (1913-    ) is a character actor who has appeared in a wide variety of movies, television and radio programs. He is the voice of the cartoon character, "Mr. Magoo." His wife, Henny, also acted in radio shows and films.

The Jim and Henny Backus Collection is medium-sized. Scripts and recordings of radio programs are its main strength:

1. Scripts of nineteen movies in which Mr. or Mrs. Backus acted.
2. Scripts of fourteen segments of *The Jim Backus Show* ("Hot Off the Line"), a radio program.
3. Script of the 1967 television version of *Damn Yankees*.
4. Approximately fifteen phonograph records of the early 1940s War Department "Jubilee" radio programs. These featured Bing Crosby, Bob Hope and Jack Benny as well as Jim Backus.
5. Three phonograph records of the Allan Young radio show (1947).
6. Phonograph records of approximately twenty-five miscellaneous radio programs in which Jim or Henny Backus participated.

7. Miscellaneous items: original drawings of Mr. Magoo; a bust of Jim Backus; program from *It's a Mad, Mad, Mad, Mad World*; program from the 28th Academy Awards; scrapbook and pictorial illustrations relating to Mr. Backus' book, *What Are You Doing After the Orgy?*.

## The Fay Bainter Collection

Fay Bainter (1892-1968) acted in many movies, as well as stage plays and television programs. She received the Academy Award for Best Supporting Actress in *Jezebel* (1938).

The Fay Bainter Collection is large and contains a variety of materials:

1. Stills and photographs from approximately fifteen films.
2. Scripts of fifteen stage plays.
3. Stills and photographs from approximately twenty stage plays.
4. Clippings covering approximately twenty stage plays, 1912-1960.
5. Ten stage play programs.
6. Scripts of six television programs.
7. Correspondence, 1917-1967, primarily concerning dramatic performances.
8. Miscellaneous publicity clippings and magazine articles dating from 1906.
9. Miscellaneous photographs—Miss Bainter's early years in the theatre, publicity photos, photos of her family and friends.
10. Personal items and documents—U.S. Passport, Screen Actor's Guild Membership card, receipts, financial statements and expenses, contracts, etc.
11. Miscellaneous items pertaining to the Academy Awards. A photograph of Miss Bainter receiving her Oscar in 1938 is included.

## The Jay Burton Collection

Jay Burton is a writer who has worked on a number of television shows.

The Jay Burton Collection consists entirely of scripts and sketches written for various television programs. The items are grouped according to the particular program for which they were written.

1. "The Texaco Star Theatre" (1948-53)—Approximately 150 sketches and scripts.
2. "The Buick-Berle Show" (1954-55—Thirty-six sketches and scripts.
3. "The Perry Como Show" (1955-59)—Seventy-six scripts.
4. "The Julius LaRosa Show" (1957)—Four scripts.
5. Eleven bound volumes of monologues, written mostly for Milton Berle.

## The Gladys Cooper Collection

Gladys Cooper (1888-1971), a distinguished British stage actress, began her Hollywood career in *Rebecca* (1940). Subsequently, she appeared in many films including *Now Voyager* (1942) and *My Fair Lady* (1964).

The Gladys Cooper Collection is a huge assortment of theatrical and filmic materials:

1. Items relating to approximately ninety plays which Miss Cooper optioned or appeared in—scripts, correspondence, memos, contracts, playbills, brochures, scrapbooks, clippings, etc.
2. Items relating to approximately twenty-five films (1916-1960)—scripts, programs, clippings, correspondence, contracts, publicity, etc.
3. Items relating to five radio programs—contracts, scripts, brochures, etc.
4. Items relating to approximately thirty television shows (mainly "The Rogues" series, 1964-65)—scripts, call sheets, shooting schedules, correspondence, contracts, clippings, etc.
5. Papers relating to the management of the Playhouse Theatre, London, 1922-1934—correspondence, contracts, playbills, financial statements, memos, etc.
6. Programs of forty-five benefit performances given between 1908 and 1956 for such organizations as

"The Church of England Waifs and Strays Society" and "The Princess Beatrice Hospital."
7. Materials relating to twelve plays and one film in which Philip Merivale appeared as a principal actor—programs, playbills, clippings, etc.
8. Playbills for three plays in which Sally Cooper appeared.
9. Materials relating to nine plays in which Joan Buckmaster appeared—playbills, programs, clippings, etc.
10. Miscellaneous clippings, playbills, etc. from twenty-nine plays dating back to 1888.
11. Approximately thirty unsolicited dramatic scripts.
12. Approximately fifty magazines and periodicals containing relevant articles (1934-1964).
13. Fifty miscellaneous music scores.
14. Approximately seventy-five photos and fourteen stills.

## The Mack David Collection

Mack David is a composer and lyricist who has scored a number of films and television programs. *To Kill a Mockingbird* (1962), *Hud* (1963) and *The Dirty Dozen* (1967) are among the films featuring David's music.

The Mack David Collection is large and contains many items of interest to the student of film music.

1. Sheet music dating from 1924. There are approximately 550 items arranged chronologically.
2. Miscellaneous items relating to several films: scripts, correspondence, budgets, advertising brochures, memos, contracts, etc.
3. Fourteen reels of audio tape containing a wide variety of music. The tapes also contain interviews from radio and television programs.

## The Don Defore Collection

Don Defore (1917-    ) is an actor with movie, radio and television experience. His screen credits include *My Friend Irma* (1949) and *Battle Hymn* (1957), and he starred in the "Hazel" television series.

The Don Defore Collection is large and contains a wide variety of materials:
1. Scripts of thirty-one films in which Mr. Defore appeared.
2. Ten films (mostly from television programs). Included is the 1953 segment of "This is Your Life" which honored Mr. Defore.
3. Sixteen phonograph records of late 1940s radio programs. Most are from "Lux Radio Theatre" and the "Family Theatre."
4. Seventeen magazines ("Movie Life," "Screen Stars," etc.) with pertinent articles.
5. Miscellaneous publicity materials—press books, playbills, clippings, photos, over 250 stills.
6. Contractual and other business papers, personal items.

## The William C. DeMille Collection

William C. DeMille (1875-1955) was active in the movie industry, primarily for Paramount Studios, from 1914 through the late 1930s. Although overshadowed by his younger brother, Cecil B. DeMille, William distinguished himself as a director, writer and producer. In addition, Mr. DeMille worked in the Broadway theatre, usually in association with David Belasco, during the first decade of the twentieth century.

The William C. DeMille Collection consists primarily of scripts and essays by Mr. DeMille and by his wife, Clara Beranger. It is a relatively large collection:
1. Approximately sixty film scripts. Some of these are from the silent era, and many were written by the DeMilles.
2. Seventeen stage plays written between 1903-1940. Most are by William C. DeMille.
3. Approximately thirty-five articles written by DeMille between 1909-1940. Most of these deal with cinema or drama.
4. Biographical clippings covering Mr. DeMille's career from 1920 to 1949.
5. More than 800 playbills from various theatres, 1900-1953.

6. Miscellaneous materials: correspondence, treatments, outlines, clippings, etc.

## The William Dieterle Collection

William Dieterle began as an actor in such German films as Paul Leni's *Waxworks*. He came to Hollywood in 1930 and soon established himself as a director of prestige movies. Among his more famous films: *The Life of Emile Zola* (1937) and *The Hunchback of Notre Dame* (1939).

The William Dieterle Collection is medium-sized and contains many items relating to the following films:

*The White Angel* (1936)
*The Life of Emile Zola* (1937)
*Juarez* (1938)
*The Hunchback of Notre Dame* (1939)
*Dr. Ehrlich's Magic Bullet* (1940)
*Dispatch from Reuters* (1940)
*September Affair* (1950)

Stills *only* are available for *The Story of Louis Pasteur* (1936), *Blockade* (1938), *All that Money Can Buy* (1941), *Tennessee Johnson* (1942), *Kismet* (1944).

## The Philip Dunne Collection

Philip Dunne (1908-    ) worked both as a screenwriter and a writer-director. His credits include *How Green Was My Valley* (1942), *The Robe* (1953) and *Ten North Frederick* (1958).

The Philip Dunne Collection contains many valuable items. Scripts and other materials relating to writing are the major strength of this large collection, which contains:

1. Scripts of fifty feature films (some unproduced). Many of these contain stills and others (those directed by Dunne) are shooting scripts with notes and sketches.
2. Working copies of fifteen novels adapted by Mr. Dunne for the screen. Included are *Forever Amber*, *The Robe*, *How Green Was My Valley*, *The View from Pompey's Head*.
3. Manuscript of *Mr. Dooley Remembers: The Informal Memoirs of Finlay Peter Dunne*, edited with an intro-

duction and commentary by Philip Dunne. Also, clippings related to this book.
4. Miscellaneous production items pertaining to approximately thirty-five different films or projects: correspondence, treatments, memos, notes, estimates, budgets, research materials, synopses, etc.
5. Five reels of taped self-interviews by Mr. Dunne. Among the topics discussed: "the function of the writer," "censorship," "on working with directors, producers, writers," *The Robe, The Agony and the Ecstacy*, etc.
6. Publicity materials and clippings concerning Dunne and several of his films.
7. Miscellaneous magazines (some containing articles or stories by Dunne).
8. Miscellaneous items: speeches, story ideas, "Screen Writers Guild" data, "Screen Producers Guild" notices, congratulatory letters, etc.

**The Dan Duryea Collection**

Dan Duryea (1907-1968) was a prominent American actor. Often cast in the role of villain, he appeared in many movies and television programs.

The Dan Duryea Collection is particularly strong in script materials. It is a large collection:

1. Eight scrapbooks dealing with Mr. Duryea's life and career, 1924-1967.
2. Scripts of approximately seventy films, 1941-1966.
3. Scripts of approximately fifty episodes of the television series, "The Affairs of China Smith," 1952-1956.
4. Scripts of approximately seventy-five miscellaneous television programs in which Mr. Duryea acted.
5. Scripts and call sheets from approximately sixty episodes of the "Peyton Place" television show, 1967-1968.
6. Scripts of six stage plays, 1952-1956.
7. Miscellaneous items—correspondence, publicity booklets, articles, story treatments, call sheets for "The Affairs of China Smith," programs, notices, family Bible, etc.

## The Nelson Eddy Collection

Nelson Eddy (1901-1967), an actor-singer, made his film debut in 1933. His most famous roles came in a series of 1930s musicals co-starring Jeanette MacDonald. These included *Naughty Marietta* (1935), *Maytime* (1937) and *The Girl of the Golden West* (1938).

The Nelson Eddy Collection, particularly strong in still photographs and phonograph records, includes:

1. Over 2200 publicity and personal stills. Included are stills from approximately twenty-five movies.
2. Approximately fifteen scrapbooks dealing with Mr. Eddy's career, 1933-1967.
3. Scripts of sixteen films and twenty-nine television programs.
4. Phonograph records of the "Nelson Eddy Radio Show," 1944-1949. Approximately 118 different programs are represented; forty-one of these are from the "Kraft Music Hall," 1947-1949.
5. Booklets filled with concert programs, 1928-1950.
6. Approximately 100 personal photographs.

## The Morton Fine Collection

Morton Fine is a writer and producer whose major experience has been in television work. He co-produced (with David Friedkin) the "I Spy" television series (1964-1968).

The materials in the Morton Fine Collection are all related to "I Spy":

1. Scripts of approximately forty different episodes of the "I Spy" show. Some were co-written by Morton Fine.
2. Miscellaneous production items from "I Spy": correspondence, staff and cast lists, call sheets, production reports, shooting schedules, memos, rough drafts, notes, revisions, etc.

## The Richard Fleischer Collection

Richard Fleischer (1916-    ) has been a prolific motion picture director since 1946. His films include *Twenty Thousand Leagues Under the Sea* (1954), *The Boston Strangler* (1968) and *Soylent*

*Green* (1973). He is the son of Max Fleischer, the cartoonist and producer, who created"Betty Boop."

The Richard Fleischer Collection is large and will undoubtedly grow in size as Mr. Fleischer adds to it in coming years:

1. Scripts of thirty-three feature films.
2. Miscellaneous items (mostly clippings and sketches) related to twenty-one films.
3. General publicity items and contracts.
4. A multitude of items is available for each of the following films:
   *Fantastic Voyage* (1966)
   *Dr. Dolittle* (1967)
   *The Boston Strangler* (1968)
   *Che!* (1969)
   *Tora! Tora! Tora!* (1970)
   *The Seven Minutes* (1971)

## The Fred Freiberger Collection

Fred Freiberger is a writer and producer. He was one of the producers of the highly acclaimed "Star Trek" television series.

The Fred Freiberger Collection consists of scripts and production items:

1. Scripts of seven feature films written (or co-written) by Fred Freiberger. Some of these were never produced.
2. Scripts from fifty-eight episodes of the "Ben Casey" television program, 1961-1963.
3. Miscellaneous production items pertaining to approximately twenty-five episodes of the "Star Trek" television series: scripts, cast lists, memos, shooting schedules, call sheets, production reports, outlines, articles, correspondence, etc.

## The Tay Garnett Collection

Tay Garnett (1898- ) began his career as a director-writer in 1920. He directed some silents, many "talkies," and also worked in television. Perhaps his most famous film was the 1946 version of the James M. Cain novel, *The Postman Always Rings Twice*.

The Tay Garnett Collection is medium-sized and consists almost entirely of scripts:

1. Scripts for approximately twenty episodes of *Three Sheets to the Wind*, a half hour radio series created, produced and directed by Mr. Garnett in 1942. It starred John Wayne.
2. Two scrapbooks containing reviews, articles, posters, programs, etc. These relate to Tay Garnett's career from 1928 to 1937.
3. Scripts of thirty-nine feature films. Some were written (or co-written) by Garnett, and most are shooting scripts, heavily annotated.

## The Arthur P. Jacobs Collection

Arthur P. Jacobs (1922-1973), a producer, created the highly successful *Planet of the Apes* series of feature films.

The Arthur P. Jacobs Collection is small. It contains budgets, script drafts, stills and photos, correspondence and publicity materials from the Arthur P. Jacobs' production, *The Chairman* (1969).

## The Arthur Knight Collection

Arthur Knight (1916-    ), a Professor in the Division of Cinema at the University of Southern California, is a distinguished film critic-historian. He is the author of a work on the history of the movies, *The Liveliest Art*.

The Arthur Knight Collection contains the manuscript and illustration layouts of his book, *The Liveliest Art*.

## The Ernie Kovacs Collection

Ernie Kovacs (1919-1962), a comedian whose cigar was his trademark, became an important television personality in the 1950s. Kovacs also appeared in several movies before his untimely death.

The Ernie Kovacs Collection consists largely of materials pertaining to his television career. It is medium-sized and contains:

1. Production materials relating to the "Kovacs Unlimited" television show, 1952-1953—scripts, rundowns, prop lists, sound effects lists, music credits, guest lists, etc.
2. Production materials relating to "The Ernie Kovacs Show," another television series, 1953-1957—

The Cinema Library at the University of Southern California

approximately 400 scripts, rundowns, notes, treatments, cue sheets, etc.
3. Production materials relating to several sessions of "The Tonight Show" television program, 1955-1957—scripts, rundowns, notes, treatments, cue sheets, etc.
4. Eight scripts from miscellaneous television shows.
5. Miscellaneous scripts, cue sheets, notes for unidentified television programs.
6. Script and publicity items for *Operation Madball*, a movie Mr. Kovacs acted in.

## The Ernest Lehman Collection

Ernest Lehman (1920-    ) is an important screenwriter who has also functioned as producer and director during his career. The films written by Lehman include *North by Northwest* (1959), *The Sound of Music* (1965) and *Who's Afraid of Virginia Woolf?* (1966).

The Ernest Lehman Collection is large and especially rich in scripts and script materials:

1. Approximately 130 miscellaneous scripts from Mr. Lehman's personal film library.
2. Approximately 120 synopses of potential properties.
3. An outstanding collection of production materials dealing with the following films:
   *The Prize* (1963)
   *The Sound of Music* (1965)
   *Who's Afraid of Virginia Woolf?* (1966)
   *Hello, Dolly!* (1969)

## The Sol Lesser Collection

Sol Lesser (1890-    ) is one of the pioneers of the film industry. He began as a film exhibitor in silent days and later became a producer. Mr. Lesser is an Adjunct Professor in the USC Division of Cinema.

The Sol Lesser Collection is large and particularly strong in items relating to the history of motion pictures:

1. Glass plate and chromatrope slides and early motion picture equipment: cameras, projectors, etc.
2. Scripts of thirty-five films produced in the period 1933-1940.

3. Scenarios of fourteen stage plays produced between 1905 and 1920.
4. Miscellaneous production materials: correspondence, contracts, scrapbooks, production books, clippings, etc.
5. Approximately 230 stills from more than thirty films. Many are "classic" films: *Greed, Metropolis, The Covered Wagon*, etc.
6. Approximately fifty items relating to the history of motion pictures: pamphlets, booklets, magazines, clippings, glass transparencies, correspondence, etc.
7. Approximately 100 books. Most deal with show business and movies.
8. Thirty-six volumes of miscellaneous periodicals, yearbooks, etc., dated 1903-1967.

**The Cesar Romero Collection**

Cesar Romero (1907-    ) is a Latin actor who made his film debut in *Metropolitan* (1935). He has since appeared in many movies and television shows, often as a leading man.

The Cesar Romero Collection is made up primarily of scrapbooks and assorted memorabilia:

1. Thirty-one scrapbooks of assorted sizes documenting Mr. Romero's career.
2. Twenty-one envelopes containing miscellaneous items: stills, clippings, letters, periodicals, programs, etc.
3. Three boxes of stills from Romero's films.

**The Harry Ruby Collection**

Harry Ruby ( ? -1974), a composer, wrote music for stage plays and movies including the Marx Brothers' production, *Animal Crackers* (1930). For many years, he teamed with Bert Kalmar.

The Harry Ruby Collection is small and consists entirely of sheet music and correspondence:

1. Sheet music for five songs composed by Ruby: "I Want to Be Loved by You" (1928), "Nevertheless" (1931), "Money Doesn't Grow on Trees" (1967), "Do All Your Living Today" (1968), "I Love You But I don't Like You" (1968).

2. Approximately eighty-five pieces of correspondence dated 1929-1968.

## The Stanley K. Scheurer Collection

Stanley K. Scheurer worked as script supervisor on a number of famous films including *West Side Story* and *Cleopatra*.

The Stanley K. Scheurer Collection is small and consists of scripts and publicity materials:

1. Miscellaneous items pertaining to the film, *Cleopatra* (1962): scripts of Act I and Act II (it was originally to be two films), two notebooks filled with Scheurer's notes on the individual shots and a pressbook.
2. Shooting scripts (heavily annotated and containing still photographs) from five other films.
3. Approximately sixty copies of "movie" magazines, dated 1912-1932. Included are: *Photoplay, Screen, Motion Picture Magazine*.
4. Publicity booklets for United Artists (1930-1931) and Fox Film Corporation (1930-1931).
5. Scrapbook containing publicity clippings for many old (mostly silent) films.
6. Miscellaneous movie-oriented clippings.

## The Joseph Schildkraut Collection

Joseph Schildkraut (1895-1964), an Austrian actor, appeared in many American films between 1920 and 1960. He won an Academy Award for his portrayal of Dreyfus in *The Life of Emile Zola* (1937).

The Joseph Schildkraut Collection is very small. It consists of approximately 100 still photographs of Mr. Schildkraut. Most of these are from various screen performances.

## The Robert Sisk Collection

Robert Sisk produced feature films at RKO, Warner Brothers and MGM in the 1930s and 1940s. In the early 1950s, he left theatrical film production for television. He created a series, "The Life and Legend of Wyatt Earp," starring Hugh O'Brien.

The Robert Sisk Collection is a large assortment of materials that spans the career of the producer from the early 1920s to the early 1960s.

1. Scripts of approximately 225 episodes of "The Life and Legend of Wyatt Earp" television series, 1955-1960.
2. Miscellaneous materials related to the "Wyatt Earp" television show: production reports, cost reports, cast lists, credit sheets, residual payment schedules, estimated negative costs, publicity materials, etc., 1955-1963.
3. Scripts of approximately sixty episodes of "The Californians" television series, 1957-1959.
4. Personal scrapbooks: 1920-1922, 1924-1926, 1927, 1930-1931.
5. Catalogs of unproduced properties: 1939 (Paramount), 1942 (MGM), 1945 (MGM).
6. Publicity photographs: 200 from thirteen motion pictures, thirty from "Wyatt Earp," twenty-five from various stage productions.
7. Scripts of sixty feature films.
8. Seventeen screen treatments.
9. Scripts or synopses of five stage plays.
10. Fifty-five group photos of Robert Sisk with show business personalities: Louis B. Mayer, John Ford, Ginger Rogers, etc.
11. Thirty-seven miscellaneous photographs. Most are of Actors and actresses such as John Barrymore, Jr. and Lynn Fontanne.
12. Eleven plaques, medals, etc., won by Mr. Sisk and his productions.
13. Programs of five stage plays produced 1924-1938.
14. Souvenir booklets for one film (*The Informer*) and two stage plays.
15. Miscellaneous personal correspondence and memos, dated 1924-1963. The catalog description of these items is reasonably complete.
16. Miscellaneous movie production papers: budget estimates, contracts, options, etc.
17. Manuscripts of rejected feature film and television pilot outlines.
18. Assorted papers relating to the Screen Producers' Guild: newsletters, membership roster, reports, ar-

rangements for Producers' Guild forums held at USC and University of California at Los Angeles.

19. Sixteen miscellaneous magazines, 1928-1953. Included are: *Hollywood Spectator, The Screen Writer.*
20. Ninety books (mostly historical novels) from Sisk's library.
21. Manuscripts of four books including *Hollywood in Transition* by Richard Dyer MacCann and *Viva Gringo!*, a novel by Borden Chase.

**The John M. Stahl Collection**

John M. Stahl (1886-1950) began his career as a stage actor. He became a movie director during the silent era and made the transition to sound films. His credits include *Magnificent Obsession* (1935) and *The Keys of the Kingdom* (1944).

The John M. Stahl Collection is medium-sized and consists largely of scripts and clippings:

1. Scripts of twenty different films.
2. Publicity clippings and reviews for many of Mr. Stahl's movies.
3. Approximately twenty books (mostly novels).
4. Miscellaneous correspondence.
5. Miscellaneous synopses and treatments.
6. Approximately fifty photos and stills (mostly of movie personalities).
7. Sketchbooks from *Immortal Sergeant* (1943) and *The Keys of the Kingdom* (1944); research book for *Parnell* (1937), still album from *Leave Her to Heaven* (1945).

**The King Vidor Collection**

One of America's most distinguished directors, King Vidor (1894-    ) began his work in Hollywood in 1915. His many important films include *The Crowd* (1928), *Our Daily Bread* (1933) and *Duel in the Sun* (1946). Mr. Vidor is Artist-in-Residence in the Division of Cinema at the University of Southern California.

The King Vidor Collection is large and contains many items of value:

1. Scripts of fifteen films.
2. General production correspondence. Letters and mem-

oranda from David O. Selznick, Samuel Goldwyn, Pare Lorentz and other famous individuals are included.
3. Miscellaneous newspaper and magazine clippings and reviews.
4. Biographical data.
5. The following films are well represented in the collection:
   *An American Romance* (1944)
   *The Citadel* (1938)
   *Duel in the Sun* (1946)
   *H.M. Pulham, Esq.* (1941)
   *Northwest Terrace* (1940)
   *Our Daily Bread* (1933)
   *So Red the Rose* (1935)
   *Stella Dallas* (1939)
   *The Texas Rangers* (1936)
   *Witch in the Wilderness* (n.d.)
6. Miscellaneous items relating to: *The Big Parade, Broken Soil, The Champ, Comrade X, The Fountainhead, Hallelujah, National Velvet, The Patsy, Sam Houston, Solomon and Sheba, These Crazy People, Three Wise Fools, The Wizard of Oz.*

## The Lawrence Weingarten Collection

Mr. Weingarten (1893-    ), a producer, began working in the movie business around 1917. Among the multitude of films he produced were *A Day at the Races* (1937), *Adam's Rib* (1949) and *Cat on a Hot Tin Roof* (1958).

The Lawrence Weingarten Collection consists primarily of scrapbooks and accolades. It is medium-sized and contains:

1. Thirteen scrapbooks mainly containing press clippings. Also included are stills, letters, advertisements, etc., relating to Mr. Weingarten's films. The scrapbooks cover the years 1929-1940, 1945-1949 and 1958-1964. Two are devoted to single films: *The Unsinkable Molly Brown* (1964) and *Don't Go Near the Water* (1957).
2. Approximately forty accolades, awards, or prizes won by Lawrence Weingarten and his productions.
3. Daily production reports from four films produced in 1930, including Buster Keaton's *Forward March.*

4. Detailed budget estimates from eleven films, including the Marx Brothers *A Day at the Races* (1937).

## The David Weisbart Collection

David Weisbart (1915-1967) entered the motion picture business in 1935. After fifteen years as an editor, he began producing movies. His films include *Rebel Without a Cause* (1955) and *Valley of the Dolls* (1967).

The David Weisbart Collection consists largely of materials pertaining to the films he produced. It is a large collection and contains:

1. Miscellaneous materials (mostly scripts and treatments) relating to fifty-six films and television shows that were never produced.
2. Synopses of approximately thirty properties, 1950-1960.
3. Extensive materials (memos and correspondence) from the story department at Twentieth-Century Fox, 1950-1959.
4. Materials relating to the production of the following films may be found in the collection:
   *Love Me Tender* (1956)
   *Between Heaven and Hell* (1956)
   *The Way to the Gold* (1957)
   *April Love* (1957)
   *These Thousand Hills* (1959)
   *A Private's Affair* (1959)
   *Holiday for Lovers* (1959)
   *Flaming Star* (1960)
   *Goodbye Charlie* (1964)
   *Rio Conchos* (1964)
   *The Pleasure Seekers* (1964)
   *Valley of the Dolls* (1967)

## The Robert Wise Collection

Robert Wise (1914-    ) began his career as a film cutter at RKO where he edited *Citizen Kane* (1941) and *The Magnificent Ambersons* (1942). In 1943, he directed *The Curse of the Cat People* and has functioned as a director and, at times, director-producer ever since. Wise is perhaps best known for *West Side Story* (1961) and that financial blockbuster, *The Sound of Music* (1965). The Robert Wise Collection contains:

1. A large potpourri of worthwhile material about these films:
   *West Side Story* (1961)
   *Two for the Seesaw* (1962)
   *The Haunting* (1963)
   *The Sound of Music* (1965)
   *The Sand Pebbles* (1966)
   *Star!* (1968)
   *The Andromeda Strain* (1971)
2. Miscellaneous materials (mostly sketch books) relating to *I Want to Live*; *Run Silent, Run Deep*; *Somebody Up There Likes Me*; *Tribute to a Bad Man*; *Two Flags West*; *Three Secrets*; *The Set-up*; *Odds Against Tomorrow*; and *Executive Suite*.
3. Other material on *Battle!*, a film that never came to fruition. It was to deal with the life of photographer Robert Capa. Several drafts of the script, research materials, tapes of Capa's voice, Capa's photos, correspondence, budgets, treatments, etc.
4. Scripts of twenty-eight different films from *The Curse of the Cat People* (1943) to *The Andromeda Strain* (1971). Most are shooting scripts with copious annotations and some have appendices containing memos, budgets, sketches, etc.

The following individuals and organizations have donated materials and have collections either in storage or as yet not itemized. The materials are by no means inaccessible. Their contents are available to a student or scholar who intends to use them for legitimate research.

Steve Allen
Fred Astaire
John J. Anthony
Mischa Bakaleinikoff
Biltmore Theatre
John Brahm
Irving Brecher
George Burns & Gracie Allen
Marvin & Mary Carlock
Saul Chaplin
Samuel Colt
George Cukor
Luther Davis
Andy Devine
Walter Doniger
Dorr Historical
Jimmy Durante
Roger Edens
Sally Eilers
William Farnum
Theodore J. Flicker
Arthur Freed
Y. Frank Freeman

Hal Goodman &
Larry Klein
Freeman Gosden &
Charles Correll
Walter Grauman
Greg Garrison Prod.
Mrs. Otto Haebel
Robert Hamner
Betty Harte
George James Hopkins
Hal Humphrey
Roger Imhoff
Maurice Jarre
Millard Kaufman
Ernest Laszlo
Jerry Lewis
Constance Littlefield
Jack Lord
Abby Mann
Jimmy McHugh
Alfred Newman

Jack Oakie
Ole Olsen
Pacific Pioneer
  Broadcasters
Parker Advertising Inc.
Louella Parsons
Joe Pasternak
Eleanor Peters
Eleanor Powell
Johnny Rivers
Hal Roach
Howard Rodman
Benny Rubin
Walter Seltzer
Richmond Shepard
Edward Small
Ann Sothern
Leonard Spigelgass
Dimitri Tiomkin
Claire Windsor
Fay Wray

## Note

1. Inquiries about specific holdings and their availability to researchers should be addressed to Dr. Robert Knutson, Head, Department of Special Collections, University Library, University of Southern California, Los Angeles, California 90007.

L. Terry Oggel

# A Short Title Guide to the Edwin Booth Literary Materials at The Players

The oldest theatre collection in the United States, housed at The Players in New York and now known as The Walter Hampden-Edwin Booth Theatre Collection and Library, was founded by Edwin Booth in 1888 as a part of The Players, the association he had established for raising the dramatic arts to the level of the other arts in America. On New Year's Day 1889, the day after the formal opening of the Club, Booth directed a letter to the Board of Directors of The Players:

> Dear Sirs—
> I beg to present to you herewith all the books furniture and pictures belonging to me and now contained in the building No 16 Gramercy Park, New York.

A Short Title Guide to the Edwin Booth    99
Literary Materials at the Players

Apparently no list was made of the books in Booth's library at the time. Its exact size and nature, therefore, remain a mystery. However, as Richardson Wright has recorded in his history of the early years of the Players ("The New Tenants at No. 16," in *The Players' Book*, Henry W. Lanier, ed. [New York: The Players, 1938], p. 107), Booth's library apparently numbered 1000 volumes and clearly it included material he had been collecting throughout his 40-year professional career.

From the beginning, the library was to be at the center of The Players' concerns. Louis Rachow, librarian and curator, has pointed out ("The Players," *Performing Arts Review*, II [1971], 717-718) that the club members were formally charged with the "primary duty of building up 'a library relating especially to the history of the American stage . . .'—to form a continuing repository where the great and colorful personalities who molded the American theatre, and who continue to direct its destinies, should live for future generations." Chartered as a research library by the State of New York in 1957 and by the federal government in 1962, The Walter Hampden-Edwin Booth Theatre Collection and Library has grown impressively since its inception. In addition to the Edwin Booth literary materials hereafter listed, it includes, in approximate numbers, 4500 autograph letters signed, 800 manuscripts, 35,000 playbills, 25,000 photographs, 12,000 printed volumes, 3000 items of stage memorabilia, and 185 paintings, sculptures and other *objets d'art*, all of this material being related to the stage and most of it related to the American stage. In addition it includes the most extensive magic collection in the United States, the John Mulholland collection, which has approximately 6000 volumes, 4000 letters, 1000 photographs, 400 stage items, 250 playbills and posters, 75 drawings and 25 manuscripts.

The Edwin Booth portion of the library, including that which is extant from Booth's 1888 bequest and that material of Booth's which the library has acquired subsequently, reveals a scholar-actor. Especially noteworthy, besides the promptbook collection of course, are the rich holdings of editions of Shakespeare and of works relating to stage effects, many of which contain marginalia by Booth. Indeed, Rachow is correct when he says, in his "The Walter Hampden Memorial Library" (*Wilson Library Bulletin*, 38 [April 1964], 656), that "Booth was quick to realize that his art... demanded documentation.... With this thought in mind he nourished and preserved... a collection that today bears eloquent evidence of the owner's reading and reflection."

Although the Booth literary material has for the most part been kept separate from the rest of the library through the years, there has never been an attempt to draw it all together and to describe its nature and scope in such a way as to provide a tool for researchers on Edwin Booth or in the history and literature of American stage and drama. What follows is a short title listing which meets that need. It covers all the *literary* material (holograph and printed material excepting playbills) housed in The Walter Hampden-Edwin Booth Theatre Collection and Library which is known, or is reasonably thought, to have been Booth's at one time or another, including many items not yet cataloged by the library which the author discovered during the preparation of this Guide. It does not include those non-literary items—playbills, photographs, stage memorabilia and the like—which were or might have been Booth's and are now at the Library. Although the Library is continually acquiring Booth material and thereby rendering any such listing tentative, the following Guide is as complete as it is possible to be now.

The collection is best described in eight categories: Holograph Messages, Promptbooks, Scrapbooks, Ledgers, Manuscripts, Legal Documents, Miscellaneous, and Printed Volumes. Since the methods of listing such a wide assortment of material must vary according to the material, explanations of method are included as headnotes for each category. Special attention should be paid to the various uses of brackets throughout the Guide, however, since they indicate different things in nearly every category. Abbreviations used in the Guide follow those established in the second edition of *The MLA Style Sheet*, New York, 1970.

A final note of gratitude is in order since the author is particularly indebted to others for completion of the Guide. Most of all, Mr. Louis A. Rachow, Curator and Librarian, and Mr. Carl Willers, his assistant, graciously supplied a great amount of personal and professional assistance and without their cooperation the Guide could not have been completed. The support and advice of my colleague, Mr. William R. DuBois of the bibliography department of the Swen F. Parson Library at Northern Illinois University, has made completion of the Guide quicker and its usability more certain. The Council of Academic Deans of Northern Illinois University supplied funds in the form of grants for travel and manuscript preparation.

# I. Holograph Messages to or by Edwin Booth (total = 2485)

This list of all "messages" to or by Booth includes both complete messages and consequential fragments, whether or not they have been cataloged. Generally they are letters, but in a few cases they are postcards, telegrams, notes, or miscellaneous other forms of communication. The messages by Booth are all originals except when noted. The years, or the span of years, of the messages are indicated within brackets following the name of the correspondent. Additional information about the messages is also included within these brackets. In all cases, brackets here are used only as a device for showing units of information, not for indicating editorial interpolation. Information supplied by the author, in the relatively few cases when it has occurred, has been added silently.

There has been no attempt to include letters to or by other members of the Booth family, even though they may have been in Edwin Booth's possession at some time.

Every effort has been made to present the most accurate and most complete information in a way that will provide the greatest service to the researcher. The author has tried to decipher and to identify names and to combine all messages from the same person within the same entry regardless of the variations in signatures. Mrs. Robert M. Hooper, for example, signed most of her letters to Booth "Lucy." But all letters certainly identified as hers are listed below under "Mrs. Robert M. Hooper" regardless of the fact that she used both "Lucy" and "Lucy Hooper." It may be, however, that there are still other letters from her written over still other names (or initials). If such letters exist, they are listed under the other names or under the grouping "from Anon., or unidentifiable or undecipherable signatures, or obvious pseudonyms." If she used only a single initial, the letter is listed in this grouping. Obviously, if Mrs. Hooper had written Booth without signing the letter in any way whatsoever, the letter would be in this grouping also.

In most cases, the identification like that of "Lucy" and "Mrs. Robert M. Hooper" has not been made, however. In fact, I have been quite conservative in making this sort of identification in the belief that such a policy will keep confusion and obstruction of scholarly investigation resulting directly from inaccurate identification to a minimum. Hence, by way of illustration, among the letters to Booth, those from "A. A.," "Ada A.," and "Mrs. H. A. A." may indeed be from the same person, but in the absence of evidence establishing such an identification beyond doubt they have been entered as three separate entries and the uncertainty of their proper identification indicated by quotation marks. As a rule only the most certainly identified names have been used. Occasionally other identifying names have been added and set off within parentheses following the entry-name. Thus, to be sure all avenues of investigation are followed, users of the Guide should consult every possible listing for a correspondent: nicknames, maiden/married names, favorite pseudonyms, initials and the like.

In some cases the problem of identification has been compounded by the illegibility of a signature. In cases where there is doubt about either the accuracy of the deciphering of some element of a signature, as little as one or two characters or as much as a whole name, or where there is doubt about the identification of a name, question marks have been used. I have been somewhat more willing to hazard a guess on the translation of a signature, however, since usually only a character or two are questionable and a letter entered under a partially incorrectly spelled name is of inestimably more use to a researcher than it is entered under the "undecipherable signature" heading. Placing it here would be safer since it would keep the Guide from being technically inaccurate but would do so at the expense of scholarly assistance. Hence, here too the user should consult other possible listings: for example, the letter to Booth from the questionable signature "George W. Boynton" may in truth be from G. H. Boughton.

In addition, the "undecipherable signature" category has also been used for those letters signed with "obvious pseudonyms" (i.e., facetious or semifacetious pseudonyms) like "Ophelia." The problem is in determining just when the pseudonym is facetious. The author has tried to separate those pseudonyms which were intended to disguise the identity of the writer—like "Ophelia" and "Honorine" and "Admiralion"—from those names which are probably pseudonyms but which might reveal the identity of the writer, such as "Mary V. Belle" and "Kate." Letters of the first kind are listed in the grouping "obvious pseudonyms" and those of the latter kind are listed individually and set off by quotation marks.

Finally, the Special Letters category which heads the list of letters to Booth includes letters recently found and not yet cataloged. The other special letters in the Guide have been cataloged and are entered alphabetically in the listing.

## A. By Booth
(total = 556)

11 to Unknown [1858-1887; 2 copies; 1 completed form; 6 undated]; 9 to Albaugh, John W. [1885-1888; 3 undated]; 1 to Aldrich, Thomas B. [undated]; 1 to Allaise, Mr. [1890]; 1 to Allen, Mrs. [1876; handwritten copy]; 67 to Anderson, David C. [1873-1884; 9 undated, 1 of which is a group of cards in an envelope addressed to Anderson]; 27 to Anderson, Mrs. David C. [1884-1892; 22 undated]; 2 to Andrews, A. [1861, 1887; 2 photocopies].

11 to Badeau, Adam [1861-1866; 1 undated]; 1 to Baker, Mrs. George [undated]; 1 to Ballenberg, Samuel [1885; telegram]; 53 to Barrett, Lawrence [1860-1891; 25 undated]; 1 to Barrett, Mrs. Lawrence [1891]; 1 to Bell, Clark [1876]; 5 to Benedict, Elias C. [1877-1884; 1 undated]; 94 to Booth, Edwina [1870-1892; 36 undated]; 1 to Booth, Dr. Joseph A. [1889]; 3 to Bromley, Theodore [1890-1891; 1 undated]; 1 to Bruorton, William (?) [1876]; 1 to Bryan, M. T. [1875].

1 to Carnes, Mrs. [1876]; 12 to Carryl, Charles [1890; 11 undated]; 2 to Carryl, Constance [1889-1891]; 10 to Cary, Emma [1864-1866; 2 undated]; 1 to Chase, Arthur Brisbane [undated]; 1 to Clarke, Frank W. [1890]; 1 to Collyer, Dr. Robert [1881]; 1 to a Costumer ("Dear Sir") [1887].

1 to Daly, Mrs. Charles F. [1888]; 1 to Dunlap, George L. [undated].

4 to Ewer, Ferdinand C. [1877-1883; all are handwritten copies]; 1 to Ewer, Mrs. Ferdinand C. [undated].

1 to Felton, Mrs. C. C. [1861]; 1 to Fisher, Stephen (co-addressee with D. H. Harthus, below) [1878]; 1 to Furness, H. H. [1874].

1 to Gayler, Charles [1870; handwritten copy]; 1 to Goldsmith, A. B. [1870]; 1 to Goodale, George [1886]; 1 to J. B. Goodman & Company [1890]; 1 to Grant, Ulysses Simpson [1867]; 1 to Grossmann, Ignatius R. [1890]; 1 to Grossmann, Mildred [1886].

1 to Halpine, C. Graham [undated; typescript copy of a transcript]; 1 to Harthus, D. H. (co-addressee with Stephen Fisher, above) [1878]; 1 to Hazlitt, Lena [1871]; 1 to Hicks, Thomas [1861]; 1 to Hoffendahl, Dr. H. L. H. [1866]; 2 to Hoyt, Goold [1869; 1 undated]; 3 to Hutton, Laurence [1886; 2 undated, 1 of them a facsimile].

1 to Irving, Henry [1879].

1 to Jefferson, Joseph [1858]; 1 to Johnson, Andrew [1869; photocopy of a handwritten copy].

1 to Kauffman, S. H. [1874; typewritten copy]; 1 to Kellogg, Gertrude [1882].

1 to LaFollette, Robert M. [1879; facsimile postcard]; 1 to Lancaster, A. E. [1878]; 1 to Laurence, Col. [undated]; 2 to Lockwood, Mr. [1881; undated].

1 to Magonigle, J. Henry [1875?]; 93 to McEntee, Jervis [1866-1888; 14 undated, 1 of them a postcard]; 2 to McVicker, James H. [1881]; 11 to Miller, Wynn E. [1881-1885; 6 undated]; 1 to "Monsieur" [1862; copy]; 1 to Moreau, Charles C. (?) [1869]; 32 to Murray, John B. [1865-1874; 1 undated]; 1 to Myers, Mrs. [1888].

3 to "Nat" [1859, 1876; 1 undated; 1876 letter accompanied by envelope addressed to "N. Levin, Esq."]; 1 to Nidell, Rev. Dr. [1880].

1 to Osgood, Rev. Samuel [1863; copy].

1 to Pardee, Dr. [1870]; 1 to People of the United States [1865; signed and slightly revised by Booth; composed and written for Booth by J. B. Murray]; 1 to Pierce & Snyder [1884]; 1 to Placide, Thomas [1865; bank draft]; 2 to The Players, Members of [1888; 1 undated]; 1 to The Players, Board of Directors of [1889].

1 to Robb, J. Hampden [1891].

A Short Title Guide to the Edwin Booth 105
Literary Materials at the Players

1 to Sanger, Frank [1891]; 1 to Sefton, Mr. [1850]; 1 to Smith, George W. [1890]; 2 to Smith, W. H. [undated]; 1 to Stedman, Edmund C. [1879]; 2 to Stoddard, Mrs. Richard Henry [undated]; 13 to Stoddard, Richard Henry [1863-1864; 9 undated]; 1 to Sullivan, Algernon [1880].

9 to Thompson, Launt [1881-1884; 1 undated].

1 to Wallace, Mr. [1888]; 2 to Walton, F. J. [1879, 1880]; 2 to Whitman, Walt [1884; both photocopies]; 4 to Winter, William [1886-1888; 1 copy; 1 undated fragment to Winter?]; 2 to Wister, Mrs. Caspar [1867]; 1 to Whytal, Russ [1885].

**B. To Booth
(total = 1929)**

Special Letters and Petitions: 1 from 24 members of Holyoke Academy asking Booth to perform in *Richard III* [undated]; 1 from A. O. Hall, G. Bedford, W. Winter, and Lester Wallack concerning a benefit for John Brougham [undated]; 1 from 8 signatories regretting an attack on Booth at Niblo's [April 25, 1864]; 1 from Henry Barrault and J. Bernard, in French [September 13, 1865]; 1 from G. W. Harris, W. C. Hyatt, W. J. P. Amity, and O. C. Hyatt inviting Booth to join the Baptist Church of Brooklyn [February 13, 1867]; 1 from 18 citizens of Providence, R.I. requesting Booth to perform [April 16, 1867]; 1 from A. Stirling and G. Loveday, Honorary Secretaries of the Harcourt Memorial Fund [November 10, 1880]; 1 from 9 members announcing their election of Booth to honorary membership in the Junior Garrick Club of London [October 16, 1880]; 1 from G. Loveday and 2 other undecipherable signatures (from Harcourt Memorial Fund?) [November 16, 1880]; 1 from E. B. Valentine, C. D. Shepard, and G. J. Griffin announcing Booth's membership in New York Lodge #330 of the Free and Accepted Masons [December 1, 1881].

123 from Anon., or unidentifiable or undecipherable signatures, or obvious pseudonyms like "Ophelia" [1857-1892; 69 undated]; 1 from "A., A." [1865]; 1 from "A., Ada" [1858]; 1 from "A., Mrs. H. A." [1865]; 1 from "A., M. R." [1865]; 1 from "A., S. L." [1872]; 1 from Abbey, Henry E. [1882]; 1 from Abbott, Charles [1891]; 1 from Abbott, I. [1868]; 1 from Abbott, Lyman [undated]; 1 from Abney, W. H. [1867]; 3 from Adams, Edwin [1868, 1873; 1 undated]; 1 from ¹Adams, John J. [1885]; 1 from Adams, Mrs. Edwin [1877]; 2 from Agassiz, J. Louis [1863, 1866]; 1 from Agassiz, L. C. [un-

dated]; 1 from [1]Aiken, David W. [1885]; 1 from Akend, E. [1876]; 1 from [2]Albaugh, John W. [1885]; 3 from Aldrich, Mrs. Thomas B. [undated; one with postscript by Thomas B. Aldrich]; 16 from [3]Aldrich, Thomas B. [1864-1891; 3 undated; 1 post card]; 4 from Allen, E. M. [1890]; 11 from Allen, George [1864-1869; 5 undated]; 1 from [2]Allison, W. B. [1885]; 8 from Anderson, David C. [1865-1881]; 1 from Anderson, E. J. L. [1877]; 1 from Anderson, Gertrude [1891]; 2 from Anderson, Mrs. David C. [1888; 1 undated]; 1 from "Annie" [undated]; 1 from Anthony, W. J. [1890]; 1 from Arents, Isabelle [1868]; 1 from Arkins, H. E. (?) [undated]; 1 from Arnold, J. [1892]; 1 from Arnold, Matthew [1883]; 1 from [2]Arthur, Chester A. [1885]; 1 from Astor, C. A. [undated]; 1 from Astor, William B. [1869]; 1 from Atlee, Thomas S. [1868]; 8 from d'Aubigney, Isabey [undated]; 1 from Aunerley, N. F. [1879].

1 from "B., Ada" [undated]; 1 from "B., A. M." [undated]; 1 from "B., J. W." [undated]; 1 from "B., M." [1865]; 38 from Badeau, Adam [1857-1893; 17 undated]; 1 from Bain, Mrs. (?) [undated]; 1 from [2]Baird, Absolom [1885]; 2 from Baker, A. Prescott [1890]; 1 from Baker, B. A. [1865]; 2 from Baltzeles, L. M. (?) [1868]; 3 from Baltzeles, Mrs. L. M. (?) [1868]; 1 from Bancroft, George [1865]; 1 from Bancroft, S. R. [1880]; 1 from [1]Barber & Ross Co. [1885]; 1 from [2]Barbour, J. L. [1885]; 1 from Barnard, James M. [undated]; 1 from von Barndorf, Auguste [1869]; 57 from Barnett, T. J. [1866-1875; 13 undated; 5 fragments]; 1 from Barnum, Henry A. [1879]; 1 from Baron, H. [1878]; 13 from Barrett, Lawrence [1867-1889; 4 undated; 1 telegram and 1 inscription]; 1 from Barrett, Louis [1882]; 1 from Barrett, Mrs. Lawrence [undated]; 1 from Barrows, Horace G. [1857]; 5 from Bartlett, Agnes [1870-1882]; 7 from Bartlett, Frank [1865-1875; 3 undated]; 1 from Bassett, Thomas [1874]; 1 from [2]Bateman & Co. [1885]; 1 from [3]Beard, W. H. [undated]; 1 from "Beaufort" [1882]; 2 from Beaufort, M. [1865]; 1 from Beecher, Henry Ward [1863]; 1 from Bell, Clark [1875]; 1 from Bell, Sara A. (?) [1881]; 1 from "Belle, Mary V." [1867]; 1 from Bellew, J. M. [undated]; 2 from Bellows, H. W. [1863, 1866]; 1 from [1]Belmont, Perry [1885]; 1 from Bence, E. [1880]; 10 from Benedict, E. C. [1877-1885; 1 undated; 1 telegram]; 2 from Bennett, T. J. [1873; 1 undated]; 1 from Benson, Eugene [1865]; 1 from [3]Bierstadt, A. [undated]; 1 from Bigelow, Isabel C. [1881]; 1 from Birmingham, J. B. [1865]; 1 from Birrell, J. B. [1880]; 2 from Bishop, Josephine [1891; undated]; 10 from Bispham, William [1865-1889; 1 telegram]; 1 from Blanshard, E. [1881]; 1 from Block, Miss [undated]; 1 from Blodgett, Mrs. R. S. [1868]; 5 from Blossom, S. [1865-1866]; 1 from

A Short Title Guide to the Edwin Booth 107
Literary Materials at the Players

Booth, Charles H. [1870]; 6 from Booth, Edwina [1875-1882; 3 undated]; 1 from Booth, E. G. [1866]; 1 from Booth, John Wilkes [1858]; 3 from Booth, Joseph A. [undated]; 7 from Booth II, Junius B. [1862-1879; 1 undated]; 4 from Booth, Mary L. [1871-1885]; 15 from Booth, Mrs. Edwin (Mary Devlin) [1857-1861; 7 undated]; 11 from Booth, Mrs. Junius B. (Mary Ann Holmes) [1862-1877; 4 undated]; 1 from Booth, Thomas [1887]; 1 from Botta, Anne C. L. [undated]; 2 from Boughton, G. H. [1881; undated]; 1 from Boynton, George W. (?) [undated]; 1 from Bowen, Clarence [1889]; 1 from [2]Bowen, Thomas M. [1885]; 1 from Bowles, W. B. [1866]; 1 from [3]Bradford, William [undated]; 1 from Bradley, Whipple B. [1875]; 1 from [4]Brady, John R. [1880]; 1 from Brainerd, Maud L. [1876]; 1 from Brewer, Francis [1867]; 3 from Brewster, Benjamin H. [1866, 1867; undated]; 1 from Bright, Jacob [1882]; 1 from Brooks, J. W. (?) [1863-1865]; 1 from Brooks, Phillip [1890]; 1 from Brown, Carrie P. [1875]; 2 from Brown, Hall & Vanderpoel [1867]; 1 from Bryant, William C. [1870]; 1 from Bull, Ole Bourneman [1880; inscription]; 1 from [1]Burnes, James N. [1885]; 1 from Burnett, J. C. [1865]; 2 from Burns, Charles K. [1891]; 1 from Burroughs, M. L. [1887]; 2 from Burroughs, W. F. [1865]; 1 from Burton, E. [undated]; 1 from Burusteugel, K. [undated]; 1 from Butler, Cyrus [1880]; 1 from Butler, Mrs. Anna M. [1882]; 1 from Bysam, E. R. (?) [1881].

1 from "C., B." [1869]; 1 from Cagin, Dr. J. (?) [1869]; 1 from Calhoun, Eleanor [undated]; 1 from Calvert, Adelaide [1882]; 1 from Campbell, Archibald M. [1874]; 1 from Campbell, Muriel [1880]; 1 from Candler, E. Stuart (?) [1865]; 1 from [1]Cannon, Joseph G. [1885]; 1 from [1]Carlisle, J. Griffin [1885]; 2 from Carlotta, Dr. C. [1880, 1881]; 1 from Carter, A. B. [1877]; 1 from Carty, Harriet W. [1881]; 12 from Cary, Emma F. [1864-1881; 4 undated]; 6 from Cary, Helen [1862-1866; 2 undated]; 1 from Cary, Richard [1862]; 1 from [1]Cassidy, George W. [1885]; 1 from Chadwick, Mary [undated]; 2 from Chamberlin, E. V. [1882; undated]; 2 from Chamberlin, W. H. [1882, 1888]; 1 from Chambers, E. V. [1888]; 1 from Chapman, Julia [undated]; 1 from Chase, Arthur B. [undated]; 1 from Chase, Eva C. (?) [1866]; 1 from Cherry, Charles H. [1867]; 1 from Child, George W. [undated]; 5 from Chilton, R. S. [1857-1881]; 2 from Cist, L. J. [1877]; 1 from Clandine, Annie [1866]; 1 from "Clara" [undated]; 1 from Clarence, Nellie A. [1867]; 1 from Clark, C. C. [undated]; 1 from Clark, Fanny S. [1866]; 2 from Clark, Frank P. [1881; 1 form]; 1 from [1]Clark, John T. [1885]; 2 from "Clarke" [1879, 1881; 1 telegram]; 1 from Clarke, Creston [1892]; 1 from [2]Clarke, Daniel B. [1885]; 1 from Clarke, George [1881]; 7

from Clarke, John S. [1889-1892; 3 undated]; 11 from Clarke, Mrs. John S. (Asia Booth) [1867-1886; 3 undated, 1 of them a copy]; 1 from Clarke, Mary B. [1890]; 1 from Clarkson, Joseph P. [1875]; 1 from Clay, Henry [1867]; 1 from Clayton, G. M. [1879]; 3 from Cleveland, Henry W. [1870-1874]; 1 from Clifford, Jeanie [undated]; 1 from Clive, Mrs. Carrie [1878]; 3 from Coates, Elmer R. [1865; 2 undated]; 1 from Coggerhall, Thomas [1891]; 2 from Collier, Laird [1868, 1880]; 2 from Collyer, Robert [1879; 1 undated]; 1 from ²Conger, Frank B. [1885]; 2 from Conrad, Lou L. [undated]; 2 from Cook, Martha [undated]; 1 from Cooke, Rev. Horace [1867]; 1 from Coolidge, H. H. [1865]; 1 from ²Coon, Charles E. [1885]; 1 from Cooper, Cornelia R. [undated]; 1 from ²Corcoran, William W. [1885]; 1 from ¹Cosgrove, John [1885]; 1 from Couldock, Charles W. [1886]; 1 from Cox, Mary I. (?) [undated]; 1 from ¹Cox, Samuel S. [1885]; 4 from Creswick, William [1871-1872]; 1 from ²Crowell, R. F. [1885]; 1 from ¹Curtin, Andrew G. [1885]; 13 from Cushman, Charlotte [1861-1876; 1 undated]; 1 from Cushman, Edwin C. [1892]; 2 from Cushman, Emma [1863; undated]; 3 from Cutter, Mrs. G. H. (Elizah?) [1880; 2 undated].

1 from ²Dalton, W. N. [1885]; 4 from Daly, Charles F. [1865-1879]; 1 from Daly, Judge [undated]; 3 from Daly, M. L. [undated]; 1 from Danforth, Felicia H. [1865]; 3 from Davenport, Edward L. [1868-1869]; 1 from Davenport, Mrs. E. L. [1879]; 1 from Davidge, William P. [1887]; 1 from Davidson, Garrison [undated]; 1 from Davidson, Mrs. Garrison [undated]; 1 from Davis, L. Clarke [1892]; 1 from Davis, S. Clark [1857]; 5 from Dawison, Bogumil [1867; 1 undated]; 1 from Dehan, William [1865]; 1 from Delafield, E. [undated]; 1 from Detonas, Jules [1868]; 1 from ¹Deuster, P. V. [1885]; 1 from Devlin, Mrs. H. [1879]; 1 from Devrient, Ludwig [1883]; 2 from Dickens, Charles [1867, 1868]; 1 from Dilks, S. Levin [1868]; 1 from ¹Dingman, H. [1885]; 1 from Doremus, Estelle E. (?) [1865]; 3 from Doremus, R. Ogden [1868-1869]; 1 from Douglas, Byron [1892]; 1 from Douglas, Olga (?) [undated]; 1 from ¹Dowling, Thomas [1885]; 1 from Drenker, Emil [1883]; 1 from Duncan, P. [1875]; 1 from Dunlap, Emma B. [1892]; 1 from Dunn, Fanny [undated]; 1 from Dwight, Charles [1865].

3 from "E., L." [1882]; 1 from "E., Mrs. L." [1882]; 1 from Edgers, Webster [1887]; 1 from "Edith" [1866]; 3 from Edmonds, J. W. [1865-1866]; 15 from Edmonds, Laura [1865-1869; 6 undated]; 1 from Edward, E. [1869]; 1 from Edwards, H. [1889]; 1 from Edwards, Maze [1881]; 1 from Edwards, Mrs. G. W. [undated]; 1 from "Effie" [undated]; 1 from Egbert, Ellen [1867]; 1 from Elicott, Y. Z.

A Short Title Guide to the Edwin Booth **109**
Literary Materials at the Players

[1877]; 1 from Ellery, Kate [1865]; 1 from Elliott, Maude H. [undated]; 1 from Ellsler, John A. [1877]; 1 from "Elvira" [1867]; 2 from Emerson, Kate [1869; 1 undated]; 1 from English, Jane [undated]; 1 from ¹Ermentrout, Daniel [1885]; 1 from ²Evans, Walter [1884]; 1 from Eve, Mrs. Philoclea E. [1871]; 1 from Everitt, L. H. [1882]; 17 from Ewer, Ferdinand C. [1877-1881; 6 undated]; 1 from Ewer, Mrs. Ferdinand C. [1884].

1 from "F., Bel." [1867]; 1 from "F., G. D." [1888]; 1 from "F., P. A." [1870]; 1 from "F., R. N." [1865]; 1 from Fabrio, Katharine S. [undated]; 1 from Fairfield, Amy [undated]; 1 from ¹Fall, R. A. [1885]; 1 from Fanyon, Dr. Joseph (?) [1875]; 1 from Fardel, J. W. [1867]; 1 from Farjeon, B. L. [1880]; 1 from Farman, G. (?) [1880]; 1 from Farnsworth, Lucy P. [1865]; 2 from Faust, A. Jerome [1866]; 1 from Fawcett, Owen [1885]; 1 from Fay, J. D. [1866]; 2 from Fechter, Charles [1869; 1 undated]; 2 from Felton, Mary [1863; undated]; 1 from Fenn, Charles A. [1879]; 2 from Fenn, Mrs. Charles A. (Fannie) [1879]; 1 from Fenost, Charles (?) [1880]; 3 from Field, Margret [1869; 1 undated]; 1 from Fields, James L. [undated]; 1 from Fields, Osgood & Co. [1869]; 2 from Fish, A. I. [1868, 1874]; 1 from Fish, James D. [1883]; 1 from Fisher, J. A. (?) [1866]; 1 from ²Fisher, Thomas J. [1885]; 1 from Fiske, Daniel W. [undated]; 3 from Fiske, Harrison G. [1881-1892]; 7 from "Fitz" [1863; 4 undated]; 1 from Flack, Binnie [1868]; 1 from Flears, Charles [1882]; 1 from Flohr, W. Henry [1877]; 3 from Flower, C. E. [1876-1879]; 1 from Foote, M. [1868]; 1 from Foote, Mary N. [1868]; 8 from Ford, John T. (?) [1858-1877; 4 undated]; 1 from Foster, Annie R. [1875]; 1 from Foster, Augusta [1891]; 1 from Foster, L. F. S. [1864]; 1 from Fox, Henry J. [1865]; 1 from Francis, M. [1879]; 1 from Francis, Saul W. [1885]; 1 from "Frank" [undated]; 1 from ²Franzoni, J. D. [1885]; 1 from Frazier, Mrs. J. W. [1878]; 1 from Fredericks, William S. [1865]; 1 from French, Fanny [1868]; 1 from French, Mrs. Mary L. [1875]; 1 from French, Wilfred A. [1880]; 1 from Friedberger, Alfred [1867]; 2 from Fronde, J. A. [undated]; 1 from Frothingham, O. B. [1881]; 1 from ²Frye, William P. [1885]; 1 from Fulkerson, A. [1867]; 1 from Fuller, George F. [1867]; 1 from Fuller, John [1866]; 1 from Fulton, Henry K. [1872]; 13 from Furness, H. H. [1875-1892; 5 undated]; 1 from Furnivall, F. J. [1881].

1 from "Gabrille" [1860]; 1 from Gage, N. H. [1879]; 1 from Gage, W. L. [undated]; 6 from Game, Mateo [1877-1882]; 1 from Garber, Davis [1875]; 1 from Garrett, R. B. [1877]; 1 from Garrett, R. P. [1880]; 1 from Garrington, R. M. [1882]; 1 from ²Geare, Randolph I.

[1885]; 2 from Gebhard, M. L. [1869; 1 undated]; 1 from George C. Parker & Son [1890]; 1 from Gibland, M. L. (?) [undated]; 1 from Gilder, Richard W. [1889]; 1 from Gill, Minnie [1877]; 1 from Gilmore, James (?) [1867]; 1 from Giltg, Annie (?) [1865]; 1 from [1]Glascock, J. R. [1885]; 3 from Godwin, Parke [1865; 2 undated]; 3 from Gooch, Walter E. [1880-1881]; 1 from [2]Goode, George B. [1885]; 1 from Goodrich, Frances B. [1869]; 1 from Goodrich, Sallie B. [1865]; 2 from Gould, Thomas [1860, 1866]; 1 from Gouldson, June (?) [undated]; 1 from Gray, Barry [1865]; 1 from Gray, L. [1878]; 1 from Gray, Mrs. Henry P. [1869]; 1 from Greenwood, J. [1888]; 1 from "Grey, Alice" [undated]; 1 from Griffin, Antonia [1891]; 1 from Griffin, G. W. [1867]; 1 from Griffith, Kate [undated].

1 from "H., Evelyn" [undated]; 1 from Haase, Friedrich [1887]; 1 from Habicht, C. E. [1867]; 1 from Hackett, C. C. [1885]; 5 from Hackett, James H. [1868-1871]; 1 from Hadaway, T. H. [1882]; 1 from Haight, Amanda [1865]; 3 from Hale, Edward E. [1883; 1 undated]; 3 from Hall, A. Oakley [1869-1870; 1 undated]; 2 from Hallam, Mrs. William L. [1872]; 1 from Halpine, Charles [1864]; 2 from Hamerick, Astger [1876, 1879]; 1 from Hamilton, Mary M. [1881]; 1 from Hanley, J. G. [1866]; 1 from "Hardinge, Wylde" [undated]; 1 from Harkins, D. H. [undated]; 1 from Hart, Lucius [1881]; 2 from Hart, William [1860, 1871]; 2 from Harte, Bret [undated]; 1 from Harvard University [1857]; 1 from [1]Harvey & Holden Co. [1885]; 1 from Harwood, Edwin [undated]; 1 from [3]Haseltine, William S. [undated]; 3 from Hastings, Thomas S. [1878-1881]; 1 from [2]Hatton, Frank [1885]; 1 from Hawes, Charlotte [1865]; 1 from [2]Hawley, J. R. [1885]; 1 from Hawthorne, Julian [1887]; 3 from Hazard, E. H. [1882]; 1 from [2]Hazen, William B. [1885]; 1 from Hebbard, Ellery [1865]; 1 from Hedge, James B. [1879]; 1 from Heffelfinger, James [1884]; 1 from Heiser, Henry [1878]; 1 from Helmer, N. [1876]; 1 from Henderson, Ettie [1891]; 1 from Henderson, Mrs. Sara (?) [undated]; 1 from [1]Henley, Barclay [1885]; 6 from Hennessy, W. J. [1868-1872; 1 undated]; 1 from [1]Hepburn, W. P. [1885]; 5 from Hepworth, George H. [1865-1889; 2 undated]; 2 from Hepworth, Wheldon [1881]; 1 from Hess, C. D. [1866; telegram]; 1 from [1]Hewitt, Abram S. [1885]; 1 from Hicks, Thomas [1865]; 1 from Highton, E. Gilbert [1881]; 1 from Hillard, G. S. [1868]; 1 from Hind, Thomas J. [1870]; 1 from [1]Hiscock, Frank [1885]; 1 from Hobbs, J. H. [1891]; 2 from Hoffman, John [1867, 1869]; 1 from Hollnook, W. A. (?) [undated]; 1 from [1]Holman, William S. [1885]; 1 from Holmes, Oliver W. [1886]; 1 from Holt, Mrs. N. N. [1875]; 7 from Hooper, Mrs. Robert M. [undated]; 1 from

Hope, James [1867]; 1 from Hopkins, Mary [1865]; 1 from Horton, E. R. [undated]; 1 from Houghton, J. C. [1878]; 2 from House, E. H. [1880, 1881]; 1 from Houston, M. H. [1879]; 7 from Howe, Julia Ward [1881, 1886; 5 undated]; 1 from Howells, William Dean [undated]; 1 from Howland, Marie [1875]; 1 from Hoxsie, Mrs. Anna P. [undated]; 1 from Hoym, Otto [1864]; 1 from Hoyt, Edward N. [1878]; 3 from Hoyt, Goold [1869; 2 undated]; 1 from Hubbell, Walter [1891; telegram]; 1 from Hughes, Ball [1863]; 1 from Hummel, A. H. [1892]; 1 from Hunter, Josephine [1880]; 4 from Huntington, W. H. (?) [1862-1866]; 4 from [4]Hutton, Laurence [1880-1882]; 2 from Hyde, Susan [1879, 1881].

1 from [2]Ingalls, John J. [1885]; 1 from "Ingersoll, Maude" [undated]; 9 from Irving, Henry [1882; 1 undated; 1 telegram].

1 from Jackson, Joseph [1871]; 1 from Jackson, Mrs. C. [1881]; 1 from Jackson, Spencer [1880]; 1 from James, M. P. [1890]; 4 from Janauschek, Francesca [1868-1889; 1 undated]; 1 from Jardine, Joseph P. [1866]; 1 from [2]J. C. Ergood & Co. [1885]; 12 from Jefferson, Joseph [1879-1891; 7 undated]; 1 from Jeffery, William S. [1871]; 2 from Jenkins, C. C. [1879]; 1 from "Jennie & May" [1867]; 1 from Jewett, Grace E. [1874]; 1 from "Joe" (Joseph A. Booth?) [1882]; 1 from Johannes, The Count [1867]; 2 from "John" (McCullough?) [1891; 1 undated]; 1 from [2]John F. Ellis & Co. [1885]; 1 from Johns, James T. [1877]; 1 from Johnson, Eastman [undated]; 1 from [2]Johnson, H. L. [1885]; 1 from Johnson, V. W. [undated]; 3 from Johnston, Christopher [1881]; 1 from [1]Jones, James [1885]; 1 from Jones, Margaret P. (?) [1891]; 1 from Jones, Melinda [1875]; 1 from Jones, Walker W. [1881]; 1 from Joshua, Marie [1883]; 1 from Joshua, Sam (?) [1882]; 1 from Joyce, Mrs. Thomas [1873].

1 from "K., C. M." [undated]; 1 from "K., V. W." [undated]; 1 from Kadlitz, F. H. [1882]; 1 from [2]Karr, W. W. [1885]; 4 from "Kate" [1867-1881; 1 undated]; 1 from Kaufmann, S. H. [1874]; 1 from Kean, Mrs. Ellen Tree [undated]; 1 from Keeley, Mary Anne [undated]; 3 from Keleltas, C. W. (?) [1860-1863]; 1 from Kellar, Harry [1885]; 1 from Kelley, John [1877]; 22 from Kellogg, A. O. [1864-1881; 4 undated]; 1 from Kellogg, Clara L. [undated]; 1 from Kellogg, Gertrude [1890]; 1 from Kemble, G. (?) [1869]; 1 from Kemble, W. [undated]; 1 from [3]Kensett, J. F. [undated]; 2 from Kent, R. B. (?) [1867; undated]; 1 from King, David [1877]; 1 from van Kleek, William [1865]; 1 from Knerr, C. B. [1879]; 1 from Knight, J. [1880]; 1 from Knight, Mable M. [1880]; 1 from [2]Knox, George W. [1885]; 1 from van Kommeritz, C. R. [1880]; 1 from Kuntze, Edward F. [1868].

1 from "L., M." [1869]; 1 from Lander, Jean M. [undated]; 1 from Lane, Edwin F. [1881]; 1 from [3]Lang, Louis [undated]; 1 from Lathrop, A. G. [1875]; 1 from [1]Latimer, M. B. [1885]; 1 from Lawrence, Philip [1868]; 5 from Lawrence, Samuel [1890-1892]; 1 from Lawson, Flora M. (?) [undated]; 1 from Lazarus, Henry [1881]; 2 from Leake, Lydia W. [1865-1866]; 1 from Leaverns, Fanny P. [1866]; 2 from [3]LeClear, Thomas [1868; undated]; 1 from Lee, William S. [1881]; 1 from Lee, L. H. [1892]; 1 from Leff, Jr., Charles H. [1878]; 1 from Lemote, N. (?) [undated]; 1 from Lentee, L. (?) [1882]; 1 from Lerey, S. (?) [1879]; 1 from Lester, Carrie C. [1865]; 1 from L'Estranger, J. F. [undated]; 2 from [3]Leutze, Emmanuel [undated]; 2 from LeVert, Octavia W. [1857]; 1 from Lewis, Nellie [1881]; 1 from [2]Lincoln, Charles P. [1885]; 1 from Liven, Charles J. B. [1875]; 1 from Livingston, C. [1869]; 1 from Lock, M. F. [1878]; 6 from Lockwood, Luke A. [1881-1892]; 1 from [1]Long, John D. [1885]; 1 from Longstreet, Mrs. A. B. (?) [undated]; 3 from Lowell, J. R. [1881-1882]; 3 from Lowndes, Charles [1876-1878]; 1 from Lowne, E. T. [1881]; 2 from Ludlow, Fitz Hugh [1864]; 1 from Ludlow, H. [1865]; 2 from Ludlow, Rosalie O. [1865, 1866]; 1 from Lyde, Dora L. [1892]; 3 from Lyon, Mark G. [1879-1881]; 1 from Lyon, Mrs. M. A. [undated]; 4 from Lytton, Edward Bulwer [1867].

1 from "M., H." [1875]; 1 from "M., J. B." [1866]; 2 from Macauley, B. (?) [undated]; 1 from Mace, Benjamin T. [1866]; 1 from MacGowan, A. B. [1882]; 1 from Mack, Henry Q. [1866]; 1 from Mackay, Charles [1880]; 1 from Mackaye, Steele [1880]; 1 from Mackenzie, Morell [1881]; 1 from Madox, G. W. [1875]; 1 from "Mag" [1877]; 1 from Magnay, William [1881]; 2 from Majeroni, E. [1880]; 1 from Majeroni, G. P. [1880]; 1 from "Margaret" [undated]; 8 from "Marie" (Marie Booth Douglass?) [1881; 5 undated]; 1 from Markens, Isaac [1865]; 1 from Martel, Adele F. [1882]; 1 from Martin, B. E. [undated]; 3 from Martin, Helena F. [1881; 2 undated]; 1 from Martin, J. [1872]; 1 from Martin, Theodore [1881]; 1 from "Mary" [undated]; 1 from Masely, H. C. [1860]; 1 from Mason, Emma [1880]; 1 from Mason, J. W. [1880]; 1 from Mason, Mrs. Kent [1881]; 1 from Mathews, Charles J. [1862]; 1 from Matthews, William [1881]; 1 from Matthison, Arthur [undated]; 1 from Mau, W. Lionel [1880]; 1 from "May, Daisy" [1890]; 3 from McAuley, Rachel (?) [1890; 2 undated]; 1 from McCarthy, Justin [1881]; 3 from McComb, Jennie (?) [1882; 2 undated]; 1 from McConony, A. I. (?) [1866]; 1 from [2]McCulloch, Hugh [1885]; 2 from [4]McCullough, John [1876, 1880]; 46 from [3]McEntee, Jervis [1864-1890; 2 undated]; 1 from McEwen, George C. [1865]; 1 from McGaffey, Ernest [1888]; 1 from

McKeon, Annie [undated]; 1 from McVay, George P. H. [1890]; 9 from McVicker, Horace [1870-1882; 3 undated]; 23 from McVicker, James H. [1870-1879; 2 undated; 1 telegram]; 1 from Merivale, Herman [1882]; 1 from Messerve, Theodore (?) [undated]; 1 from Methua, D. I. [1865]; 4 from Methua, J. G. [1860-1866]; 1 from Michel, Carl [1883]; 1 from Miles, Frank [1866]; 1 from Miles, George [1870]; 1 from ¹Millard, S. C. [1885]; 1 from Miller, Wynn E. [1881]; 1 from Mills, John G. [1869]; 1 from Mills, Luther L. [1879]; 4 from Miln, George C. [1878-1882; 1 undated]; 2 from ¹Mitchell, John [1869, 1885]; 3 from Modjeska, Helena [1881, 1882; 1 undated]; 1 from Montgomery, Walter [1871]; 1 from Moore, Clara J. [undated]; 2 from Moran, E. [1866, 1873]; 2 from Morgan, Dellie [undated]; 1 from ²Morgan, John T. [1885]; 1 from Morrell, Y. A. [1866]; 1 from Morris, Hester [undated]; 1 from ²Morrison, William R. [1885]; 1 from ¹Morse, Leopold [1885]; 1 from Mounor, Col. F. B. (?) [1882]; 1 from Muller, Gertrude C. [1868]; 1 from ¹Muller, N. [1885]; 2 from Murdock, James E. [1884, 1888]; 1 from Murray, G. [1876]; 13 from Murray, John B. [1865-1869]; 3 from Murray, Mrs. John B. [1867; 2 undated]; 1 from Murray, Sarah E. [1867]; 1 from Myrtle, Mrs. M. A. [1867].

1 from ²Nailor, Jr., Allison [1885]; 1 from "Narrow" [1891]; 3 from Nash, Charles [1857-1882]; 1 from Nash, E. Adele [undated]; 2 from "Ned" [undated]; 1 from "Nellie" [1867]; 1 from Nione, John F. [1857]; 1 from ²Norris, James L. [1885].

1 from Oakes, James [1857]; 1 from Oasly, Haight (?) [1881]; 1 from ¹Ochiltie, Thomas P. [1885]; 1 from O'Connor, J. [1867]; 1 from Olcampan, Adele (?) [1865]; 1 from Olcott, H. S. [1869]; 3 from Oliver, Marshal [1866-1868]; 1 from ²Olmstead, J. F. [1885]; 1 from ¹O'Neill, J. J. [1885]; 1 from ¹Orme, James W. [1885]; 1 from Osgood, Ellen H. [1881]; 1 from ⁴Osgood, George [1880]; 10 from Osgood, Samuel [1862-1880]; 1 from Owen, Catherine [1867]; 1 from Owen, Robert D. [1867]; 1 from Owens, John [1859].

1 from Pagny, S. H. (?) [undated]; 1 from Palacin, Edward L. [1878]; 1 from Palmer, Albert M. [1890]; 3 from Palmer, E. D. [1864-1877]; 1 from Palmer, Nettie C. [1868]; 1 from ²Parke, John G. [1885]; 1 from Parker, A. [1875]; 1 from Parker, Henry G. [1881]; 1 from ²Parker, Jr., Peter [1885]; 1 from Parmly, Lucy [1865]; 1 from Parr, Thomas [1880]; 1 from Parsons, Mrs. T. W. (Anna) [1863]; 3 from Parsons, T. W. [1865; 2 undated]; 1 from Parsons, Sara [undated]; 1 from Paulding, Frederick [1882]; 1 from Peckham. E. Truman [1882]; 1 from Pember, Arthur [1869]; 1 from ²Pendleton,

George H. [1885]; 3 from Perabo, Ernest [1867-1881]; 1 from ²Peters, Norris [1885]; 1 from ²Phillips, F. J. [1885]; 1 from Phillips, George [1867]; 1 from Phillips, Watts [undated]; 1 from Phillmore, William [1880]; 4 from Pierce, Benjamin [1857-1879; 1 undated]; 4 from Pierce, James M. [1875-1884; 1 undated]; 1 from Pierce, M. [1881]; 1 from Piercy, Mary [1880]; 2 from Pike, Samuel N. [1866; 1 telegram]; 1 from Piker, Horace L. [1870]; 1 from Plank, P. W. and Jean M. [1882]; 1 from Platt, J. H. [1875]; 1 from Ploszczgnski, Edwin [undated]; 1 from ²Plumb, Preston B. [1885]; 1 from ¹Poland, Luke P. [1885]; 1 from Pollock, Walter [1881]; 1 from Pomrow, Dr. T. W. [undated]; 1 from Porter, William V. [1867]; 1 from Possart, Ernest [undated]; 6 from Potter, Marie (Mrs. Launt Thompson?) [1869]; 1 from ¹Potter, Orlando B. [1885]; 1 from Powers, James T. [1864]; 1 from Presh, M. Redde (?) [undated]; 5 from Preston, D. [1875-1879]; 1 from Proctor, Joseph [1890]; 1 from Purey, D. J. (?) [1882]; 1 from Pyne, R. L. [1866].

1 from Quinlan, Francis J. [1891].

1 from Rainey, John [1879]; 1 from ¹Randall, Sam [1885]; 1 from Rasch, Elsie [1879]; 1 from ²Rathbun, Richard [1885]; 1 from ²Rau, Charles [1885]; 1 from Ravlin, Rev. N. F. (?) [1875]; 1 from Read, E. A. [1876]; 1 from Reade, Charles [undated]; 1 from Reader, Maj. William [1867]; 1 from ¹Reagan, John H. [1885]; 1 from Real, A. E. [undated]; 1 from ¹Reed, Thomas B. [1885]; 1 from Rich, Belle [1878]; 1 from Rich, Helen H. [1888]; 1 from Richards, T. Addison [1865]; 1 from ²Ridgway, Robert [1885]; 1 from ²Riggs & Co. [1885]; 1 from Rivers, Lillie [1882]; 2 from Ristori, Adelaide [1885]; 1 from Ritchie, Anna C. [1858]; 7 from Robertson, Richard A. [1863-1871]; 1 from Robinson, S. [1875]; 1 from Robitaille, R. W. [1876]; 1 from deRosset, Mrs. Louis H. (Maria F. deRosset) [1867]; 2 from Runnian, James B. [1875, 1879]; 1 from Russell, Albert C. [1877]; 1 from Russell, Caroline N. [1881]; 1 from Russell, Charles [undated]; 4 from Russell, John E. [1871-1881; 1 undated]; 1 from Ryan, Daniel J. [1878]; 1 from ¹Ryan, Thomas [1885]; 1 from Ryers, Abbie H. [1878]; 1 from Ryerson, George W. [1871].

1 from ²Sacket, D. B. [1885]; 1 from ²Saks, I. [1885]; 1 from Salvini, A. [undated]; 3 from Salvini, Tommaso [1886; 1 undated inscription]; 1 from Sanderson, William [1874]; 1 from Sandon, Mary [1864]; 1 from Sanford, Mrs. R. M. [1867]; 1 from Sap, G. Herbert (?) [1876]; 1 from "Sara" (Sara C. Bull?) [undated]; 12 from Sargent, Epes [1866-1867; 4 undated]; 1 from Savage, M. J. [1881]; 1 from Saybrook, E. L. [1865]; 1 from Schaad, D. [1869]; 1 from

## A Short Title Guide to the Edwin Booth Literary Materials at the Players

[1]Schneider, L. H. [1885]; 1 from Scholl, Edward [1873]; 1 from Schonberg, James [1881]; 1 from Schreiner, H. A. [1879]; 1 from Scott, Clement [undated]; 1 from Sesser, W. F. [1892]; 3 from Seville, John D. [1865-1866]; 1 from Seymour, C. B. [1868]; 1 from Seymour, L. S. [1867]; 1 from Shackleford, J. W. [1871]; 1 from Shakspeare, Stephen H. [1866]; 1 from Shanks, William F. G. [1874]; 1 from Shaw, Parsons [1881]; 1 from Shear, Edwin H. [1881]; 1 from Shenk, Jane [1883]; 1 from [2]Sheridan, Philip H. [1885]; 1 from Sherman, William T. [undated]; 1 from Sherrill, A. F. [1888]; 1 from Siddons, J. H. [1860]; 1 from "Silas" [1865]; 1 from Simmonds, Morris [1880]; 1 from Simon, Louis M. [undated]; 1 from Simpson, Emmanuel [1881]; 2 from Sims, Richard [1880, 1881]; 1 from Sinding, Paul [1872]; 1 from [1]Singleton, Otho R. [1885]; 1 from Singley, Georgie [1867]; 1 from Sloane, M. P. [1865]; 1 from Smalley, H. A. [1881]; 1 from Smith, Arden R. [1879]; 1 from Smith, E. Oakes [1867]; 1 from Smith, J. Hyatt [undated]; 1 from Smith, Mark [1871]; 1 from Smith, Richard M. [1874]; 1 from Smith, Sara F. [1875]; 10 from Smith, St. Clair [1893; 9 medical bulletins relating to Booth's final illness]; 1 from Smith, William L. [1873]; 1 from Spicon, Leearn [undated]; 1 from Spies, A. W. [1865]; 1 from [2]Spofford, C. W. [1885]; 1 from [2]Spofford, H. W. [1885]; 1 from Staats, Anable (?) [1877]; 1 from Stanton, Effie C. [1869]; 1 from Stanton, Kay [1868]; 2 from Stark, James [1871, 1873]; 1 from Starrwood, R. W. [1867]; 1 from Staye, L. M. [1881]; 1 from St. Clair, Addie [1861]; 14 from Stedman, E. C. [1865-1891]; 1 from Stedman, Frederick S. [1879]; 2 from Stephens, Mrs. Ann [1857, 1858]; 1 from Sterns, E. E. [1875]; 1 from Stevens, B. F. [undated]; 1 from Stewart, R. L. (?) [1876]; 7 from Stoddard, R. H. [1862-1865; 1 undated]; 1 from "Stokenstrum, I." [undated]; 5 from Stoker, Bram [1881]; 1 from Stone, R. M. [1873]; 1 from [3]Stone, William O. [undated]; 1 from Stoughton, Kate [undated]; 1 from Sturgis, Russell [1881]; 2 from Sturtevant, Mary C. [1880, 1892]; 1 from [4]Sullivan, Algernon S. [1880]; 1 from Sutton, W. R. [1863]; 2 from Sweeny, J. G. [1866, 1867]; 1 from Swing, David [1882].

1 from "T., C." [1865]; 1 from "T., L." (Launt Thompson?) [undated]; 1 from [1]Talbott, J. F. C. [1885]; 1 from Tarnell, Mrs. G. C. [1881]; 1 from Tayleine, C. W. (?) [1889]; 1 from Taylor, A. B. [1881]; 2 from Taylor, Bayard [1863, 1866]; 1 from Taylor, Charles [1867]; 4 from Taylor, Col. James [1874-1877]; 1 from Templeton, Mrs. Zuluka E. [1892]; 1 from [2]Tenney & Co. [1885]; 1 from Tennyson, Alfred [1869]; 2 from Thayer, C. C. [1877]; 1 from Thayer, George F. [1868]; 1 from Thompson, Frank [1883]; 1 from Thompson, G. (?)

116 PERFORMING ARTS RESOURCES

[1868]; 28 from [3]Thompson, Launt [1863-1883; 5 undated]; 7 from Thompson, Marie L. (Mrs. Launt Thompson) [1890-1891; 2 undated]; 1 from [2]Thompson, W. S. [1885]; 1 from Thorndike, Henrietta D. [undated]; 1 from Thorp, Amelia C. [undated]; 1 from Tilden, M. H. [1865]; 1 from Tisdale, Archibald (?) [undated]; 1 from Tisdale, K. B. [undated]; 1 from [2]Todd, R. S. [1885][5]; 2 from Toole, J. L. [1881, 1882]; 1 from [1]Towles, H. O. [1885]; 1 from Townsend, John D. [1881]; 1 from Townsend & Weed [1881]; 1 from [1]Townshend, R. W. [1885]; 1 from [2]T. Roessle & Son [1885]; 1 from Trowbridge, Adelaide [undated]; 1 from [2]True, Frederick W. [1885]; 1 from [1]Tucker, John B. [1885]; 1 from Tucker, Mary M. [1880]; 1 from Tucker, Mrs. James 1886]; 1 from Tuckerman, Charles K. [1863]; 1 from Tuckerman, Henry T. [1868]; 1 from [2]Turnbull, Thomas R. [1885]; 1 from [1]Turner, H. G. [1885]; 1 from [2]Tweedale, J. [1885].

1 from Ulman, H. Charles [1887]; 1 from Urquhart, Isabel C. [undated].

1 from Vanderhoff, George [1865]; 2 from [3]Vaux, Calvert [1881; 1 undated]; 3 from Vaux, Downing [1882; 1 undated fragment]; 1 from Vermilye, J. D. [1878]; 1 from Vernon, George [1869]; 1 from LeVerrier, Genevieve [1867]; 1 from Vurauth, W. F. [1866].

1 from "W., B." [1882]; 1 from "W., H. M." [1865]; 2 from Wagner, Clinton [1881]; 1 from Wahs, Isabella (?) [undated]; 1 from Walker, James [undated]; 1 from Wallack, Emily [undated]; 1 from Wallack, Lester [undated]; 4 from Waller, D. W. [1865-1873]; 1 from Waller, Emma [undated]; 1 from Walls, Alfred [1891]; 1 from Walter, James [undated]; 1 from Ward, E. Burke [1890]; 1 from [2]Ward, Lester F. [1885]; 1 from Ward, Quincy [1866]; 1 from Warner, Charles D. [1885]; 1 from Warren, Theodore D. [1877]; 4 from Warren, William [1857-1886]; 1 from Washburn, John S. [1865]; 1 from [2]Washington, Richard [1885]; 1 from Waters, A. [undated]; 1 from Waterworth, C. [undated]; 1 from Watkins, Harry [1891]; 2 from Watson, W. Argyle [1879]; 1 from Way, Jennie M. (?) [1864]; 3 from Webster, Charles [1881-1891]; 1 from Westno, S. H. (?) [1881]; 3 from Wetmore, Mrs. Eliza Jane [1871]; 1 from Wheeler, Fred M. [1866]; 1 from Whilian, J. (?) [1880]; 1 from White, Horace [1879]; 2 from White, Richard G. [1862, 1869]; 1 from Whitehead, John [1865]; 2 from Whitman, Walt [1884]; 2 from Wiggin, Mrs. L. M. (Mattie H.?) [1881; undated]; 1 from Wikoff, H. (?) [undated]; 1 from Wildson, W. H. (?) [1882]; 1 from "Wilfred" (Clarke?) [1892]; 1

A Short Title Guide to the Edwin Booth 117
Literary Materials at the Players

from [1]Wilkins, Beriah [1885]; 1 from Wilkinson, Warring [undated]; 1 from "Will" (Bispham?) [1881]; 1 from Willard, Louise B. [1879]; 1 from [2]Willett & Ruoff Co. [1885]; 1 from "William" [1866]; 1 from Williams, Barney [1871]; 1 from Williams, Edward [1874]; 1 from Williams, Mrs. Marshall [1891]; 1 from Williams, M. T. [1875]; 1 from [2]Wilson, A. A. [1885]; 3 from Wilson, Caroline C. [1880; 1 undated]; 1 from Wilson, Francis [1892]; 1 from Winchester, M. E. [1865]; 1 from Winter, E. C. [1869]; 7 from [4]Winter, William [1879-1880; 1 undated]; 1 from Winters, William H. [1888]; 1 from Wood, Maltide [undated]; 1 from Wood, Ralph [1868]; 1 from Wood, Sara A. [1889]; 1 from Wood, Mrs. W. [1865]; 1 from Woodruff, Henry [undated]; 1 from Woolf, Jacob [1880]; 1 from Worcester, Samuel [1867]; 1 from [2]Wyman, A. N. [1885]; 1 from Wyndham, Rose [undated].

1 from Yates, Edmund [1881]; 1 from [2]Yeates, William S. [1885]; 1 from Young, C. E. [1867]; 1 from Young, J. Russell [1881]; 1 from Young, Mrs. William [1889].

12 from Zayas, H. C. and L. C. [1879-1881; 1 undated]; 1 from von Zglinzka, Maria [undated].

## II. Promptbooks (total = 89)

This list is of all of Booth's promptbooks (including partbooks, cutbooks, etc.) now at The Players. The major part of the collection is of books made for or by Booth, and many were actually used by him in his productions. There are actually 157 separate books, but they are listed under 89 entries here since several of them (represented in 2 of the *Lears*, 1 *Richard II*, 3 *Richard III*s, and 1 *Ruy Blas*) are housed together and are obviously meant to be used together.[6] Brackets here indicate information which I have supplied. The number following each title indicates the number of promptbooks of that play in the collection.

### A. by Shakespeare (total = 52)

*Hamlet* 6; *Henry VIII* 1; *Julius Caesar* 2; *King Lear* 6; *Macbeth* 2; *Measure for Measure* 1; *Merchant of Venice* 4; *Othello* 9; *Richard II* 8; *Richard III* 12; *Romeo and Juliet* 1.

**B. By Others**
**(total = 37)**

Unknown: *Sylvain* 1; Banim, John: *Damon and Pytheas* 1; de Bellow, Pierre-Laurent B.: *Gabrielle de Vergy* 1; [Dawes, Rufus?]: *Nix's Mate, or Boston in 1689* 1; Colman, The Younger, George: *The Iron Chest* 2; Dumanoir, Philippe F. P. and Adolphe Philippe Dennery: *Don Caesar de Bazan* 1; Gordon, George [Lord Byron]: *Werner* 1; Holcroft, Thomas: *A Tale of Mystery* 1; Hugo, Victor: *Ruy Blas* 7; von Kotzebue, Augustus F. F.: *The Stranger* 1; Lytton, Edward Bulwer: *The Lady of Lyons* 2, *Richelieu* 5; Massinger, Philip: *A New Way to Pay Old Debts* 1; [Moore, Edward]: *The Gamester* 1; Payne, John Howard: *Brutus* 3; Shiel, Richard L.: *The Apostate* 2; Talfourd, Thomas N.: *Ion* 2; Taylor, Tom: *The Fool's Revenge* 4.

## III. Scrapbooks

This list includes all of Booth's scrapbooks, albums, journal books and the like, cataloged or not, which are not concerned with financial matters. In so far as possible, they are arranged chronologically. Information in brackets following some entries indicates physical appearance and/or location of scrapbooks which have no identifying lettering on spine or front cover.

1. "Scrapbook" on spine of oversize volume; collection of odds and ends, some notes by Booth; no indication of year.
2. "Journal Book No. 2" on front cover; newspaper clippings, 1857-1858.
3. No lettering on spine or front cover; photo album of Booth family given by Edwin Booth to Mary Devlin Booth about 1860. [ornamental, simulated-wood front cover; Winslow Purchase]
4. No lettering on spine or front cover; newspaper clippings, 1861-1867. [Booth Case No. 2]
5. "Booth Newspaper Clippings 1866-1869" on spine.
6. "Scrapbook" on spine; memorabilia of opening night at Booth's Theatre, February 3, 1869.
7. No lettering on spine or front cover; newspaper clippings, 1869-1870. [Booth Case No. 2]
8. "Scrapbook" on spine; newspaper clippings, 1870-1871.

A Short Title Guide to the Edwin Booth
Literary Materials at the Players

9. Clipping from New York *Tribune* regarding Booth with notes by William Winter, December 5, 1871. [Miscellaneous file]
10. "Booth Newspaper Clippings 1871-1873" on spine.
11. "Edwin Booth by Hennessy, Linton and Winter. Illustrated. Boston, 1872" on spine; extra-illustrated edition of a published volume with letters, playbills, and memorabilia inserted.
12. "Scrapbook" on spine; newspaper clippings, March, April, and May, 1873.
13. No lettering on spine or front cover; album of photos, clippings and memorabilia from Booth's Theatre compiled by Lena Hazlitt, 1874. [blue velvet; Winslow Purchase]
14. Clipping from New York *Tribune* regarding Booth with notes by William Winter, August 17, 1876. [Miscellaneous file]
15. "Booth Newspaper Clippings" on spine; 1880-1881.
16. "Edwin Booth 1881-82 Season Henry E. Abbey Manager" on spine; notices of plays, memorabilia.
17. "Booth Newspaper Clippings 1882" on spine.
18. No lettering on spine or front cover; clippings from German Tour of 1882-1883 and from Booth's return to the United States in the spring of 1883. [Booth Case No. 2]
19. "Booth Memorial. Vol. I" on front cover; clippings and memorabilia dating for the most part no later than 1884.
20. "Booth's Theatre Moreau 1884" on spine; material related to Booth's Theatre collected and prepared by Charles C. Moreau.
21. "To Edwin Booth, Esq." on front cover; album of 66 letters signed by 111 Washingtonians collected by John B. Albaugh, 1885. [see footnotes 1 and 2]
22. "Scrapbook" on spine; record of Booth's United States tour, 1886-1887.
23. "Edwin Booth Season 1886-1887 Under the management of Lawrence Barrett Arthur B. Chase, Director" on front cover; daily playbills and memorabilia.
24. "Booth-Barrett Season 1887-1888 Under the management of Lawrence Barrett Director Arthur B. Chase" on front cover; daily playbills and memorabilia. [Winslow Purchase]
25. "Autographs" on front cover; "A memorial of the inauguration of The Players. Dec. 31st 1888" on first page.

120 PERFORMING ARTS RESOURCES

26. "Edwin Booth" on spine and front cover; playbills and memorabilia of Booth-Barrett tour of 1888-1889. [Winslow Purchase]
27. No lettering on spine or front cover; newspaper clippings concerning Booth, 1888-1893. [Booth Case No. 2]
28. "Autograph Letters Dramatic" on spine; a collection of letters by 36 people presented to The Players by Daniel B. Fearing May 4, 1889.
29. "To Edwin Booth From Augustin Daly and A. M. Palmer" on front cover; souvenir collection of excerpts from speeches delivered in honor of Booth in March, 1889; presented compliments of H. W. McVicker, June 30, 1889.
30. "The Stage Season 1889-90" on spine; clippings and memorabilia.
31. "Autograph Letters" on spine and front cover; 131 letters collected by Booth probably in late 1889.
32. "The Stage 1890-91" on spine; daily record of last Booth-Barrett tour.
33. "Edwin Booth from Mr. & Mrs. Kendal 1891" embossed on lower right corner of metal front cover; 5 holograph letters from Charles Kean, March and April 1867.
34. "Theatrical Agreements" on front cover; a collection of 15 Articles of Agreement between Charles Kemble and players in his company between 1822 and 1831 presented to Booth by Frederick Burgess, June 9, 1891.

## IV. Ledgers

This list includes all of those books of Booth's which deal with financial matters—ledgers, receipt books, account books and the like—cataloged or not and arranged chronologically as far as possible. Within the brackets following some entries is indicated the location and/or physical appearance of ledgers which would otherwise be particularly difficult to identify.

1. No lettering on spine or front cover; a book of thumb-index pages from a financial record book; undated. [Booth Case No. 2]
2. "Cashbook—1856 B. A. Baker" on front cover; "Booth Record" on spine of slip-box; many entries for "Mr. Booth" for 1857-1858.

3. A folder of fragments of 3 cash books: 1) an account book, with many entries for Booth, 1857-1858; 2) an account book with entries for Mrs. Booth, 1876-1878; 3) a book of Booth's check stubs, 1881-1883. [Documents file]
4. An envelope of fragments of ledger books with entries for Booth for 1863, 1864, and 1865 and of record books with references to Booth for 1872 and 1874. [Booth Case No. 2]
5. "Booth-Clarke Ledger Walnut St. Theatre 1863-70" on all spines; 2 vols.: Vol. 1 is record of performances and receipts; Vol. 2 is record of disbursements.
6. "Ledger Winter Garden 1864-66" on spine; record of receipts and disbursements.
7. A bundle of 42 cancelled checks, receipts, and pages from ledger books, 1865-1890. [Miscellaneous file]
8. "Booth-Clarke Ledger Boston 1866-69" on spine; record of receipts and disbursements.
9. "Journal" on spine and "Booth & Clarke Boston" on front cover; financial records from 1866 to 1873.
10. A bundle of 23 cancelled checks, receipts, and pages from ledger books, 1867-1892. [Miscellaneous file]
11. No lettering on spine or front cover; "McVicker's Theatre Chicago, Illinois" on first page; Booth's personal daily receipt and expense book for 1867-1868 (including many checks to Joe Booth to pay for construction of Booth's Theatre in New York). [Booth Case No. 2]
12. Binding missing and no lettering on front cover; an account book for the construction of Booth's Theatre, July 1867-1869. [Booth Case No. 2]
13. "Ledger Booth's Theatre" on all spines; 3 vols.: Vol. 1 is related to mortgage retirement, May 29, 1867-January 2, 1874; Vol. 2 lists debits and credits, 1867-1870; Vol. 3 lists debits and credits, 1871-1874.
14. "Ledger" on spine; account book for Booth, his theatre, and his company for 1867, 1868, 1869, 1870.
15. "Cashbook Booth's Theatre 1869-70" on spine; record of receipts and expenditures.
16. "Nightly Receipts Booth's Theatre" on all spines; 4 vols.: Vol. 1 covers February 3, 1869-January 21, 1870; Vol. 2 covers January 22, 1870-April 29, 1871; Vol. 3 covers May 1, 1871-May 22, 1872; Vol. 4 covers May 27, 1872-June 4, 1873.

17. "Salaries and Expenses Booth's Theatre" on all spines; 3 vols.: Vol. 1 covers February 6, 1869-March 12, 1870; Vol. 2 covers April 12, 1870-May 4, 1872; Vol. 3 covers May 11, 1872-August 16, 1873.
18. Binding missing and no lettering on front cover; expense book for tour, January 6, 1872-January 4, 1873. [Booth Case No. 2]
19. Binding missing and no lettering on front cover; expense book for tour, November 1872-January 1873 (similar to #18 except that entries are arranged differently). [Booth Case No. 2]
20. 1872, 1874; see #4 above.
21. "Salaries Booth's Theatre 1873" on spine.
22. Booth's checkbook with stubs for "RAR" (Richard A. Robertson) and "JHM" (J. Henry Magonigle) from July to November, 1873. [Booth Case No. 2]
23. 1876-1878; see #3 above.
24. Binding missing and no lettering on front cover; cash book-check book for 1876-1879; some stubs, 1876-1889, in Booth's handwriting. [Booth Case No. 2]
25. "Booth's Theatre Expense Book Season Jan. 7th, 1878-July 16th" on front cover; expenses, advertising costs, and salaries.
26. Binding missing and no lettering on front cover; "1880 Royal Princess's Theatre London Lessee and Manager Mr. Walter Gooch" on first ledger page; receipts for performances from November 6, 1880 to March, 1881; then for Lyceum (London) May, 1881; then for season in the United States, 1881-1882 under management of Henry E. Abbey. [Booth Case No. 2]
27. A folder of box office receipts for Booth's performances at various theatres during tour of 1881-1882. [Documents file]
28. 1881-1882; see #3 above.
29. No lettering on spine or front cover; "Preliminary Expenses" on first page; account book for the 1882-1883 season including trip abroad. [Booth Case No. 2]
30. 1882-1883; see #13 in "Legal Documents" below.
31. 1882-1883; see #14 in "Legal Documents" below.
32. "'83-'84" marked very faintly on front cover; bank book of Booth's receipts for 1883-1884 and 1884-1885 seasons, the

A Short Title Guide to the Edwin Booth 123
Literary Materials at the Players

latter including those for Booth-Salvini performances. [Booth Case No. 2; small red book, soft covers]

33. No lettering on spine or front cover; "Edwin Booth E. T. Peckham 1884" on first page; account book for Peckham's work for and charges to Booth, 1884-1885. [Booth Case No. 2]

34. "Booth Tours—1886-91" on spine; receipts and some notes by Booth.

35. Two pages from Boston Theatre ledger for Booth's performances of *Hamlet* and *Richelieu* on February 1, 1890. [ALS Miscellaneous file #5]

# V. Manuscripts

These nine items are the only substantial, completely handwritten items in the collection which are not included in other, obvious categories like letters, promptbooks and ledgers. Information in brackets following entries is to assist identifying and locating the material.

1. Handwritten copy of "Booth's interpretation of the part of Shylock differed greatly from that which was popular on the stage of his day"; undated; 4 pp. [Miscellaneous file]

2. Handwritten copy of *Hamlet, Altered from Shakespear*; undated; 98 pp.; inscribed to Booth from William Bispham, 18[90]. [Booth Case No. 2]

3. Handwritten pencilled copies of "A Recollection of Bogumil Dawison" and "A Recollection of Dawison" by W. Winakler (?); undated; the latter is a rough form of the former. [Miscellaneous file]

4. Booth's handwritten copy of verses "There's no such word as fail"; undated. [Miscellaneous file]

5. An envelope containing John Wilkes Booth's "Allow me a few words..." holograph; 8 leaves; on a separate sheet, in Edwin Booth's writing: "This was found long after his death among some old play books and clothes left by J. W. B. in my house. E. B."; undated. [Booth Case No. 2]

6. Handwritten notes by Edwin and Mary McVicker Booth as Mary's reason was beginning to return; undated. [Miscellaneous file]

7. Handwritten copy of *Shakespeare Amoureaux*, by Alexandre

Duval, 1804; 60 pp. "J. B. Booth Nouvelle Orleans 1828" on front cover; very few markings. [Booth Case No. 2]

8. Handwritten verses titled "John Brougham" by William Winter; April 4, 1869. [Miscellaneous file]
9. Handwritten verses title "A Bridal Song" by Richard H. Stoddard; May 14, 1885. [Miscellaneous file]

## VI. Legal Documents

This list includes all the legal documents—for the most part, contracts and theatrical agreements—of Booth's. They are arranged here in chronological order, and unless otherwise indicated by the information in the brackets following some entries all are located in the Documents file.

1. Agreement to perform between William E. Burton and Booth, 1857.
2. Receipt for payment of $1,500 by Booth for 11 original portraits by Neagle; signed by seller, Mary C. Owens, 1858.
3. Passport, 1861.
4. Memorandum of lease agreement between Booth and Mary Dupleix, November 7, 1861. [Miscellaneous file]
5. Agreement between William Stuart, John S. Clarke, and Booth concerning Winter Garden Theatre, 1863.
6. Subpoena for Booth to appear in Common Pleas Court, February 4, 1865. [Miscellaneous file]
7. Attached to #4 above, renewal of agreement, 1866.
8. Agreement of co-partnership between John S. Clarke and Booth, 1867.
9. Property deed to 368 6th Avenue, New York, from Margaret King to Booth, 1867.
10. Agreement between J. Augustus Page and Booth for property, May 17, 1867. [Miscellaneous file]
11. Lease between Levi P. Rose and Booth, September 30, 1867. [Miscellaneous file]
12. Agreement between Mutual Life Insurance Co. of New York and Booth, 1868.
13. Mortgage for Walnut Street Theatre, Philadelphia, in names of John S. Clarke and Booth, 1869.

14. Lease for Walnut Street Theatre, Booth to John S. Clarke, 1870.
15. Lease for Booth's Theatre, Booth to Oliver and Oakes Ames, 1877.
16. Agreement to perform between Booth and Henry E. Abbey, 1881.
17. Four 25-share stock certificates in the Cooperative Dress Association, 1881.
18. Agreement between E. T. Peckham and Booth for construction of dwelling near Newport, R.I., July 31, 1882. [Miscellaneous file]
19. An envelope of incomplete legal agreements and financial records from England, Ireland, and Scotland, 1882-1883.
20. An envelope of incomplete legal agreements and financial records from German and Austrian tour, 1882-1883.
21. Theatrical management agreement between Lawrence Barrett and Booth for 1886-1887 season, 1885.
22. Theatrical management agreement between Lawrence Barrett and Booth for 1887-1888 season, 1886.
23. A financial guarantee from Lawrence Barrett to Booth for $20,000, 1887.
24. Theatrical management agreement between Lawrence Barrett and Booth for 1888-1889 season, 1887.
25. Theatrical management agreement between Lawrence Barrett and Booth for 1891-1892 season, 1890. [Miscellaneous file]
26. Last Will and Testament, June 15, 1892.

# VII. Miscellaneous

This list includes various materials closely connected with Booth and either certainly or probably owned by him at one time or another. They are arranged chronologically as much as possible, and within the brackets is information to assist in identifying and locating them.

1. Edwin Booth's memorandum book, undated. [soft black leather covers]
2. Pp. 163-168 of "Spelling Bcok" owned by W. C. Drummond, undated. [Miscellaneous file]

3. Copy of one-act dramatic sketch "Phantoms" by "Elcho" dedicated to Booth; undated. [Miscellaneous file]
4. An envelope of Booth and Wilkes genealogy from 16th century. [Booth Case No. 2]
5. "Pages from the journal of J. B. Booth 1814-1815" on spine of black slip-box; 9 leaves of journal kept during tour in Belgium and Netherlands.
6. J. B. Booth's pocket memorandum book for 1822. [soft red leather covers; Booth Case No. 2]
7. Edwin Booth's copybook dated July 10, 1845.
8. St. Louis, Missouri Petition (of appreciation from 34 young players), January 28, 1851. [ALS file]
9. "Daily Journal for 1860" on front cover; Mary Devlin's diary. [Winslow Purchase]
10. Scroll, presented to Booth on second anniversary of the opening of his theatre; 88 signatures of the ladies and gentlemen under his management. [Documents file]
11. "Directory Booth's Theatre" on front cover; for 1873. [Booth Case No. 2]
12. "Letters" on spine of book in black slip-box; a book of onionskin copies of business letters signed by J. Henry Magonigle from September 4, 1872 to January 7, 1874. [Booth Case No. 2]
13. Acknowledgement of Booth's gift to Library of Congress of an 1882 New York edition in German of *Richelieu*, dated May 12, 1882 and signed by A. R. Spofford, Librarian of Congress. [Documents file]
14. Acknowledgement of Booth's gift to Library of Congress of an 1882 German edition of *Des Narren Rache*, dated May 16, 1882 and signed by A. R. Spofford, Librarian of Congress. [Documents file]
15. In envelope, a certificate of gratitude signed by 12 members of the Berlin Press Association thanking Booth for his tour, dated February 12, 1883. [Bookcase III]

# VIII. Printed Volumes

This list is of all the printed volumes, with hard or soft covers, bound volumes or pamphlets, contained in the collection excluding the printed volumes among the promptbooks. The list is divided into eight subject categories, some with sub-divisions:

A Short Title Guide to the Edwin Booth
Literary Materials at the Players

A. Editions of Shakespeare's works
   1. Individual plays
   2. Collected editions

B. Works relating to Shakespeare and his works
   1. Works relating to Shakespeare's life, personality, etc.
   2. Works relating to examinations of Shakespeare's works, characters, texts and art
   3. General reference works and miscellanies relating to Shakespeare

C. Individual or collected/selected editions of plays by authors other than Shakespeare

D. Works on acting, acting styles, elocution and oratory

E. Works relating to stage effects
   1. Works on costuming
   2. Works on heraldry
   3. Works relating to the history of aristocracies
   4. Works relating to miscellaneous stage effects

F. General reference works, including histories of nations, theatre, stage, drama and literature

G. Editions (individual/collected/selected) of fiction, verse and assorted forms of writing other than drama by authors other than Shakespeare

H. Works of autobiography (including memoirs), biography, critical studies (including commentaries and appreciations) of authors other than Shakespeare and memorial volumes

In all eight subject categories these practices have been followed: for the sake of less complicated entries, normal name order has been preserved; brackets indicate my interpolations, although in minor matters information has been supplied silently; and references within an entry to number of volumes refer only to the number of volumes in the Booth collection at the Walter Hampden, not to the number of volumes in the original issue.

A. **Editions of Shakespeare's works**

1. Individual plays:

   1. *As You Like It* (see #4 below).
   2. *Hamlet*, [London?], [T. Caldcott?], [1819?].

3. *Hamlet*, New York: Baker and Godwin, 1866.
4. *Hamlet and As You Like It* ..., London: John Murray, 1819.
5. *Hamlet, by William Shakespeare, 1603; Hamlet ... 1604*, Samuel Timmins, ed., London: Sampson Low, Son, and Co., 1860.
6. *Mr. William Shakespeare's Tragedie of Hamlet* ..., London: W. Ludlow, 1884.
7. *Shakespere's Hamlet: ... 1603* ..., W. Griggs, ed., London: W. Griggs, [1880].
8. *Shakespere's Hamlet; ... 1604* ..., W. Griggs, ed., London: W. Griggs, [1880].
9. *King Lear*, Booth-Winter edn., New York: Francis Hart, 1878. (2 copies)
11. *Love's Labor's Lost*, [New York], Augustin Daly, 1891.
12. *Macbeth*, de Chatelain, trans., Paris: Poulet-Malassis, 1862.
13. *The Tragedy of Macbeth* ..., Glascow: 1758.
14. *Merchant of Venice*, Booth-Hinton edn., New York: Henry L. Hinton, 1867. (3 copies)
15. *The Comedy of A Midsummer Night's Dream*, [New York], Augustin Daly, 1888.
16. *Much Ado About Nothing*, C. E. Flower, ed., London: Samuel French, [1879?].
17. *The True Tragedy of Richard the Third* ..., London: The Shakespeare Society, 1844.
18. *Twelfth Night* ..., C. E. Flower, ed., London: Samuel French, n.d.
19. *Shakespeare's Play A Winter's Tale*, H. Staunton, ed., New York: Henry L. Hinton, 1870.

2. Collected editions:

1. *The Comedies, Histories, and Tragedies of Mr. William Shakespeare* ..., A. Morgan, ed., 20 vols., New York: The Shakespeare Society of New York, 1888-1892.
2. *The Complete Works of Shakespeare*, B. Cornwall (pseud. for B. W. Proctor), ed., 3 vols., London: The London Printing and Publishing Company, [1875-1880].
3. *Complete Works of W. Shakspeare*, V. Hugo, trans., 15 vols., Paris: Pagnerre, 1859-1865.

A Short Title Guide to the Edwin Booth
Literary Materials at the Players

4. *The Dramatic Works of W. Shakespeare*, G. Steevens, ed., 2 vols. in 1, Boston: Phillips, Sampson, & Co., 1851.
5. *Dramatic Works of W. Shakespere* ..., A. Wivell, ed., 2 vols., London: George Virtue, [1850?].
6. *The Leopold Shakespeare*, F. J. Furnivall, ed., London: Cassell and Co., Ltd., [1882].
7. *Mr. William Shakespeares Comedies, Histories, and Tragedies*, London: Printed by T. Cotes for R. Hawkins, 1632.
8. *A New Variorum of Shakespeare*, H. H. Furness, ed., Vols. 1, 2, 3, 4, 5, 6, 7, & 9, Philadelphia: J. B. Lippincott & Co., 1871-1892.
9. *The Pictorial Edition of the Works of Shakspere*, C. Knight, ed., 8 vols., London: C. Knight and Co., [1839, 1843].
10. *The Plays and Poems of Shakespeare*, A. J. Valpy, ed., 15 vols., London: Henry G. Bohn, 1857.
11. *The Plays and Poems of W. Shakspeare*, E. Malone, ed., 10 vols. (Vol. I in 2 parts = 11 vols.), London: H. Baldwin, 1790.
12. *The Plays of William Shakspeare* ..., S. Johnson, G. Steevens, and I. Reed, eds., 17 vols., Philadelphia: C. & A. Conrad & Co., 1809.
13. *Shakespeare.... A Reproduction in Exact Facsimile of the Famous First Folio, 1623* ..., H. Staunton, ed., London: Day and Day & Son, 1866.
14. *Shakespeare's Plays* ..., G. C. Verplanck, ed., 2 vols. (of a 3 vol. set), New York: Harper and Bros., 1847.
15. *The Works of Shakespeare*, A. Dyce, ed., 5 vols. (of a 6 vol. set), London: Edward Moxon, 1857.
16. *The Works of Shakespeare*, H. Staunton, ed., 3 vols., London: George Routledge and Sons, [1860].
17. *The Works of Shakespeare*, W. G. Clark and W. A. Wright, eds., 9 vols., Cambridge and London: Macmillan and Co., 1863-1866.

B. **Works relating to Shakespeare and his works**

1. Works relating to Shakespeare's life, personality, etc.: James Boaden, *An Inquiry into the Authenticity of various pictures and prints ... of Shakespeare* ..., London, 1824; Thomas De

130 PERFORMING ARTS RESOURCES

Quincey, *Shakspeare: A Biography*, Edinburgh, 1864; Francis Douce, *Illustrations of Shakspeare and Ancient Manners*, London, 1839; Nathan Drake, *Shakespeare and His Times...*, 2 vols., London, 1817; Walter R. Furness, *Portraits of Shakespeare*, Philadelphia, 1855; J. O. Halliwell-Phillips, *Outlines of the Life of Shakespeare*, London, 1882; Louis K. Harlow, *The Home of Shakespeare...*, [Boston], 1888; Franklin H. Head, *Shakespeare's Insomnia...*, Chicago, 1886; [J. A. Heraud?], *Shakspere, his Inner Life*, London, 1860; Victor Hugo, *William Shakespeare*, Chicago, 1887; Thomas Kermy, *Life and Genius of Shakespeare*, London, 1864; Frederick Madden, *Observations on an Autograph of Shakespeare*, London, 1838; [J. R. Smith?], *Shakespeare's Will*, London, 1838; G. W. Thornbury, *Shakspere's England...*, 2 vols., London, 1856; George Tweddell, *Shakspere: His Times and Contemporaries*, London, 1852; Robert Waters, *William Shakespeare Portrayed by Himself*, New York, 1888; [R. F. Williams?], *The Youth of Shakspeare*, 3 vols., Philadelphia, 1840; George Wise, *The Autograph of William Shakespeare...*, Philadelphia, 1869; John R. Wise, *Shakspere: His Birthplace and its neighborhood*, London, 1861; H. E. Wiseman, *William Shakespeare*, Boston, 1865.

2.  Works relating to examinations of Shakespeare's works, characters, texts, and art: Anon., *The Exegesis of Shakespeare...*, Edinburgh, 1859; Anon., *Richard the Third and the Primrose Criticism*, Chicago, 1887; Martin W. Cooke, *The Human Mystery in Hamlet*, New York, 1888; William H. Cox, *Analyses of Othello, Hamlet, Macbeth, King Lear*, Baltimore, 1886; William Dodd, *The Beauties of Shakspeare*, Boston, 1845; Edward Dowden, *Shakspere. A Critical Study of His Mind and Art*, New York, 1881; G. G. Gervinus, *Shakespeare Commentaries*, 2 vols., London, 1863; R. S. Guernsey, *Ecclesiastical Law in Hamlet...*, New York, 1885; James H. Hackett, *Notes, Criticisms, and Correspondence upon Shakespeare's Plays and Actors*, New York, 1863; N. E. S. A. Hamilton, *An Inquiry into the Genuineness of the Manuscript Collections in Mr. J. Payne Collier's Annotated Shakespeare...*, London, 1860; George P. Hansen, *The Legend of Hamlet...*, Charles B. Simons, ed., Chicago, 1887; William Hazlitt, *Characters of Shakspeare's Plays*, New York, 1845; Frank Howard, *The Spirit of the Plays of Shakspeare*, 5 vols., London, 1833; H. N. Hudson, *Lectures on Shakespeare*, 2 vols., New York, 1848; W. H. Ireland, *An Authentic Account of the Shaksperian Manu-*

scripts..., London, 1796; W. H. Ireland, [*Shakspeare Forgeries:*] *Vortigern; an Historical Play*, London, 1832; William P. Johnston, *The Prototype of Hamlet*..., New York, [1890]; A. O. Kellogg, *Shakespeare's Delineations of Insanity, Imbecility, and Suicide*, New York, 1866 (2 copies); J. P. Kemble, *Macbeth and King Richard the Third: An Essay*..., London, 1817; P. Macdonell, *An Essay on the Tragedy of Hamlet*, London, 1843; Mrs. E. M. Montagu, *An Essay on the Writings and Genius of Shakspeare*..., London, 1810; Michael H. Rankin, *The Philosophy of Shakspere*, London, 1841; William Richardson, *Essays on some of Shakespeare's Dramatic Characters*..., London, 1797; Henry I. Ruggles, *Method of Shakespeare as an Artist*, New York, 1870; E. H. Seymour, *Remarks ... Upon the Plays of Shakspeare*..., 2 vols., London, 1805 (2 copies); Samuel W. Singer, *The Text of Shakespeare Vindicated*, London, 1853; Walter Skeat, *Shakespeare's Plutarch*..., London, 1875; [George A. Stringer], *Shakspere's Draughts from the Living Water*, n.p., 1883; Edward P. Vining, *The Mystery of Hamlet*, Philadelphia, 1881; William S. Walker, *Shakespeare's Versification*, London, 1854; William S. Walker, *A Critical Examination of the Text of Shakespeare*..., 3 vols., London, 1860; Thomas Whatley, *Remarks on Some of the Characters of Shakspeare*, Oxford, 1808; Richard G. White, *Shakespeare's Scholar*..., New York, 1854.

3. General reference works and miscellanies relating to Shakespeare: John Campbell, *Shakespeare's Legal Acquirements*, New York, 1859; Charles and Mary Cowden Clarke, *The Shakespeare Key*..., London, 1879; Mrs. Cowden Clarke, *The Complete Concordance to Shakspere*..., Boston, [1853?]; J. Payne Collier, *Shakespeare's Library*..., 2 vols., London, [1843]; L. Clarke Davis, *The Story of the Memorial Fountain to Shakspeare*..., Cambridge, [Mass.], 1890; Thomas Dawes, *Dramatic Miscellanies*..., 3 vols., London, 1784-1785; Thomas Dolby, *The Shakespearian Dictionary*, London, 1832; Frederick D. Huntington, *Religious and Moral Sentences culled from the Works of Shakespeare*..., Boston, 1859; Francis Jacox, *Shakspeare Diversions*..., London, 1876; Francis Jacox, *Shakspeare Diversions*..., Second Series, London, 1877; Charles and Mary Lamb, *Tales from Shakspere*..., New York, 1870; Moritz Retzsch, *Gallerie zu Shakspeare's dramatischen werken*, Leipzig, 1828; Moritz Retzsch, *Gallerie zu Shakspeare's dramatischen werken*, New York, 1849; Alexander Schmidt, *Shakespeare-Lexicon*..., 2 vols., London,

1886; *The Shakspeare Calendar* ..., William C. Richards, ed., New York, 1850; *Shakespeare Jest-Books*, W. Carew Hazlitt, ed., London, 1864; *Shakespeare Jest-Books*, W. Carew Hazlitt, ed., London, 1881; *Shakespeare's Songs and Sonnets*, John Gilbert, illus., London, [1863?]; J. H. Siddons, *The Shakespearian Referee* ..., Washington, [D.C.], 1886.

## C. Individual or collected/selected editions of plays by authors other than Shakespeare

Anon., *The Latin Play at Saint Francis Xavier's*, New York, 1890; Anon. or unknown, *Thomas A. Becket: A Tragedy*, New York, 1863; Vittorio Alfieri, *The Tragedies of Vittorio Alfieri*, Charles Lloyd, trans., 3 vols., London, 1815; *American Dramatic Library* (containing Rufus Dawes, *Athenia of Damascus*, New York, 1839; N. P. Willis, *Bianca Visconti*, New York, 1839; and [N. P. Willis], *Tortesa the Usurer*, New York, 1839), New York, n.d.; Francis Beaumont and John Fletcher, *The Dramatick Works of Beaumont and Fletcher*, 10 vols., London, 1778; George H. Boker, *Plays and Poems by George H. Boker*, 2 vols., Boston, 1858; [Arthur W. Bruyley?], *Beatrice: A Tragedy* ..., Boston, 1892; George H. Calvert, *Brangonar: A Tragedy*, Boston, 1883; George Chapman, *The Works of George Chapman*, Richard H. Shepherd, ed., and Algernon C. Swinburne, introd., 3 vols., London, 1874-1875; George Colman, The Younger, *John Bull* ..., *Sylvester Daggerwood* ..., and *Ways and Means* ..., Boston, 1833; [W. Congreve], *Love for Love: A Comedy*, n.p., 1753; Charles Cotton, *Scarronides* ..., Durham, N.C., 1807; Mrs. H. Cowley, [*Cowley's Comedies*] (containing *The Runaway*, *The Belle's Stratagem*, *Which is the Man?*, *A Bold Stroke for a Husband*, *More Ways Than One*, and *A School for Greybeards*), London, [1786?]; John Dennis, *The Comical Gallant* ..., London, 1702[7]; F. Donaldson, Jr., *Two Comedies: An Ill Wind*; *An Abject Apology*, Boston, 1887; *The Drama* (containing Thomas Morton, *Speed the Plough*, London, n.d.; W. B. Bernard, *The Nervous Man*, London, n.d.; J. O'Keefe, *The Poor Soldier*, Baltimore, 1827; Unknown, *Of Age To-Morrow*, New York, 1808; John Home, *Douglas*, New York, 1828; Unknown, *Three Weeks After Marriage*, n.p., n.d.; Mr. Jackman, *All the World's a Stage*, Washington, D.C., 1822; and Benjamin Webster, *The Golden Farmer*, New York, [1835?]), n.p., n.d.; John Dryden, *Dramatic Works of John Dryden*, London, 1762; John Dryden, *The Tempest* ..., London, 1690; [Raymond Eshobel], *How Much I Loved Thee*, Washington, D.C., 1884; John Ford, *The Dramatic*

## A Short Title Guide to the Edwin Booth 133
Literary Materials at the Players

*Works of John Ford*, 2 vols., New York, 1831; Clara Gazul, *The Plays of Clara Gazul*, London, 1825; Oliver Goldsmith, *Poetical and Dramatic Works of Oliver Goldsmith*, London, 1793; Karl Gutzkow, *Uriel Acosta* ..., "M. M.," trans., New York, 1860; Joseph Hatton, *The Scarlet Letter*..., London, [1876]; Aaron Hill, *The Dramatic Works of Aaron Hill*, 2 vols., London, 1760; G. H. Hollister, *Thomas A' Becket* ..., Boston, 1866; John Home, *The Dramatic Works of John Home*, London, 1760; G. E. Howard, *The Siege of Tamor*, Dublin, 1773[8]; Victor Hugo, *Le Roi S'Amuse!*..., F. L. Slous, trans., London, 1877; Ben Jonson, *The Works of Ben Jonson*, biography by William Gifford, Boston, 1853; Thomas Legge, *Richardus Tertius*, Barron Field, introd., London, 1844[9]; Henry W. Longfellow, *The New England Tragedies*, Boston, 1868; Edward Bulwer Lytton, *Money*, New York, 1845; Edward Bulwer Lytton, *Richelieu*, as performed by Edwin Booth, New York, 1866; Edward Bulwer Lytton, *Richelieu*, Edwin Booth-William Winter Promptbook Edition, New York, 1878; Malcolm MacColl, *The Ammergau Passion Play*, London, 1870; Philip Massinger, *The Plays of Philip Massinger*, William Gifford, ed., New York, 1860; Jean Baptiste Moliere, *The Dramatic Works of Moliere*, Henri van Laun, trans., 3 vols., New York, 1880; Hannah More, *Sacred Dramas* ..., Edinburgh, [1825?]; Arthur Murphy, *The Orphan of China*, Dublin, 1787[8]; Alfred de Musset, *Comedies et Proverbes*, 2 vols., Paris, 1861; Laughton Osborn, *Cavalry* and *Virginia*, New York, 1867; Laughton Osborn, *Dramatic Works*, 2 vols., New York, 1868-1870; Laughton Osborn, *Ugo da Esta*, *Uberto*, and *The Cid of Seville*, New York, 1869; Thomas Otway, *The Works of Thomas Otway*, 2 vols., London, 1712; John H. Payne, *Brutus*, Edwin Booth-William Winter Promptbook Edition; New York, 1878; James Rush, *Hamlet: A Dramatic Prelude*..., Philadelphia, 1834; Frederick Schiller, *The Works of Frederick Schiller*, Henry G. Bohn, trans., London, 1849; Joseph Alan Scofield, *Alwynne* ..., London, 1887; Walter Scott, *The Doom of Devorgoil and Auchindrane*, New York, 1830; Walter Scott, *Dramatized Works of Sir Walter Scott*, London, [1824]; Richard B. Sheridan, *The Dramatic Works of Richard Brinsley Sheridan*, Richard G. White, introd., 3 vols., New York, 1883; Sophocles, *Sophocles*, Thomas Francklin, trans., New York, 1834; Sophocles, *The Tragedies of Sophocles*, E. H. Plumptre, trans., 2 vols., London, 1865; Robert Southey, *Wat Tyler*, London, 1852; Charles A. Swinburne, *Chastelard: A Tragedy*, New York, 1866; Tom Taylor, *Des Narren Rache: A Tragodie*, as performed by Edwin Booth, Lilian Taylor, trans., [New York], 1882; Alfred Tennyson, *Queen Mary: A Drama*, Boston, 1875; John

Vanbrugh, *Plays* ..., 2 vols., London, 1759; [Charles Whurtors?], *Fortune in her Wits* ..., London, 1705[7]; [W. B. Wood?], *Touch and Take*, Philadelphia, n.d.; John Wynne, *Three Original Plays*, London, 1853.

### D. Works on acting, acting styles, elocution, and oratory

Anon., *The Thespian Dictionary* ..., [London], 1805; Anon., *The Whole Art of the Stage* ..., London, 1684; *Actors and Actresses of Great Britain and the United States*, Brander Matthews and Laurence Hutton, eds., New York, 1886; Henry Alford, *The Queen's English* ..., London, 1864; Henry B. Baker, *Our Old Actors*, London, 1881; Charles Bell, *The Anatomy and Philosophy of Expression* ..., London, 1865; [Denis Diderot], *Paradox of Acting*, Walter H. Pollock, trans., Henry Irving, pref., London, 1883; Edward S. Gould, *Good English* ..., New York, 1870; George H. Lewes, *On Actors and the Art of Acting*, New York, 1878; G. Washington Moon, *The Dean's English* ..., New York, [1865]; Edward G. Parker, *The Golden Age of American Oratory*, Boston, 1857; William H. Phyfe, *How Should I Pronounce?* ..., New York, 1885; William H. Phyfe, *Seven Thousand Words Often Mispronounced*, New York, 1889; Charles J. Plumptre, *King's College Lectures on Elocution*, London, 1881; Peter Mark Roget, *Thesaurus* ..., Barnes Sears, ed., New York, 1861; Richard C. Trench, *The Study of Words* ..., London, 1867.

### E. Works relating to stage effects

1. Works on costuming: Anon., *The Costume of the Russian Empire* ..., London, 1804 (2 copies); Anon., *The Costume of Turkey* ..., London, 1804; Anon., *The Military Costume of Turkey* ..., London, [1818]; T. A. Day and J. H. Dines, *Illustrations of Medieval Costume in England* ..., London, [1851]; F. W. Fairholt, *Costume in England* ..., London, 1860; Charles A. Herbe, *Costumes Francais* ..., Paris, [1837?]; Henry L. Hinton, *Select Historical Costumes*, New York, 1868; Thomas Hope, *Costumes of the Ancients*, 2 vols., London, 1841; George H. Mason, *The Costume of China* ..., London, 1804; [G. H. Mason?], *The Punishments of China* ..., London, 1804; Betrand d'Moleville, *The Costume of the Hereditary States of the House of Austria*, R. C. Dallas, trans., London, 1804; *Old England: A Pictorial Museum* ..., Charles Knight, ed., 2 vols., [London], 1845, [-1846]; William Y. Ottley, *A Collection of Thirty-Nine Fac-similes of Rare Etchings* ..., London, 1828; [H. L. E. and P. J. C. Pauquet], *Modes et Costumes Historiques*, Paris, [1864]; B. Pinelli, *Twenty-seven*

*Etchings Illustrative of Italian Manners and Costume,* Rome, 1844; J. R. Planche, *History of the British Costume,* London, 1847; A. Welby Pugin, *Glossary of Ecclesiastical Ornament* ..., Bernard Smith, ed., London, 1846; W. H. Pyne, *The Costume of Great Britain* ..., London, 1804; Henry Shaw, *Illuminated Ornaments* ..., descriptions by Frederick Madden, London, 1833; Henry Shaw, *The Encyclopedia of Ornament,* London, 1842; Henry Shaw, *Dresses and Decorations of the Middle Ages,* 2 vols., London, 1843; Henry Shaw, *The Decorative Arts Ecclesiastical and Civil of the Middle Ages,* London, 1851; F. B. Solvyns, *The Costume of Indostan* ..., London, [1804?].

2. Works on heraldry: Anon., *The Book of Family Crests,* 2 vols., London, 1854; Hugh Clark, *An Introduction to Heraldry* ..., London, 1854; Samuel R. Meyrick, *A Critical Inquiry Into Antient Armour* ..., 3 vols., London, 1842.

3. Works relating to the history of aristocracies: J. Bernard Burke, *Romantic Records of Distinguished Families* ..., 2 vols., London, 1851; Bernard Burke, *The Romance of the Aristocracy* ..., 3 vols., London, 1855; Hugh Clark, *A Concise History of Knighthood* ..., 2 vols., London, 1784; G. Lillie Craik, *The Romance of the Peerage* ..., 2 vols., London, 1847-1849; T. William Parsons, *The Old House at Sudbury,* Cambridge, [Mass.], 1870.

4. Works relating to miscellaneous stage effects: Anon., *Designs for Gold and Silversmiths,* London, 1836; Anon., *Gothic Furniture of the Fifteenth Century,* London, 1835; M. E. Chevreul, *Laws of Contrast of Colour* ..., John Spanton, trans., London, 1861; G. Scharf, Jr., *Recollections of the Scenic Effects of Covent Garden Theatre,* London, 1839; [Charles W. Schumann], *Art and Gems,* [New York], 1891; Henry Shaw, *Specimens of Ancient Furniture* ..., descriptions by Samuel R. Meyrick, London, 1836; Henry Shaw, *The Handbook of Medieval Alphabets and Devices,* London, 1856; Henry Shaw, *Handbook of the Art of Illumination as Practiced during the Middle Ages* ..., London, 1866.

**F. General reference works, including histories of nations, theatre, stage, drama, and literature**

Anon., *The Abridgement or Summarie of the Scots' Chronicles,* Edinburgh, 1633; Anon., *Booth's Theatre. Behind the Scenes,* New York, 1870; Anon., *Catalogue of the Collection of Books and*

136 PERFORMING ARTS RESOURCES

*Manuscripts Belonging to Mr. Brayton Ives of New York*, New York, 1891; Anon., *Companion to the Playhouse* ..., 2 vols., London, 1764; Anon., *The German Theatre*, Benjamin Thompson, trans., 6 vols., London, 1811; Anon. or unknown, [*A History of England*], place and date of publication unknown; Anon., *The History of Masonry* ..., Edinburgh, 1772; Anon., *Lights of the Old English Stage*, New York, 1878; Anon., *The Mirror of Taste and Dramatic Censor*, 2 vols., Philadelphia, 1810; Anon., *The Old English Drama* ..., London, 1825; Anon., *The Players*, New York, 1889; Anon., *Politeuphuia* ..., London, 1707; *Adventures of an Actor* ..., 2 vols., Theodore Hook, ed., London, 1842; J. Keith Angus, *A Scotch Playhouse* ..., Aberdeen, 1878; [David E. Baker and] Stephen Jones, *Biographia Dramatica* ..., 3 vols., London, 1812; J. Bartholomew, *Philips' Series of Traveling Maps: Europe*, n.p., n.d.; W. A. Becker, *Charicles* ..., Frederick Metcalfe, trans., New York, 1866; W. A. Becker, *Gallus, or Roman Scenes* ..., Frederick Metcalfe, trans., New York, 1866; John Bernard, *Retrospections of the Stage*, 2 vols. in 1, Boston, 1832; *The Bill of the Play*, J. Higden Thornell, ed., London, 1881; Alfred Bunn, *The Stage* ..., Philadelphia, 1840; F. Caffaro, *A Defense of the Drama* ..., New York, 1826; William W. Clapp, Jr., *A Record of the Boston Stage*, Boston, 1853; John Coleman, *Players and Playwrights I Have Known* ..., 2 vols., Philadelphia, 1890; Jeremy Collier, *A Short View of the ... English Stage* ..., London, 1699; Dutton Cook, *A Book of the Play* ..., 2 vols., London, 1876; *The Cyclopedia of Wit and Humor* ..., William E. Burton, ed., 2 vols., London, 1859; William Dunlap, *History of the American Theatre*, 2 vols., London, 1833; John Ebers, *Seven Years of the King's Theatre*, Philadelphia, 1828; John Florio, *A Worlde of Wordes*, [London, 1598]; John Foxe, *The Acts and Monuments of the Church* ..., M. Hobart Seymour, ed., London, [1838]; John Froissart, *Chronicles* ..., Thomas Johnes, trans., 2 vols., London, 1839; F. P. G. Guizot, *General History of Civilization in Europe* ..., C. S. Henry, ed., 2 vols., New York, 1846; [Joseph Haselwood], *The Secret History of the Green-Room*, 2 vols., London, 1795; George Hogarth, *Memoirs of the Musical Drama*, 2 vols., London, 1838; William Hone, *The Every Day-Book* ..., 2 vols., London, [1827]; William Hone, *The Table Book* ..., London, [1831]; William Hone, *The Year Book* ..., London, [1832]; Francis Hueffer, *The Troubadours*, London, 1878; Laurence Hutton, *Literary Landmarks of Edinburgh*, New York, 1891; Basil Kennett, *Romae Antiquae Politia* ..., Philadelphia, 1822; ["J. B. M.?"], *Events in the History of New York City* ..., New York, 1880; ["J. B. M.?"], *Events in the History of New York*

A Short Title Guide to the Edwin Booth 137
Literary Materials at the Players

City . . . , Second Series, New York, 1881; George Mackenzie, *The Lives of the Scot's Nation* . . . , 3 vols., Edinburgh, 1708-1722; Henry Morley, *The Journal of A London Playgoer* . . . , London, 1866; [T. H. Morrell?], *Shakespeare: Ward's Statue in Central Park, New York*, New York, 1873; W. C. Oulton, *A History of the Theatres of London* . . . , 3 vols., London, 1818; *Our Actors and Actresses* . . . , Charles E. Pascoe, ed., London, 1880; H. P. Phelps, *Players of A Century* . . . , Albany, 1880; William H. Rideing, *Dramatic Notes* . . . , London, 1881; *Sensible Etiquette of the Best Society* . . . , Mrs. H. O. Ward, comp., Philadelphia, 1878; Thomas B. Shaw, *A Complete Manual of English Literature*, William Smith, ed., with a sketch of American Literature by Henry T. Tuckerman, New York, 1878; John T. Smith, *Nollekens and His Times* . . . , 2 vols., London, 1828; Joseph Strutt, *Sports and Passtimes of the People of England* . . . , London, 1810; H. A. Taine, *History of English Literature*, H. van Laun, ed., 2 vols., London, [1871]; Charles Varle, *Moral Encyclopedia* . . . , New York, 1831; Benjamin Victor, *The History of the Theatres of London and Dublin* . . . , 2 vols., London, 1761; Benjamin Victor, *The History of the Theatres of London from . . . 1860* . . . , London, 1771; Benjamin Victor, *The History of The Theatres of London from 1760* . . . , London, 1771; Noah Webster, dictionary, place and year of publication unknown; William Winter, *The Press and the Stage*, New York, 1889.

**G. Editions (individual/collected/selected) of fiction, verse, and assorted forms of writing other than drama by authors other than Shakespeare**

Anon., *The Modern Apollo* . . . , Philadelphia, 1811; Anon., *Monsieu Tonson*, n.p., n.d.; Anon., *Ravenswood*, n.p., n.d.; P. Abailard and Heloise, *Lettres et Epitres Amoureuses D'Heloise et Abailard*, [R. de Bussy-Rabutin, trans.?], Paris, 1861; *The Actor's Budget* . . . , W. Oxberry, ed., London, [1820]; Joseph Addison, *The Spectator*, A. Chalmers, ed., 6 vols., New York, 1853-1854; Thomas B. Aldrich, *Mercedes* . . . , Boston, 1884; Thomas B. Aldrich, *A Midnight Fantasy* . . . , Boston, 1877; Thomas B. Aldrich, *The Sisters' Tragedy* . . . , Boston, 1891; Dante Alighieri, *Seventeen Cantos of the Inferno of Dante Alighieri*, T. W. Parsons, comp., Boston, 1865; John Arbuthnot, *Miscellaneous Works of the late Dr. Arbuthnot*, 2 vols., London, 1770; Henry Austin, *Vagabond Verses*, Boston, 1890; *A Book of Roxbughe Ballads*, John P. Collier, ed., London, 1847; Thomas Browne, *Pseudodoxia-Epidemica* . . . , and *Urn*

*Burial,* and *Garden of Cyrus,* London, 1658; Robert Burns, *The Works of Robert Burns* ..., biography by John Lockhart, New York, 1857; Robert Burns, *The Works of Robert Burns*..., biography by J. Wilson, 2 vols., Glascow, 1863; Miguel de Cervantes, *Don Quixote de la Mancha,* New York, 1860; George Colman, The Younger, *Broad Grins,* London, 1819; [John Cooper?], *The Italian Bride,* Savannah, [Georgia?], 1856; Charlotte Cushman, *Charlotte Cushman: her letters and memoirs of her life,* Emma Stebbins, ed., Boston, 1878; Charles Dickens, *Letters of Charles Dickens to Wilkie Collins,* Laurence Hutton, ed., New York, 1892; Charles J. Dunphie and Albert King, *Free Lance*..., London, 1881; Thomas D'Urfey, *New Operas*..., London, 1721; George Eliot, *The Spanish Gypsy*..., Boston, 1868; John Evelyn, *Diary and Correspondence of John Evelyn*..., William Bray, ed., 4 vols., 1862-1863; Henry Fielding, *The Miscellaneous Works of Henry Fielding,* 4 vols., New York, 1859; Henry Fielding, *The Works of Henry Fielding,* biography by Arthur Murray, 5 vols., [London], 1813-1814; Jean Baptiste La Fontaine, pseud., *Fables of La Fontaine,* J. J. Grandville, illus., Elizur Wright, Jr., trans., New York, 1860; Catherine V. Gasparin, *The Near and Heavenly Horizons,* New York, 1862; Oliver Goldsmith, *The Miscellaneous Works of Oliver Goldsmith,* James Prior, ed., 4 vols., New York, 1859; George Gordon, *The Works of Lord Byron*..., biography by J. W. Lake, Philadelphia, 1856; George Gordon, *The Works of Lord Byron,* New York, 1825; John Henderson, *Letters and Poems by the late John Henderson,* John Ireland, ed., London, 1786; [*History on the Stage: Tracts on C. Cibber*], [W. E. Burton, ed.?], London, 1718 [1743]; Homer, *The Illiad and Odyssey of Homer,* Alexander Pope, trans., W. C. Armstrong, ed., New York, 1848; *The Humbler Poets* ..., Slason Thompson, ed., Chicago, 1887; Samuel Johnson, *The Rambler,* 4 vols., Princeton, N.J., 1828; Flavius Josephus, *The Works of Flavius Josephus,* William Whiston, trans., London, 1874; Charles Lamb, *The Life and Letters of Charles Lamb,* Thomas N. Talfourd, ed., 5 vols., New York, 1858-1859; John Locke, *An Essay Concerning Human Understanding,* 2 vols. in 1, New York, 1825; Nicholas Lockyer, *A Divine Discovery of Sincerity,* London, 1640; *The Loves and Heroines of the Poets,* Richard H. Stoddard, ed., New York, 1861; [Jane H. Marcet], [*Conversations on Natural Philosophy*], [John L. Blake, ed.], [Boston], [1841]; Charles Mathews, The Elder, *Mr. Mathews At Home,* London, 1822; Adam I. Mencken, *Infelicia,* Philadelphia, 1887; Chester G. Miller, *Chihuahua* ..., Chicago, 1891; Richard M. Milnes, *The Life, Letters, and Friendships of Richard Monckton Milnes*..., T.

A Short Title Guide to the Edwin Booth 139
Literary Materials at the Players

Wemyss Reid, ed., Richard H. Stoddard, introd., 2 vols., New York, 1891; Michael de Montaigne, *Works of Michael de Montaigne*, notes by W. Hazlitt, O. W. Wright, ed., 4 vols., New York, 1859; [W. W. Newton], *The Priest and the Man* ..., Boston, 1883; Christopher North, *Noctes Ambrosianae*, John Skelton, ed., New York, [1876]; Ossian, *The Poems of Ossian*, James Macpherson, trans., Boston, 1858; Samuel Pepys, *Diary and Correspondence of Samuel Pepys*, biography and notes by Richard Brabrooke, 4 vols., London, 1865; *The Pictorial Book of Ballads, Traditional & Romantic*, J. S. Moore, ed., London, 1849; *The Poetic Remains of Some of the Scottish Kings*, George Chalmers, ed., London, 1824; Francis Rabelais, *The Works of Francis Rabelais*, J. Ozell, ed., 2 vols., London, 1738; Francis Rabelais, *The Works of Francis Rabelais*, Thomas Urquhart and [P. A.] Motteux, trans., 2 vols., London, 1851; Henry C. Robinson, *Diary, Reminiscences, and Correspondence of Henry Crabb Robinson*, Thomas Sadler, ed., 2 vols. in 1, Boston, 1880; Nicholas Rowe, *The Works of Nicholas Rowe*, 2 vols., London, 1766; Alain René le Sage, *The Adventures of Gil Blas* ..., [Tobias Smollett, trans.?] and Tobias Smollett, *Sir Launcelot Greaves* [London], [1816]; Richard Savage, *The Works of Richard Savage* ..., Samuel Johnson, ed., 2 vols., London, 1777; James and Horace Smith, *Rejected Addresses, and Other Poems*, Epes Sargent, ed., New York, 1860; Tobias Smollett, *The Miscellaneous Works of Tobias Smollett*, memoir by Thomas Roscoe, 6 vols., New York, 1857; Edmund Spenser, *The Works of Edmund Spenser*, J. Payne Collier, ed., 5 vols., London, 1862; A. L. G. de Stael-Holstein, *Corrine; or, Italy*, Isabel Hill, trans., New York, 1859; A. L. G. de Stael-Holstein, *Germany*, O. W. Wright, ed., 2 vols., New York, 1860-1861; [P. D. Stanhope], *The Beauties of Chesterfield* ..., Alfred Howard, ed., Boston, 1828; [P. D. Stanhope], *Letters Written by the Earl of Chesterfield to his Son*, New York, 1860; E. C. Stedman, *Poets of America*, Boston, 1885; Richard Steele and Joseph Addison, *The Tatler and Guardian*, with an account of the authors by Thomas B. Macaulay, New York, 1858; Laurence Sterne, *A Sentimental Journey* ..., New York, 1859; Joseph Story, *Selections from the Works of Joseph Story*, James Burns, ed., Boston, 1839; Torquato Tasso, *Jerusalem Delivered* ..., John Hoole, trans., 2 vols., London, 1803; Bayard Taylor, *The Poet's Journal*, Boston, 1863; Bayard Taylor, *Life and Letters of Bayard Taylor*, Marie Hansen-Taylor and Horace E. Scudder, eds., 2 vols., Boston, 1884; John Wilkes, *The Correspondence of the late John Wilkes* ..., John Almon, ed., 5 vols., London, 1805; [Henry L. Williard?], *Cardinal Richelieu*, London, n.d.; William Winter, *My*

*Witness*..., Boston, 1871; William Winter, *English Rambles*..., Boston, 1884.

**H. Works of autobiography (including memoirs), biography, critical studies (including commentaries and appreciations) of authors other than Shakespeare, and memorial volumes**

Anon., *Baconian Facts* ..., Boston, 1890; Anon., *The Bryant Festival at The Century*, New York, 1865; Anon., *In Memory of John McCullough*, New York, 1889; Anon., *Twelfth Night at The Century Club*, New York, 1858; George Anne Bellamy, *An Apology for the Life of George Anne Bellamy*, 2 vols., Dublin, 1785; George Anne Bellamy, *An Apology for the Life of George Anne Bellamy*, 2 vols., London, 1785; James Boswell, *The Life of Samuel Johnson* ..., 4 vols. in 2, London, 1859; John Brougham, *The Life, Stories, and Poems of John Brougham*, William Winter, ed., Boston, 1881; Frances Anne Butler, *Journal of Frances Anne Butler*, 2 vols., Philadelphia, 1835; Thomas Campbell, *Life of Mrs. Siddons*, New York, 1884; Colley Cibber, *An Apology for the Life of Mr. Cibber* ..., London, 1740; Asia Booth Clarke, *The Elder and the Younger Booth*, Boston, 1882; [Asia Booth Clarke], *Passages, Incidents, and Anecdotes in the Life of Junius Brutus Booth, "The Elder,"* New York, 1866 (2 copies); George Colman, The Younger, *Random Records*, 2 vols., London, 1830; Moncure D. Conway, *The Wandering Jew*, New York, 1881; George F. Cooke, *Memoirs of George Fred. Cooke*, William Dunlap, ed., 2 vols., London, 1813; [Barry Cornwall, pseud.], *The Life of Edmund Kean*, 2 vols., London, 1835; J. R. Darley, *The Grecian Drama* ..., London, 1840; Thomas Dibdin, *The Reminiscences of Thomas Dibdin*, 2 vols. in 1, New York, 1828; Robert W. Elliston, *Memoirs of Robert William Elliston, Comedian*, George Raymond, ed., London, 1845; Robert W. Elliston, *Memoirs of Robert William Elliston, Comedian*, George Raymond, ed., 2 vols., London, 1846; Samuel Foote, *Memoirs of Samuel Foote* ..., William Foote, ed., 2 vols., New York, 1806; Edwin Forrest, *Oration Delivered at the Democratic Republican Celebration*, New York, 1838; Thomas E. Garrett, *The Masque of the Muses*, St. Louis, Mo., 1885; David Garrick, *Memoirs of David Garrick*, Thomas Davis, ed., 2 vols., London, 1780; Johann Wolfgang von Goethe, *Auto-Biography of Goethe*, John Oxenford and A. J. W. Morrison, trans., 2 vols., London, 1849; Thomas R. Gould, *The Tragedian* ..., New York, 1868 (2 copies); Zadel B. Gustafson, *Genevieve Ward*, Boston, 1882; [J. O. Halliwell-Phillips], *New

*Lamps or Old?* ..., Brighton, [England], 1880; John S. Harford, *The Life of Michael Angelo Buonarroti* ..., 2 vols., London, 1858; Gabriel Harrison, *John Howard Payne* ..., Philadelphia, 1885; William Hazlitt, The Elder, *Criticisms and Dramatic Essays of the English Stage*, William Hazlitt, The Younger, ed., London, 1854; William Hone, *Ancient Mysteries Described* ..., London, 1823; W. H. Ireland, *The Confessions of W. H. Ireland* ..., London, 1805; Mrs. A. Jameson, *Characteristics of Women* ..., Boston, 1858; John W. Jarvis, *The Glyptic*, London, 1875; Joseph Jefferson, *The Autobiography of Joseph Jefferson*, New York, 1890; Samuel Johnson, *Lives of the Most Eminent English Poets* ..., Peter Cunningham, ed., biography by Thomas B. Macaulay, 2 vols., New York, 1859; Michael Kelly, *Reminiscences of Michael Kelly* ..., 2 vols., London, 1826; John P. Kemble, *Memoirs of the Life of John Philip Kemble*, James Boaden, ed., 2 vols. in 1, New York, 1825; [Louis Kossuth], *Kossuth in New England* ..., Boston, 1852; Robert M. LaFollette, *Oration by Robert M. LaFollette* ..., n.p., 1879; Charles L. Lewes, *Memoirs of Charles Lee Lewes* ..., London, 1805; Charles Macklin, *Memoirs of the Life of Charles Macklin* ..., James T. Kirkman, ed., 2 vols., London, 1799 (2 copies of vol. 1); Charles Macklin, *Memoirs of Charles Macklin*, William Cooke, ed., London, 1806; Charles Macready, *Macready's Reminiscences* ..., Frederick Pollock, ed., New York, 1875; Benjamin E. Martin, *In the Footprints of Charles Lamb*, New York, 1890; R. Osgood Mason, *Sketches and Impressions* ..., New York, 1887; Charles Mathews, *Memoirs of Charles Mathews, Comedian*, Mrs. A. Mathews, ed., 4 vols., London, 1838-1839; *Memorials of Thomas Hood* ..., [Frances F. Broderip and Thomas Hood, eds.], 2 vols., Boston, 1860; John O'Keefe, *Recollections of the Life of John O'Keefe*, 2 vols. in 1, Philadelphia, 1827; Samuel Osgood, *Bryant among his Countrymen* ..., New York, 1879; Wallie C. Oulton, *The Beauties of Kotzebue* ..., London, 1800; [Otto Peltzer], *The Moralist and The Theatre* ..., with a criticism on "Moses and Pharaoh" by John Fraser, Chicago, 1887; [J. Quin?], *The Life of Mr. James Quin, Comedian* ..., London, 1766; *The Repository* ..., [I. Reed, ed.], 4 vols., London, 1790; Frederick Reynolds, *Life and Times of Frederick Reynolds*, 2 vols. in 1, Philadelphia, 1826; D. Terry, [*British Theatrical Gallery?*], [London], 1825; Lester Wallack, *Memories of Fifty Years*, Laurence Hutton, introd., New York, 1889; Alfred Walls, *The Oldest Drama in the World* ..., New York, 1891; William Winter, *Ada Rehan* ..., New York, 1891; William Winter, *The Life and Art of Edwin Booth*, New York, 1893; Charles M. Young, *A Memoir of Charles Mayne Young, Tragedian* ..., Julian C. Young, ed., New York, 1871.

## Notes

1. Signature only on one of three petitions, dated January 8, 1885, January 8, 1885, and January 12, 1885, asking Booth to perform again in Washington, D.C. These three petitions are bound with 63 individual letters into a scrapbook titled "To Edwin Booth, Esq."

2. One of 63 individual letters written to Booth in December 1884 and January 1885 asking him to perform again in Washington, D.C. Bound into a scrapbook titled "To Edwin Booth, Esq."

3. One of 13 signatories of a letter, undated, consoling Booth after Lincoln's assassination. Letter is handwritten by Thomas B. Aldrich.

4. Signature on letter dated May 22, 1880 regarding the breakfast party at Delmonico's in Booth's honor.

5. Letter is actually addressed to John W. Albaugh regarding the collection of autograph letters for Booth, but it was intended for Booth's eyes.

6. For a complete description of these books, see L. Terry Oggel, "The Edwin Booth Promptbook Collection at The Players: A Descriptive Catalog," *Theatre Survey*, XIV, 1 (May 1973), 72-111.

7. These two plays are bound together.

8. These two plays are bound together.

9. Appended to Shakespeare's *Richard the Third*, listed above.

Llewellyn H. Hedgbeth

# The Chuck Callahan Burlesque Collection

In vaudeville and burlesque the comic was king. Whether it was a courtroom scene with a stupid judge, a dumb cop and a pretty lady defendant or a hotel scene with an old man and his young wife being spied upon by guests peeking through the keyhole, the comics made jokes and stale humor come alive. Employing words of more than two syllables and words like *machacha*, *gondola*, *box* and *paddle* for their humorous and sexual meanings, these comedians developed a pool of material so vast that only the pros could master it. Old comics used to brag of knowing more than three hundred skits. Simply by the title, the premise or the props to be used, they could reconstruct these skits from memory. It was an oral tradition. Few scripts were committed to paper. It is a wonder, then, that one man moved out of his tradition just a bit and began to record these skits. His name was Chuck Callahan.

Callahan, born in 1891, began his show business career as a street-corner dancing bootblack in Toledo, Ohio. From there he graduated to candy butcher at a movie theatre, then starred in a vaudeville tap dancing act with his brother Emmett. From that time on, he worked in various dancing acts and finally switched over to burlesque comedy, eventually becoming a burlesque doctor or fix-it man for others' sketches. Throughout his career, Callahan gathered comic bits and sketches, collected scripts, wrote material and locked all this away in an old, battered suitcase.

When television began, Callahan envisioned a show to be known as "Burlesque Hall of Fame" which would bring burlesque stars together to perform in their old skits, each week using a different theatre in a different town. A preliminary shooting script was made for a first program with Smith and Dale, well-known burlesque comics, and Callahan tried for weeks to get a hearing about his new show. He received no encouragement from New York television producers who were eager to bring in California film stars with important names but were wary of the musty burlesque comic.

Not able to find a market for his old scripts, Callahan moved them to the trunk of his car for storage, but he never had the heart to throw them away. Friends constantly ribbed him about being a junk collector and a man attempting to find life in a dead art form.

When Callahan died in 1964, his widow, Virginia Meyers Callahan, was about to destroy the scripts. For countless hours she had helped her husband update and retype old scripts for the proposed television show and then for a possible nightclub act. She had watched as time and time again he had returned home without finding any buyer for their work. At his death Mrs. Callahan saw no point in storing her husband's show business junk any longer. A friend passing by noticed the scripts and asked Mrs. Callahan to donate them to The Walter Hampden-Edwin Booth Theatre Collection and Library at The Players' Club. Thus the Chuck Callahan Collection of rare vaudeville and burleycue skits came into existence. (Little has been written on the collection except for a short article by Louis A. Rachow in the *Players' Bulletin*, included here as an Appendix.)

The days of vaudeville variety acts are lost to us forever,

but we do retain records of how the shows were structured. A vaudeville bill may have listed a one-armed cornetist, bareback riders, female impersonators, Dutch imitators, Spanish novelty dancers, educated dogs and geese. The comic sketches on these bills had very thin plots and were used primarily to introduce the following number. The comics, in their ragged clothes, pork-pie hats, huge shoes and fright wigs, exchanged lines, did a song and dance number, then led up to the next act. Censorship was very strict and a comic could be fired for inserting a single "damn," much less for introducing a blue gag or allusion.

Burlesque, on the other hand, thrived on old jokes, clean or dirty. The comics were there to make the audience laugh, and any means to that end was acceptable. A typical burlesque company might include a first and second comic, a prima donna, a soubrette, an ingenue, a straight, a juvenile and the chorus girls. The first comic would often play the lazy braggart bum, resilient to every downfall, simple-minded but joyful, or perhaps a mercenary Jew. The second comic was a dialog expert, playing such stock parts as the drunken Irishman. The prima donna played the female lead, the soubrette played a frivolous young woman known for her spectacular costume, and the ingenue played the naive young woman. The juvenile was assigned to bit or character parts, often playing the homosexual "Nance" character, and the chorus girls decorated the stage.

The comedian and the chorus girls were the center of burlesque performance from about 1900 on. The comic bits were short scenes with a single premise, usually lasting for eight to twelve minutes. The written bits were only outlines, however, for comics insisted on trying new bits of business or wisecracks at each performance. Most comics would never work with any written material, in part because they knew full well that anything recorded could be stolen more easily. All of the skits, in any case, were stolen, copied and revamped by every burleycue comic on the circuit. Ralph Allen, in "Our Native Theatre," divides the burlesque sketch into two categories: the "flirtation scene," a single-joke situation performed by not more than five characters in front of the curtain, and the "body scene," an extended comic bit with a complex premise involving as many as seven or eight characters.

There is a deliberate illogical structure to these skits which allows a great deal of latitude for improvisation. There are stock characters—lecherous old men, naive young virgins, comic fools, the eunuch "Nance"—all playing out scenes with a sexual basis. Often the situations are menacing—involved with death, suicide, alcoholism, fear—but always the outcome is ludicrous.

Perhaps the most important relationship within the burlesque company was between the straight and the comics. The straight is a well-dressed city man who uses highfalutin' language and feeds lines to the comics. Often he is the sole possessor of a magical charm which he alone can make work. The grotesque first comic or top banana is a simpering fool, dressed in baggy pants and big shoes. He is not easily taught a lesson, but he falls into the right way of doing things simply by chance, often to the chagrin of the straight man.

All of these characters figure monumentally in the Callahan Collection. In the collection left by Callahan there are nearly three hundred vaudeville and burlesque skits, music in manuscript, photographs, programs, a group of about two hundred wisecracks, a water color copy of a vaudeville scenic backdrop, a typed biography of Chuck Callahan written by his widow, a rough index to the skits and various other souvenirs of burlesque days. During the ten years in which Mr. and Mrs. Callahan were updating this material for future use in nightclub and television acts, several hundred more skits existed. Unfortunately these skits were not kept with the original batch, and have been lost or destroyed.

The scripts may be divided in any number of ways, but they fall naturally into about twenty categories. Military themes, card games, racial caricatures, beggars, cars and trains, country bumpkins, and courtrooms: there are five to ten scripts in each of these categories. Ten to twenty scripts each are allotted to tough characters, foreign locations and foreigners, burlesques of plays and films, police skits, medicine skits, arguments and bets, skits relying heavily on props, and drinking scenes. Comic fools, malapropisms and word games, and rampaging mates are categories containing between twenty and thirty sketches.

Each category contains widely differing sketches, as may be indicated by a quick glance at several drinking scenes. "Bar Bit" is a Jewish-Irish skit in which both characters dupe the bartender. In "Drink Strip Bit" a doctor's strike is on, and the juvenile introduces alcohol as the drink to make any woman your slave. The comic buys the liquor and sells it for a dollar a drink to the prima donna. She quickly runs out of money and barters her hat, her skirt and her slip. A comic and an ingenue are the characters appearing in "The Drunk Scene" as well. They discuss "generosity whiskey"—one drink, and the comic gets a hug; two drinks, a kiss; three drinks, use your own judgement. A very short scene entitled "Free Drink Bit" avoids the burlesque rhetoric altogether and is a pure sight gag. The comic enters with a bottle which has a sponge in its side. He hands it to the bartender to be filled with twenty-five cents worth of whiskey. When the comic can't pay, the bartender pours the whiskey out. Breaking the bottle, the comic removes the sponge and squeezes himself a drink.

Other sketches deal with one comic selling another whiskey pills which turn out to be castor oil pills, with the comic, straight and juvenile getting drinks for attentions shown a lady bootlegger; and with uptown slickers slumming in a Bowery bar. The "Telephone Bootleg Scene" involves an atomizer which sprays alcohol to interest clients who are then led to the telephone booth for a shot. "Politics," the most complicated of the drinking scenes, is a discussion between a street cleaner who has made a bar out of his cleaning cart and the investigating policeman. The comic insults the policeman, confuses his rank, commands his service, then offers to sell him a drink. An infuriated cop chases the comic offstage.

Differences in these sketches came in length as well as in content. If a sketch needed to be lengthened, the comics could throw in extra comic bits or wisecracks, one-line exchanges between the straight and the first comic. In the drinking bits many wisecracks were introduced.

> STRAIGHT: It says in the paper that on the Weegie Island you can buy a wife and a keg of whiskey for five bucks.
> COMIC: I'll bet it's awful whiskey.
> STRAIGHT: Did you try Alcohol Anonymous?
> COMIC: I guess so. I'll drink anything.

The scenarios in the collection have now been indexed according to title (usually related to the major premise), with a list of the characters involved and a short précis of the action. At many times the skits are difficult to describe for a number of reasons. They all appear in variant formats, and most of them are peppered with misspelled words, run-on sentences, and stray punctuation marks. For these and other problems related to form and content it has often been troublesome for me to prepare a clear and concise entry.

When a skit has been written for a particular comic or comic team, that specialization has been noted. Special note has also been made of skits ending in a blackout (the stage lights black out suddenly) or skits which are known by more than one title.

Some of the sketches introduce characters other than those generally included in a comic company, and an explanation of their function may be necessary. The Tough, as the name implies, is a man who lets his muscles do the talking and is a constant threat to both Straight and comic. Luke is the country bumpkin character just off the farm. Murphy is the hot-headed Irishman, and Cohn the penny-pinching Jew.

The Callahan Collection is important because it well may be the largest collection of burlesque and vaudeville original material in the United States. It is a wellspring of humorous situations, ludicrous characters and bawdy jokes. The collection allows us all to peep through the long line of chorus girls usually associated with burlesque in order to see the comics employing ancient bits of business in a traditionally zany setting.

# Appendix

Rachow, Louis A. "Chuck Callahan Burlesque Collection," *Players' Bulletin.* Spring 1966.

In days of yore burlesque in America was an extemporaneous but natural training ground for the comedian. Those who reached the pinnacle of fame and glory in filmland, radio and television were primarily graduates *summa cum laude* of burlesque. Laughmakers Bert Lahr, Leon Errol, Bobby Clark, George Jessel, Eddie Cantor and W.C. Fields are only a few who trod the burleycue boards to stardom.

From out of the theatrical mêlée came another dedicated performer to whom the theatre library world is indebted—Chuck Callahan. Running the gamut from a Toledo, Ohio dancing bootblack and candy butcher to a burlesque and movie script writer to a featured player on television with Fred Allen, Robert Montgomery and Kate Smith, Chuck Callahan made his own indelible mark in the annals of the stage.

Talented performer that he was he will no doubt be best remembered for his abilities as script writer and composer of popular burleycue routines. *Atta Boy Petey, Old Boy* and *Two Sports from Michigan* are perhaps his two most familiar acts while the "Andy Gump" series starring Slim Summerville is representative of his work in Hollywood.

Chuck Callahan died less than two years ago but he left a legacy. Through the kindness and thoughtfulness of his widow, Virginia Meyers Callahan and through the courtesy of Player Ed Roberts, The Walter Hampden Memorial Library has become the beneficiary. During the decade prior to his death he and Mrs. Callahan updated and rewrote much of his material for future nightclub use. Although the project failed to materialize the fruits of their labors remained intact. The Players and students of the theatre are

fortunate. Authentic burlesque material is hard to come by—especially a collection such as this which consists of nearly three hundred burlesque scripts and vaudeville skits, music in manuscript, photographs, programs and a typescript biography of Chuck Callahan written by Mrs. Callahan and inscribed to "The Players in Friendship with Mr. Edward Barry Roberts."
Thank you Mrs. Callahan. Thank you Mr. Roberts.

## Bibliography

Allen, Ralph. "Our Native Theatre," *The American Theatre: The Sum of its Parts*, ed. Henry Williams. New York: Samuel French, 1971.
Cahn, William. *A Pictorial History of the Great Comedians*. New York: Grosset & Dunlap, Inc., 1957.
Gilbert, Douglas. *American Vaudeville*. New York: Whittlesey House, 1940.
Green, Abel and Joe Laurie, Jr. *Show Biz from Vaude to Video*. New York: Henry Holt and Co., 1951.
Laurie, Joe, Jr. *Vaudeville*. New York: Henry Holt and Co., 1953.
Sobel, Bernard. *A Pictorial History of Burlesque*. New York: G. P. Putnam's Sons, 1956.
———. *Burleycue*. New York: Farrar and Rinehart, Inc., 1931.
———. *A Pictorial History of Vaudeville*. New York: The Citadel Press, 1961.
Zeidman, Irving. *The American Burlesque Show*. New York: Hawthorn Books, 1967.

# Index to Volumes I & II

## Author Index

Auburn, Mark S. *Promptscripts of* The Rivals: *An Annotated Bibliography.* **II,** 41.

Bowser, Eileen. *Guidelines for Describing Unpublished Script Materials.* **II,** 1.

Browne, Ray B. and William Schurk. *The Popular Culture Library and Audio Center.* **I,** 74.

Correll, Laraine. *The Belknap Collection of Performing Arts: University of Florida Libraries.* **I,** 56.

Fletcher, James E. and W. Worth McDougald. *The Peabody Collection of the University of Georgia.* **II,** 31.

Haynes, David. *A Descriptive Catalog of the Filmic Items in the Gernsheim Collection.* **II,** 69.

Henderson, Mary C. *With the Compliments of the Raymond Mander and Joe Mitchenson Theatre Collection.* **II,** 9.

Hunter, Frederick J. *Theatre and Drama Research Sources at the University of Texas at Austin.* **I,** 43.

Johnson, Kay. *The Wisconsin Center for Theatre Research.* **I,** 66.

Kozuch, Frances Knibb and Richard Stoddard. *The Theatre in American Fiction, 1774-1850: An Annotated List of References.* **I,** 173.

Krivatsy, Nati H. and Laetitia Yeandle. *Theatrical Holdings of the Folger Shakespeare Library.* I, 48.

Kuiper, John B. *The Motion Picture Section of the Library of Congress.* I, 88.

Lee, Briant Hamor. *Theatrical Visual Arts Ephemera: Care and Protection.* I, 156.

Lichty, Lawrence W. *Sources for Research and Teaching in Radio and Television History.* I, 218.

MacCann, Richard Dyer. *Reference Works for Film Study.* II, 57.

McDougald, W. Worth and James E. Fletcher. *The Peabody Collection of the University of Georgia.* II, 31.

Pilkington, James P. *Vanderbilt Television News Archive.* I, 213.

Powers, James. *The Film History Program of the Center for Advanced Film Studies of the American Film Institute.* I, 79.

Rachow, Louis A. *Performing Arts Research Collections in New York City.* I, 1.

Schlosser, Anne G. *Film/Broadcasting Resources in the Los Angeles Area.* I, 17.

Schurk, William and Ray B. Browne. *The Popular Culture Library and Audio Center.* I, 74.

Stoddard, Richard and Frances Knibb Kozuch. *The Theatre in American Fiction, 1774-1850: An Annotated List of References.* I, 173.

Wharton, Betty. *The Chamberlain and Lyman Brown Theatrical Agency Collection.* I, 93.

Witham, Barry B. *An Index to "Mirror Interviews."* I, 153.

Woods, Alan T. *A Survey of The Ohio State University Theatre Research Institute.* I, 33.

Wortis, Avi. *The Burnside Mystery: The R. H. Burnside Collection and The New York Public Library.* I, 99.

Yeandle, Laetitia and Nati H. Krivatsy. *Theatrical Holdings of the Folger Shakespeare Library.* I, 48.

Zucker, Phyllis. *The American Film Institute Catalog Project.* **I,** 147.

Zuker, Joel. *Ralph Sargent's* Preserving the Moving Image: *A Summary Review.* **II,** 15.

# Index

NOTE: **We have tried to catch spelling errors. In the Schlosser article, page numbers in brackets have been added to indicate continuation of sections.**

"A.E.B." *See:* Berg, Albert Ellery
A.S.C.A.P. **I,** 106
Abbott, Elisabeth **I,** 118
Abington, Mrs. **I,** 53
About, Edmond Francois Valentin **I,** 118
Academie Royale de Musique (Paris) **I,** 210
Academy of Motion Picture Arts and Sciences **I,** 26, 149 *See also:* Margaret Herrick Library
Ackermann and Co. **II,** 79
Acosta, Mercedes de **I,** 118
Actors' Equity Association **I,** 103
Actors Studio **I,** 1
Adams, Maude **I,** 112, 114
Ade, George **I,** 118
Adelphi Theatre (Edinburgh) **I,** 50
Adler, Hans **I,** 118
Adler, Jacob **I,** 16
Aeschylus **I,** 43, 206
Agar, Herbert **I,** 118
Agate, James **I,** 118
Aide, Hamilton **I,** 118
Aitken Brothers **I,** 69
Aitken Collection **I,** 43, 46
Akins, Zoe **I,** 118
Alcaraz, Enrique **I,** 118
Aldrich, Louis **I,** 154
Alfieri, Vittorio **I,** 206
Allen, Fred **I,** 94, 97-98
Allen, John **I,** 89
Alonso, Alicia **I,** 59
Altman, Robert **I,** 70
Ambient, Mark **I,** 118
American Antiquarian Society **I,** 75-76
American Broadcasting Company (ABC) **I,** 13, 24, 224
American Film Institute **I,** 25-27, 69, 70, 79, 80, 83, 89, 90
American Film Institute Catalog Project **I,** 147-152
American Film Institute, Center for Advanced Film Studies **I,** 79-87 *See also:* Charles K. Feldman Library

American Museum (New York) **I,** 210
American Society for Theatre Research **I,** 94
American Theatre (New Orleans) **I,** 210
American Theatre Association **I,** 170
American Theatre Library-Museum (Florida State University) **I,** 57
Ames, Winthrop **II,** 51-52
Amos n' Andy (radio show) **I,** 23
Anderson, John **I,** 118
Anderson, Joshua R. **I,** 206
Anderson (M.D.) Foundation **I,** 44
Anderson, Maxwell **I,** 46
Andre, Major John **I,** 206
Andrews, George **I,** 206
Anger, Kenneth **I,** 2
Angus, William **I,** 3
Anhalt, Edward **I,** 23
Animated Films **I,** 81 *See also:* Walt Disney Productions Archives
Anschutz, Ottomar **II,** 85
Anstey, F. **I,** 118
Anthelme, Paul **I,** 118
Anthology Film Archives **I,** 2-3
Aqua-Dramas **I,** 41
Arch Street Theatre (Philadelphia) **II,** 54
Archer (William) Library **II,** 10
Archive of Recorded Voice **I,** 5
Arliss, George **I,** 118
Armbruster Collection **I,** 37
Armin, Walter **I,** 118
Armont, Paul **I,** 118
Armstrong, Paul **I,** 119
Arnold, Franz **I,** 119
Arnold, Victor **I,** 119
Aronson, Boris **I,** 9
Arthur, Joseph **I,** 154
Arts Council of Great Britain **II,** 74
Artus, Louis **I,** 119
Artzybashev, Mikail Petrovitch **I,** 119
Ashton, Winifred *See:* Dane, Clemence
Association for Educational Communications and Technology **II,** 35

## 154 PERFORMING ARTS RESOURCES

Astley's Amphitheatre (London) **I**, 209
Astor Place Opera House (New York) **I**, 210; **II**, 12
Athis, Alfred **I**, 119
Atkinson, Hugh **I**, 42
Audio Center (Bowling Green State University) *See:* The Popular Culture Library and Audio Center
Audio Collections (recordings and tapes) **I**, 5, 14-15, 16, 20, 23, 26, 76-77, 219, 221-222, 223; **II**, 33-34
Augusta, Mlle. **I**, 206
Austin, Mrs. Elizabeth **I**, 206
Avco Broadcasting **I**, 220
Awards: Film **I**, 18, 19, 28, 29
Awards: Radio *See:* Peabody Awards
Awards: Television *See:* Peabody Awards

Bach, Ernesta **I**, 119
Bachmann (Edward) Collection **I**, 45
Bacon-Shakespeare controversy **I**, 45
Bagby Concerts **I**, 9
Bahr, Herman **I**, 119
Baker, Benjamin **I**, 175
Baker, Elizabeth **I**, 119
Baker, Robert Melville **I**, 119
Bakonyi, Karl von **I**, 119
Bakst, Leon **I**, 9
Balimer, Orylss W. **I**, 119
Balint, Michael **I**, 119
Ballard, Frederick **I**, 119
Baltimore Theatre **I**, 10, 11
Balzac, Honore de **I**, 12, 119
Bancroft, George P. **I**, 119
Bangs, Frank C. **I**, 154
Bankhead, Tallulah **I**, 15
Barba, Sagi **I**, 119
Barde, Andre **I**, 119
Barker, Albert **I**, 119
Barker, Edwin L. **I**, 119
Barker, Harley Granville **I**, 119
Barker, Mary E. **I**, 154
Barker, Richard **I**, 119
Barker, Richard Hardinge **I**, 119
Barker, Theodore T. **I**, 119
Barks, Carl **I**, 29
Barnard, Charles **I**, 154
Barnard College **I**, 5
Barnes, J. H. **II**, 43, 51
Barnes, John **I**, 206
Barnett, John **I**, 119
Barnum, Phineas Taylor **I**, 11, 45, 206
Barre, Albert **I**, 119
Barrett, George H. **I**, 206
Barrett, Lawrence **I**, 14, 54
Barrie, James M. **I**, 44, 110, 112, 113, 119
Barrisre, Theodore **I**, 119

Barry, Thomas **I**, 206; **II**, 43
Barrymore, Ethel **I**, 112
Barrymore, Maurice **I**, 153, 154
Barthelmess, Richard **I**, 21
Bartholmae, Philip **I**, 119
Bartholomew Fair **I**, 206
Basset, Serge **I**, 119
Bataille, Henry **I**, 119
Battelle Memorial Institute **II**, 24-26
Battle, William James **I**, 43
Baum, L. Frank **I**, 119
Bavarian State Academy of Photography **II**, 72
Beahan, Charles **I**, 120
Beals, Ralph **I**, 108
Beatty-Kingston **I**, 120
Beaumont and Fletcher **I**, 206
Beauvoir, Roger de **I**, 120
Becks, George **I**, 50; **II**, 46, 48
Behrman, S. N. **I**, 67, 120
Belasco, David **I**, 97, 112, 120, 153, 154
Bel Geddes, Norman **I**, 45
Belknap Collection of Performing Arts **I**, 56-65
Belknap, Edwin S. **I**, 120
Belknap, Sara Yancey **I**, 57-58, 65
Bell, Hilary **I**, 120
Bellamy, Frank **I**, 120
Bellew, Kyrle **I**, 154
Benedetti, Sesto **I**, 207
Beneventano, Signor **I**, 207
Beniere, Louis **I**, 120
Benjamin, Burton **I**, 72
Benjamin, Walter **II**, 15
Bennett, Arnold **I**, 120
Benny, Jack **I**, 15, 20, 220
Bensman, Marvin **I**, 222
Beranger, Clara **I**, 120
Bereny, Henry **I**, 120
Berg, Albert Ellery ("A.E.B.") **I**, 153, 155
Bergerat, Emile **I**, 120
Bergeret, Gaston **I**, 120
Beringer, Oscar **I**, 120
Berkeley, Reginald **I**, 120
Berlin, Irving **I**, 120
Berman, Eugene **I**, 3
Berman, Pandro S. **I**, 26
Bernard, Octave **I**, 120
Bernard, Tristan **I**, 120
Bernauer, Rudolph **I**, 120
Bernstein, Else **I**, 120
Bernstein, Helen **I**, 120
Bernstein, Henry **I**, 120
Bernstein, Herman **I**, 120
Berr, Georges **I**, 120
Berry, William J. **I**, 120
Berte, Heinrich **I**, 120
Berton, Pierre **I**, 120

Index to Volumes I & II  **155**

Bertucca, Zerlina **I**, 207
Besier, Rudolph (misspelled as Beiser) **I**, 120
Bessie, Alvah **I**, 70
Bettis, Valerie **I**, 59
Betty, Henry **I**, 42
Biberman, Herbert **I**, 70
Bibesco, Prince Antoine **I**, 120
Bilhaud, Paul **I**, 120-121
Biograph Company **I**, 27
Bipschuetz, Leopold **I**, 121
Birabeau, Andre **I**, 121
Birdsall, Alfred Ward **I**, 120
Biro, Ludwig **I**, 121
Bisson, Alexandre **I**, 121
Black film industry **I**, 19, 149
Blackfriars Theatre (London) **I**, 51-52
Blacklist (in films) **I**, 70
Blackmore, R. D. **I**, 121
Blake, Mr. **I**, 207
Blasco Ibanez Vicente **I**, 121
Blitzstein, Marc **I**, 67-68
Bloch, Bertram **I**, 121
Bloomgarden, Kermit **I**, 68
Blossom, Henry **I**, 121
Blow, Sydney **I**, 121
Blum, Daniel **I**, 71
Blumenthal, Oscar **I**, 121
Board Alley Theatre (Boston) **I**, 207
Boar's Head Tavern **I**, 207
Bodansky, Robert **I**, 121
Boddington, E. F. (misspelled as Beddington) **I**, 120
Bogart, Humphrey **I**, 94, 95
Bogdanovich, Peter **I**, 81
Bolton, Guy **I**, 121
Bonfanti, Marie **I**, 153, 154
Boniface, George C. **I**, 154
Bonsergent, Alfred **I**, 121
Booth, Barton **I**, 53
Booth, Edwin **I**, 9, 14, 54, 55
Booth, Hilliard **I**, 121
Booth, Junius Brutus **I**, 153, 207
Booth's Theatre (New York) **I**, 14
Boretz, Alvin **I**, 72
Borge, Victor **I**, 15
Borzage, Frank **I**, 30
Boston civic repertory theatre **I**, 50
Boston Museum **II**, 49, 54
Boston Theatre **II**, 46, 48
Boucheron, Maxime **I**, 121
Bouchinet, Alfred **I**, 121
Boucicault, Dion **I**, 54, 121, 153
Boughton (E. S.), Collection of Biographies of Silent Screen Actors and Actresses **I**, 11
Bovill, C. H. **I**, 121
Bowers, Robert Hood **I**, 121
Bowery Theatre (New York) **I**, 210

Bowling Green Public Library **I**, 76
Bowling Green State University *See:* The Popular Culture Library and Audio Center
BOWSER, EILEEN **I**, 149
Boyesen, Algernon **I**, 121
Bracco, Roberto **I**, 121
Bradley, David **I**, 81
Bradley, Lillian Trimble **I**, 121
Brady, Alice **I**, 95, 97
Brady, William A. **I**, 9
Braham, David **I**, 154
Brakhage, Stan **I**, 2
Brammer, Julius **I**, 121
Brecht, Bertolt **II**, 28
Bresson, Robert **I**, 2
Bright, Addison **I**, 121
Brinton, Selwyn **I**, 121
British Broadcasting Corporation (BBC) **II**, 11
British Film Institute **I**, 7, 79
British Museum **I**, 34, 49; **II**, 22, 73
British Mutoscope and Biograph Co., Ltd. **II**, 86, 87
Broadcast Music, Inc. (BMI) **I**, 77-78
Broadcast Pioneers Library **I**, 225
Broadhurst, George Howells **I**, 122
Broadhurst, Thomas W. **I**, 122
Broadway Theatre (New York) **I**, 210
Brody, Alexander **I**, 122
Brook, Clive **I**, 83
Brookfield, Charles Hallam Elton **I**, 122
Brough Family **II**, 12
Brough, Lionel **I**, 154
Brown, Anne **II**, 75
Brown, Chamberlain and Lyman **I**, 93-98
Brown (C. and L.) Theatrical Agency Collection **I**, 93-98
Brown, Martin **I**, 122
Brown, Vincent **I**, 122
Browne, J. H. **II**, 48
Browne, Porter Emerson **I**, 122
BROWNE, RAY B. **I**, 78
Brownell, John ("Thespis") **I**, 153, 155
Brownlow, Kevin **I**, 151
Bruegger, Frederick **I**, 122
Brundage, Mary Anne **I**, 207
Buchanan, Robert **I**, 122
Buchanan, Thompson **I**, 122
Buchbinder, Bernard **I**, 122
Buffalo Bill *See:* Cody, William
Buhler, Hans **I**, 122
Bull, Lucien **II**, 95
Bull, Ole **I**, 207
Buntline, Ned **I**, 207
Bunuel, Luis **I**, 2
Burani, Paul **I**, 122

Burnand, Sir Francis Cowley I, 122
Burgtheater (Vienna) I, 35, 41
Burke, Annie Elizabeth I, 10
Burke, John D. I, 41
Burke, Joseph I, 207
Burke, Thomas I, 207
Burlesque collections I, 14, 64
Burnett, Frances Hodgson I, 122
Burns and Allen I, 23
Burns, George I, 222
Burnside, Kathryne I, 122
Burnside, Robert Hubber Thorne I, 99-108, 115-116, 122-123
Burnside (R. H.) Collection I, 99-146
Burrows, Mary Anne (Brundage) I, 207
Burton's Chambers Street Theatre (New York) I, 210
Burton's Theatre (Philadelphia) II, 48
Bury, T. T. II, 78
Busch, Adolf I, 12
Bus Fekete, Laszlo I, 123
Bussiere, Tadena I, 123
Byrne, John F. I, 123
Byron, George G., Lord I, 207
Byron, Henry J. I, 123

Cagney, James I, 15
Caillavet, Gaston Armand de I, 123
Calderon de la Barca, Pedro I, 4, 5
Caldwell, Anne I, 123
Caldwell, Glen I, 123
Caldwell, James H. I, 207
California History Collection I, 31
Callahan, Chuck I, 14
Calthrop, Dion Clayton I, 123
Campbell, Charles J. I, 123
Campbell, Lawton I, 123
Canadian Broadcasting Corporation (CBC) I, 57
Cantor, Arthur I, 72
Capus, Alfred I, 123-124
Card, James I, 149
Caree, Ben I, 151
Carleton, Henry Guy I, 124, 154
Carleton, William T. I, 154
Carnes, Mason I, 124
Carpenter and Westly II, 81, 87-89
Carpenter, Edward Childs I, 124
Carpenter, N. II, 77
Carr, Comyns I, 124
Carr, F. Osmond I, 124
Carr, Joseph William Comyns I, 124
Carr, Philip I, 124
Carre, Albert I, 124
Carre, Fabrice I, 124
Carre, Michel I, 124
Carroll, John S. I, 124
Carroll, Lewis II, 74
Carson, Murray I, 124

Carten, Audrey I, 124
Carten, Waveney I, 124
Carter, Mrs. Leslie I, 97
Carton, R. C. I, 124
Cary (Mary Flagler) Music Collection I, 12
Castellan, Jeanne I, 207
Castle Garden (New York) I, 210
Castle Square Theatre (New York) II, 51-52
Cataloging procedures I, 35, 41, 58-65; II, 1-7, 97-101.
For non-print materials I, 91-92, 147-152; II, 35
Cates, Gilbert I, 68
Cawarden, Sir Thomas I, 51
Cayvan, Georgia I, 154
Celeste, Mme. I, 207
Cella, Louis J. I, 124
Cellier, Francois I, 124
Cellini, Benvenuto I, 44
Censorship, films I, 148
Center for Understanding Media II, 67
Centlivre, Susannah I, 207
Ceram, C. W. II, 71
Chaine, Pierre I, 124
Chambers, Charles Hadoon I, 124
Chambers-Ketchum, Annie I, 154
Champlin, Charles I, 81
Chancel, J. I, 124
Chanfrau, F. S. I, 207
Charlecote Hall I, 207
Charles K. Feldman Library I, 25-27, 82
Charnay, Robert I, 124
Charvay, Robert I, 124
Chase, Ilka I, 124
Chase, Marjorie I, 124
Chase, William Cummings I, 9
Chatham Theatre (New York) I, 176, 210
Chayefsky, Paddy I, 72
Cherichetti, David I, 82
Cherry Kearton, Ltd. II, 94
Chestnut Street Theatre (Philadelphia) I, 211
Chevalier, Albert I, 124
Chevalier, Maurice I, 15
Chiarelli, Luigi I, 124
Children's programs (radio and television) II, 37, 38-39
Chilton, Eleanor Carroll I, 124
Christie Studio I, 31
Christmas, Walter I, 124
Churchill Club II, 72
Churchill, Winston I, 124
Cibber, Colley I, 53
Cibber, Mrs. I, 53
Cinematheque Francaise II, 17

Cinematheque Royale de Belgique **II**, 21
Cineteca Nazionale **II**, 21
Circus **I**, 60, 175, 207; **II**, 78, 80, 83, 84, 85
Circus collections **I**, 11; **II**, 12
Civic Repertory Theatre (New York) **I**, 10
Claretie, Jules **I**, 124
Clark, Alec **I**, 124
Clark, Alexander **I**, 124
Clarke, Annie H. **II**, 54
Clarke, Harry **I**, 124
Clarke, Macdonald **I**, 207
Clarke, Shirley **I**, 70
Clarke's Wheel of Life **II**, 81-82
Claxton, Kate **I**, 9, 154
Clay, Isobel **I**, 124
Clayton, Mr. and Mrs. Will **I**, 44
Clemens, Le Roy **I**, 124
Cleveland Public Library **I**, 76
Clint, George **II**, 12
Clinton Academy (East Hampton) **I**, 10
Clive, Jocelyn **I**, 125
Clive, Mrs. **I**, 53
Clubb, Louise **I**, 49
Cocteau, Jean **I**, 2
Cody, William ("Buffalo Bill") **I**, 153, 154
Coghlan, Rose **I**, 154
Cohan, George M. **I**, 9, 15, 125
Colbert, Claudette **I**, 95-96
Colbron, Grace Isabel **I**, 125
Cole, Florence **I**, 28
Coleby, Wilfred T. **I**, 125
College and University Arts Archives (University of Florida Libraries) **I**, 62
Collier, Constance **I**, 12
Collier, J. Palmer **II**, 50
Collier, John **II**, 12
Collier, William **I**, 125
Collins, Wilkie **I**, 54, 125
Collyer, "Doctor" **I**, 207
Colman, George (the elder) **I**, 53
Colman, George (the younger) **I**, 53
Columbia Broadcasting System (CBS) **I**, 13, 24, 219, 223, 224, 227; **II**, 20
Columbia Pictures **I**, 26, 89
Columbia University **I**, 222
Combination System **I**, 153
Comedie Francaise **I**, 35, 39
Commedia dell'Arte **I**, 3; **II**, 79
Commerce Department (U.S.) **I**, 223
Conan Doyle, Sir Arthur *See:* Doyle, Arthur Conan
Congreve, William **I**, 207
Conjuring **I**, 207 *See also:* Magic
Conland, Francis **I**, 125

Connelly, Marcus C. **I**, 125
Conroy, Frank J. **I**, 125
Cook, James Francis **I**, 125
Cooke, George Frederick **I**, 53, 207
Coolus, Romain **I**, 125
Cooper, James Fenimore **I**, 175, 180-181
Cooper, Thomas A. **I**, 207
The Cooper Union Museum *See:* Cooper-Hewitt Museum of Design
Cooper-Hewitt Museum of Design **I**, 3-4
Cooperman, Gail B. **I**, 35, 41
Copyright **I**, 207
Copyright and legal information:
  Films **I**, 32, 88-92, 148, 223-224
  Television **I**, 32, 88-92
Cormon, Eugene **I**, 125
Cornell University **I**, 222
Cornwall, Barry **I**, 207
Corporation for Public Broadcasting **II**, 15, 28, 29 *See also:* National Educational Television; Public Broadcasting Service
Corrigan, Joseph F. **I**, 99
Cort, Harry L. **I**, 125
Costume **I**, 207
Costume collections **I**, 1, 9, 108; **II**, 12 *See also:* Design
Cottens, Victor de **I**, 125
Cotton, Ben **I**, 154
Cottrell, Harry D. **I**, 125
Coudurier, Joseph **I**, 125
Couldock, Charles **I**, 10, 154
*The Country Gentleman* ("lost" play) **I**, 52
The Country Music Hall of Fame **I**, 225
Courtauld Institute of Art **II**, 72
Courtneidge, Robert **I**, 125
Covent Garden Theatre (London) **I**, 49, 54, 209
Coward, Noel **I**, 125
Cowell, Samuel **II**, 12
Cox, R. Kennedy **I**, 125
Crane, Wilbur **I**, 81
Crane, William H. **I**, 154
Craven, Frank **I**, 125
Crawford Collection **I**, 57
Cripps, Thomas R. **I**, 149, 151
*The Critic* (periodical) **I**, 11
Critics **I**, 2, 11, 69, 81, 151-152, 207
Croisset, Francis de **I**, 125
Cronin, A. J. **I**, 125
Cronin-Wilson, W. **I**, 125
Crooker, Earle **I**, 125
Crosley Broadcasting *See:* Avco Broadcasting
Cross, Richard **I**, 53
Crothers, Rachel **I**, 125
Crouse, Russel **I**, 67, 125

Croxton, R. C. **I,** 125
Cruger's Wharf Theatre (New York) **I,** 210
Cukor, George **I,** 20, 82
Cumberland, Richard **I,** 53
Curtiz, Michael **I,** 70
Curzon, Frank **I,** 125
Cushing, Catherine Chisholm **I,** 125
Cushing, Tom **I,** 125
Cushman, Asa **II,** 45
Cushman, Charlotte **I,** 54, 153, 207
Cutter, Rollin **I,** 125
Cutti, Berta **I,** 125

Dalrymple, Leons **I,** 125
Daly, Augustin **I,** 44, 50, 54, 153
Daly's Theatre (New York) **I,** 50
Dana, Richard Henry **I,** 207
Dance **I,** 175, 207
Dance collections **I,** 1, 4-5, 46, 56-65
Dancourt, Grenet **I,** 125
Dane, Clemence **I,** 125
Darnley, J. H. **I,** 125
Daudet, Alphonse **I,** 125
Dauncey, Silvanus **I,** 125
D'Avenant, Sir William **I,** 48
Davenport Family **I,** 54
Davidson, David **I,** 72
Davidson, John **I,** 126
Davies, Hubert Henry **I,** 126
Davis (Albert) Collection **I,** 44
Davis, Dorrance **I,** 126
Davis, Elmer **II,** 37
Davis, Gustav **I,** 126
Davis, Jessie Bartlett **I,** 154
Davis, Richard Harding **I,** 126
Davis, Robert Hobard **I,** 126
Dawson, Nancy **I,** 207
Dazey, C. T. **I,** 126
Dazian Library for Theatrical Design **I,** 9
Dean, Basil **I,** 126
De Angelis, Jefferson **I,** 154
De Antonio, Emile **I,** 70-71
De Belleville, Frederic **I,** 154
Decourcelle, Pierre **I,** 126
De Koven, Reginald **I,** 126, 154
Delacour, A. C. *See:* Thiboust, Lambert
Delancey, Capt. Oliver **I,** 207
De Mille, Cecil Blount **I,** 126
De Mille (Cecil B.) Collection **I,** 28
De Mille, Henry Churchill **I,** 126
De Mille, William **I,** 23
Dennery, Adolphe Philippe **I,** 126
Denny, Ernest **I,** 126
De Patie, Edmund **I,** 20
Dering Family (of Kent) **I,** 52
Design (lighting, scenery and costume) **I,** 1-2, 3-4, 9, 14, 29, 33, 35, 41, 43, 44, 45, 49, 50-51, 69, 72, 116, 156-172; **II,** 12
Deslandes, Raimond **I,** 126
Desvallieres, Maurice **I,** 126
De Sylva, George Gard **I,** 126
De Vaal, Jan **II,** 21
Deval, Jacques **I,** 126
De Wilde, Samuel **II,** 12
Diaghilev, Serge **I,** 12
Diamond, I. A. L. **I,** 70
Dickens, Charles **I,** 12, 126
Dickey, Paul **I,** 126
Dietz, Howard **I,** 9
Dillingham, Charles **I,** 101, 102, 103, 112, 115-116
Disney, Walt **I,** 29 *See also:* Walt Disney Productions Archives
Ditrichstein, Leo James **I,** 126
Documentaries and news (film and television) **I,** 24-25, 29, 70-71, 72, 76, 89, 90, 213-217, 223, 224-225; **II,** 11, 38-40
Dodson, J. E. **I,** 154
Doermann, Felix **I,** 126
Dohanos, Peter **I,** 72
Doheny Library **I,** 22-23
Dolley, Georges **I,** 126
Donnay, Maurice-Charles **I,** 126
Donnelly, Dorothy **I,** 126
Donohue, Jack **I,** 126
Donovan, Royle **I,** 126
Doremus, Elizabeth Johnson (Ward) (Mrs. Charles A. Doremus) **I,** 126
Dormann, Felix **I,** 126
Dortort, David **I,** 71
Dotter, Paul M. **I,** 126
Douglas, Kirk **I,** 70
Dowling, Eddie **I,** 126
Downing (Robert) Theatre Collection **I,** 45
Doyle, Arthur Conan **I,** 110, 126-127
Doyle, J. Neven **I,** 127
Drama collections **I,** 4, 6, 7, 15, 25, 43, 44, 45, 46, 48-49, 55, 116 *See also:* Scripts
Draper, Ruth **I,** 10
Dregely, Gabriel **I,** 127
Drew, F. C. **I,** 127
Drew, John **I,** 54, 112, 114, 141, 153, 154
Drew, Mrs. John **I,** 153, 154; **II,** 46, 50, 51, 52, 54
Dreyer, Carl Theodor **I,** 2
Dreyer, Max **I,** 127
Driesbach, Mr. **I,** 208
Drury Lane Theatre (London) **I,** 48, 49, 53-54, 209; **II,** 42-43
Drury, W. P. **I,** 127
Dryden, John **I,** 48

Dubbing of films **I**, 6
Dubourg, Augustus **I**, 127
Duff, Mr. and Mrs. John **I**, 208
Dumax, Alexandre, the elder **I**, 127
Dumas, Alexandre; the younger **I**, 127
Du Maurier, Gerald **I**, 127
Dunlap, William **I**, 10, 175, 183-184, 208
Dunning, James E. **I**, 127
Dunning, Philip Hart **I**, 127
Dunstan, Gatewood **I**, 89
Duquesnel, Felix **I**, 127
Durante, Jimmy **I**, 222
Duval, Georges **I**, 127
Dwan, Allan **I**, 26, 81, 148
Dwight, John S. **I**, 208

Eastman House *See:* George Eastman House
Ebenhack, Arthur **I**, 127
*Edison Kinetogram* (periodical) **I**, 18
Edison Kinetoscope **I**, 88
Edison, Thomas A. **I**, 27; **II**, 93
Educational programs (radio and television) **II**, 37, 38
Edwards, Harry **II**, 46-47
Edwards (John) Memorial Foundation **I**, 220
Edwards, Julian **I**, 127
Egerton, George **I**, 127
Ehrlich, Max **I**, 72
Eisenstein, Sergei **I**, 2; **II**, 21
Eldridge, Florence **I**, 15
Eldridge, Louisa **I**, 154
Electric Gyroscope Kinematograph Camera Co., Ltd. **II**, 93-94
Eliot, T. S. **I**, 44
Elisch, Ernest **I**, 127
Elkin, Mendl **I**, 16
Elkins, Hillard **I**, 68
Elliot, Mr. **I**, 97
Ellis, Edith **I**, 127
Ellis, Walter **I**, 127
Elliston, Robert W. **I**, 208
Ellsler, John A. **I**, 154
Elssler, Fanny **I**, 176, 208
Emerson, John **I**, 127
Empire Theatre (New York) **I**, 112, 114; **II**, 52
Endowed theatres **I**, 153
Englander, Victor **I**, 127
English Autograph Miscellaneous Letters Dramatic Collection **I**, 12
English, William B. **I**, 175, 185
Entertainment programs (radio and television) **II**, 37-38
Enthoven Collection (Victoria and Albert Museum) **II**, 10
Epstein, Robert **I**, 20
Erdmann, Louis Otto **I**, 41

Ernst, Louise **I**, 89
Erskine, Beatrice **I**, 127
Erskine, John **I**, 127
Esmond, Henry V. **I**, 127
Estabrook, Howard **I**, 83
Ethel, Agnes **I**, 54
Euripides **I**, 208
Evans, Edith **II**, 12
Evans, G. Blakemore **I**, 49
Evans, Maurice **I**, 15
Everson, William **I**, 81, 149
Exhibitions, photographic **II**, 72, 74, 75, 127-128
Eysler, Edmund **I**, 127

Fabre, Emile **I**, 127
Fagan, James Bernard **I**, 127
Fairbanks, Douglas **I**, 94
Falconer, Edmund **I**, 127
Fall, Leo **I**, 127
Farmington Plan **I**, 22
Farnie, H. B. **I**, 127
Farquhar, George **I**, 41, 208
Fashion Institute of Technology **I**, 1
Fauler, A. N. C. **I**, 127
Fazekas, Imre **I**, 128
Fecheimer, Richard **I**, 128
Federal Communication's Commission **I**, 223
Federal Radio Commission **I**, 223
Federal Street Theatre (Boston) **I**, 207
Federal Trade Commission **I**, 223
Federation Internationale des Archives du Film (FIAF) **I**, 21; **II**, 1, 57
FIAF Documentation Commission **II**, 1-7
FIAF *International Index to Film Periodicals* **I**, 19, 23; **II**, 2, 3
Feild, Robert **I**, 29
Fell, John L. **II**, 57
Fenn, Frederick **I**, 128
Fennell, James **I**, 208
Ferber, Edna **I**, 67, 128
Fernald, Chester Bailey **I**, 128
Ferrier, Paul **I**, 128
Festival of Britain **II**, 74
Fetchit, Stepin **I**, 151
"Fetes" and Festivals **I**, 3, 4, 35, 36, 39, 41, 60, 64 *See also:* Merry-Mount, La Meschianza
Feuillerat, Albert **I**, 52
Feydeau, Georges **I**, 128
Fiction collections **I**, 25, 75
Fiction, theatre in **I**, 173-212
Field, Joseph M. **I**, 175, 185-186
Fielding, Raymond **I**, 149
Fields, Herbert **I**, 128
Fifth Avenue Theatre (New York) **I**, 50
*Figaro* (periodical) **I**, 11

# 160 PERFORMING ARTS RESOURCES

Film Archive (Wisconsin Center for Theatre Research) I, 69-71
Film Art, Inc. I, 2
Film, avant-garde I, 2
Film: color II, 19-20
Film Effects of Hollywood (corporation) II, 19
Film equipment I, 27, 30, 31, 91; II, 28, 71, 76-95
Film History Advisory Committee I, 80, 81, 82
Film History Program (American Film Institute) I, 79-87
*The Film Index* I, 20
Film: Nitrate stock I, 30, 88, 90; II, 15, 16-17, 29, 95-97
Film research resources I, 1, 2-3, 5, 7-8, 11, 16, 17-32, 44, 46, 56, 60-61, 63, 65, 67, 69-71, 76, 79-87, 88-92, 93-98, 147-152; II, 11, 21-22, 57-68, 69-129 *See also:* Scripts, film
Film research resources, commercial dealers I, 31-32, 226-227
Film studios I, 31, 81 *See also:* Names of individual studios
Film Technology Company, Inc. II, 29
Films: collections I, 2, 5-6, 7-8, 20-21, 28, 29, 30, 69-71, 88-92; II, 21, 71, 95-97
Films: foreign language materials I, 18, 22, 23, 24, 89, 150; II, 21
Financial aspects of the theatre I, 68, 95
Finn, Henry J. I, 208
First Federal Savings and Loan Association of Hollywood (photograph collection) I, 30-31
First National Studios I, 26
Fischer, Hans I, 128
Fisher, Clara I, 154, 208
Fitch, Clyde I, 110, 112, 128
Fleck, Glen II, 29
Fleming, Carroll I, 128
Fleming, George I, 128 *See also:* Fletcher, Constance
Flers, P. L. I, 128
Flers, Robert de I, 128
Fletcher, Constance I, 128
Fletcher, (Julia) Constance *See also:* Fleming, George
Fleury I, 40
Flexner, Anne Crawford I, 128
Florence, Mrs. William J. I, 154
Florida League of the Arts I, 64-65
Florida Music Educators Association I, 64
Florida State University *See:* American Theatre Library-Museum
Folger Shakespeare Library I, 48-55
Folk plays, music and folklore I, 15, 76, 220

Fonson, Frantz I, 128
Fontanne, Lynn I, 10, 15
Foote, Samuel I, 53
Forbes, James I, 129
Ford, Corey I, 129
Ford Foundation I, 147
Ford, Harriet I, 129
Ford, John I, 26, 70
Ford, John Thomson I, 10
Foreign Broadcast Intelligence Service I, 223
Fores, S. W. II, 79
Forman, Justus Miles I, 129
Forrest, Edwin I, 52, 153, 208
Forst, Emil I, 129
Forti, Giuseppe I, 208
Forzano, Giovacchino I, 129
Foster, George G. I, 208
Foster, Norman I, 95-96
Fox Studio I, 31
France, Anatole I, 129
Francis, W. T. I, 129
Francis, William I, 208
Frank, Paul I, 129
Frank, Waldo I, 129
Frankenheimer, John I, 70
Franklin, Sidney I, 151
Franklin Theatre (New York) I, 210
Frapie, Leon Eugene I, 129
Frappa, Jean-Jose I, 129
Freedley, George I, 33, 99, 107-108, 109
Freeman, Max I, 154
Friedmann-Frederich, Fritz I, 129
Frimbley, Mr. I, 208
Frith, John Leslie I, 129
Froelich, Louis I, 107-108
Frohman, Ben I, 129
Frohman, Charles I, 9, 110-116, 118
Frohman, Daniel I, 9, 111, 113, 153, 154
Frohman, Gustave I, 111
Frondaie, Pierre I, 129
Frye, Emma Sheridan I, 129
Fulda, Ludwig I, 129
Fuller, Loie I, 129
Funt, Allen I, 222
Furneau, Michael I, 129
Furthman, Jules I, 152
Fyles, Franklin I, 129
Fyles, Vanderheyden I, 129

Gaiety Theatre (Glasgow) I, 100
Galantiere, Lewis I, 129
Galligan, Arthur I, 70
Galsworthy, John I, 44, 112, 129
Gandera, Felix I, 129
Garcia, Pauline I, 208
Gard, Alex I, 9
Garmes, Lee I, 26
Garnier, P. L. I, 129
Garren, Joseph J. I, 129

Garrick Club **II**, 12, 13
Garrick, David **I**, 45, 48, 49, 52-53, 63, 129, 208; **II**, 12
Garwood, Mr. and Mrs. St. John **I**, 44
Gassner (John) Collection **I**, 45-46
Gatti, E. V. **I**, 129
Gavault, Paul **I**, 129
Genest, John **I**, 54
George, Charles **I**, 129
George Eastman House **I**, 17, 28, 149, 225
Georges, Corwin A., Jr. **I**, 41
Gerard, Paul **I**, 129 *See also:* Sylvane, Andre
Gernsheim Collection of Photography (University of Texas at Austin) **II**, 69-129
Gernsheim, Helmut and Alison (Eames) **II**, 71, 72-74, 76
Gershwin, George and Ira **I**, 10, 129
Gibson, Lawrence **I**, 129
Gielgud, John **II**, 12
Gilbert and Sullivan **I**, 12, 100, 101 *See also:* Gilbert, William S.; Sullivan, Sir Arthur
Gilbert, Jean **I**, 129
Gilbert, John G. **II**, 41, 45-46
Gilbert, Mrs. **I**, 54
Gilbert, Victor **I**, 129
Gilbert, William S. **I**, 129 *See also:* Gilbert and Sullivan
Gilfert, Charles **I**, 208
Gillett, Burton **I**, 29
Gillette, William **I**, 110, 112, 130, 153, 154
Giroux (Alphonse) and Co. **II**, 79-80
Gish, Lillian **I**, 10
Glanz Collection (photographs) **II**, 75
Gleason, J. MacArthur **I**, 130
Globe Theatre (New York) **I**, 115
Glover, J. H. **I**, 130
Goddard, Charles **I**, 130
Godefroy, Jacques **I**, 130
Godfernaux, Andre **I**, 130
Goethe, Johann Wolfgang **I**, 12
Goetz, Curt **I**, 130
Goetz, E. Ray **I**, 130
Goldbeck Collection (photographs) **II**, 75
Golden, John L. **I**, 130
Goldfaden, Abraham **I**, 16
Goldmark, Peter **II**, 20
Goldoni, Carlo **I**, 208
Gold-schmidt, Lothar *See:* Schmidt, Lothar
Gooch, Frances Pusey **I**, 130
Goodman, Jules Eckert **I**, 130
Goodrich, Frances **I**, 68
Goodwin, J. Cheever **I**, 130, 154
Goodwin, Mr. **II**, 43-45

Gordin, Jacob **I**, 16
Gordon, Archibald **I**, 130
Gordon, Julian **I**, 130
Gordon, Leon **I**, 130
Gordon, Mack **I**, 130
Gordon, Max **I**, 15
Gordon-Lennox, Cosmo **I**, 130
Gorsse, Henry Joseph Auguste de **I**, 130
Gosselin, Louis Leon Theodore **I**, 130
Gostony, Adam **I**, 130
Graham, H. **I**, 130
Granichstaetten, Bruno **I**, 130
Grant, Cary **I**, 94
Granville-Barker, Harley *See:* Barker, Harley Granville
Green Collection of American Sheet Music **I**, 64
Greenbank, Henry **I**, 130
Greenbank, Percy **I**, 130
Greene, Clay M. **I**, 130
Gresac, Fred **I**, 130
Grimshaw, Thomas T. **I**, 130
Grisham, Frank P. **I**, 214, 217
Grisi, Giulia **I**, 208
Gronovius **I**, 43
Grosbard, Ulu **I**, 68
Gross, Franz **I**, 130
Gross, Laurence **I**, 130
Grove Theatre (New York) **I**, 210
Groves, Charles **I**, 130
Gruenwald, Alfred **I**, 130
Grundy, Sydney **I**, 130-131
Grupenhoff, Richard L. **I**, 41
Guide to the Performing Arts (Index series) **I**, 57
Guillemand, Marcel **I**, 131
Guillen de Castro y Bellvis **I**, 4
Guinon, Albert **I**, 131
Guitry, Sacha **I**, 131
Gunter, Archibald Clavering **I**, 131
Guthrie, Thomas Anstey *See:* Anstey, F.

Hackett, Albert **I**, 68
Haggart, John D. **I**, 131
Haines, Frank and Elizabeth **I**, 3
Haines Marionette Co. **I**, 3
Hal Roach Studios **I**, 89
Halevy, Ludovic **I**, 131
Hall, Owen **I**, 131
Hall, Roger Allan **I**, 41
Hallam, Lewis, Sr. **I**, 208
Hallam, Lewis, Jr. **I**, 208
Halliday, Jon **I**, 82
Halliwell-Phillips, James Orchard **I**, 43
Halton, Theo **I**, 131
Hamilton, Cicely **I**, 131
Hamilton, Cosmo **I**, 131
Hamilton, Henry **I**, 131

Hamilton, Patrick **I**, 131
Hamilton, Theodore **I**, 154
Hampden, Walter **I**, 14 *See also:* The Walter Hampden Memorial Library
Hampden (Walter) Theatrical Company **I**, 14
Hanley (T. E.) Library **I**, 44, 46
Hanser, Richard **I**, 72
Harbach, Otto **I**, 131
Harbage, Alfred **I**, 52
Harding, D. C. F. **I**, 131
Hare Collection (photographs) **II**, 75
Harkness House Library and Museum of Dance **I**, 1
Harley, Mr. **II**, 43
Harmant, Abel **I**, 131 *See also:* Hermant, Abel
Harmon, David **I**, 72
Harmount Collection **I**, 37
Harnick, Sheldon **I**, 68
Harper, Neal **I**, 131
Harrigan, Edward **I**, 154
Harrington, William **I**, 208
Harris, Augustus **I**, 131
Harrison, Gabriel **I**, 154
Hart, Moss **I**, 67
Harte, Bret **I**, 131
Harwood, H. M. **I**, 131
Hastings, Basil MacDonald **I**, 131
Hatvany, Lili **I**, 131
Haussman, John **I**, 131
Haworth, Joseph **I**, 154
Hayden, John **I**, 131
Hayes, Helen **I**, 10
Hayman, Alf **I**, 111, 114
Haymarket Theatre (London) **I**, 209; **II**, 49
HAYNES, DAVID **II**, 75, 98, 128
Hedberg, Tor **I**, 131
Hedges, Alan **I**, 42
Heijermans, Herman, Jr. **I**, 131
Hein, Sylvio **I**, 131
Heine, Heinrich **I**, 12
Heineman Foundation **I**, 12
Hellinger, Mark **I**, 131
Hellman, Lillian **I**, 46
Heltai, Eugen **I**, 131
Hemmerde, E. G. **I**, 131
Henderson, Al **I**, 131
Henderson, Isaac **I**, 131
Henderson (William) Collection **I**, 15
Hendrix, August **I**, 131
Henmyine, Maurice **I**, 131
Hennequin, Maurice **I**, 131
Henry, Mr. and Mrs. John **I**, 208
Herbein, Paul **I**, 131
Herbert, Ian **I**, 131
Herbert, Joseph **I**, 132
Herczeg, Ferenz **I**, 132

Hergesheimer, Joseph **I**, 132
Hermant, Abel **I**, 132 *see also:* Harmant, Abel
Herne, James A. **I**, 132
Herriman, H. N. **I**, 132
Herrmann, Alexander **I**, 153, 154
Hervieu, Paul **I**, 132
Herzer, Ludwig **I**, 132
Herzog, Wilhelm **I**, 132
Heyward, Dorothy **I**, 132
Hichens, Robert **I**, 132
Hicks, Seymour **I**, 132
Higgins, David **I**, 132
Hiken, Nat **I**, 71
Hill, Grace Livingston **I**, 132
Hillebrand, Fred **I**, 132
Hillian, B. C. **I**, 132
Hilliard, Robert **I**, 154
Hilson, Mr. and Mrs. Thomas **I**, 208
Hippodrome (New York) **I**, 9, 101-106, 110, 115
Hispanic Society of America **I**, 4-5
Historical Sound Recordings Program (Yale University) **I**, 222
*The Histrionic* (periodical) **I**, 11
Hitchcock, Robert W. **I**, 132
Hoare, Douglas **I**, 132
Hobart, George V. **I**, 132
Hoblitzelle Foundation **I**, 43, 44
Hoblitzelle, Karl **I**, 43
Hoblitzelle Theatre Arts Library **I**, 44-46, 222; **II**, 70
Hodges, Horace **I**, 132
Hodgkinson, John **I**, 208
Hodkinson, W. W. **I**, 20
Hogarth, William **I**, 63
Hogg, John **I**, 208
Holbrook, Hal **I**, 68
Holland, E. M. **I**, 154
Holland, Joseph **I**, 154
Hollister, Len D. **I**, 132
Hollywood Bowl (Los Angeles) **I**, 58-59
Hollywood Center for the Audio-Visual Arts **I**, 30
Hollywood (community) **I**, 31
Hollywood Democratic Committee **I**, 70
Hollywood Museum **I**, 30
Hollywood Ten **I**, 70
Hood, Basil **I**, 132
Hoover Institution **I**, 220
Hope, Anthony **I**, 132
Hopkins, Arthur **I**, 132
Hopkins, William **I**, 54
Hopper, De Wolf **I**, 154
Hopwood, Avery **I**, 132
Horn, Charles **I**, 208
Hornblow, Arthur, Jr. **I**, 132
Horner, W. G. **II**, 81

Index to Volumes I & II  **163**

Hornung, E. W. **I**, 132
Houdini, Harry **I**, 44
Houghton, Stanley **I**, 132
Houseman, John **I**, 19
Howard Athenaeum (Boston) **II**, 49
Howard, Bronson **I**, 54, 111-112, 132
Howard, Frederick **I**, 132
Howard (George C.) Collection **I**, 46
Howard, Sir Robert **I**, 52
Hoyt, Charles H. **I**, 132, 154
Hubermann, Bronislaw **I**, 12
Hughes, Elizabeth **I**, 208
Hughes, Rupert **I**, 132
Hume, Fergus **I**, 132
Hume, R. D. **I**, 52
Hungary: National Theatre **I**, 35
HUNTER, FREDERICK J. **I**, 45
Hutin, Monsieur **I**, **I**, 208
Hyatt, Donald **I**, 72

Ice shows **I**, 60
Ide, Leonard **I**, 132
Ince, Thomas **I**, 21
Inceville Studio **I**, 31
Indiana University, Audio-Visual Library **I**, 221
Indians, American **I**, 208
Infant, Vestris **I**, 208
Inman, Clarence **I**, 30
Inman, Henry **I**, 9
Institute for Education by Radio and Television (Ohio State University) **I**, 221-222
Institute of the American Musical **I**, 5-6
International Exhibition (Paris), 1937 **II**, 72
International Federation of Film Archives *See:* Federation Internationale des Archives du Film (FIAF)
International Performing Arts Archives (University of Florida) **I**, 61-62
International Theatre Institute of the United States, Inc. **I**, 6-7
Interstate Circuit (films) **I**, 44
Invisible Cinema **I**, 2
Irby, Charles C. **II**, 75
Ireland, William Henry **I**, 52
Irving, Henry **I**, 51, 53, 54; **II**, 12
Irving, Washington **I**, 175, 191-192
Irwin, Fred **I**, 132
Irwin, Wallace **I**, 132
Isham, Frederick **I**, 132
Italian Opera House (New York) **I**, 210
Ivanhoff, Nikolai **I**, 208
Ives, Alice E. **I**, 132

Jack, Henry *See:* Esmond, Henry V.
Jack, John **I**, 154

Jackson, Allan S. **I**, 41
Jackson, Fred **I**, 132
Jackson collection (photographs) **II**, 75
Jacobs, W. W. **I**, 133
Jacobson, Leopold **I**, 133
Jacoby, Carl M. **I**, 133
Jacoby, Wilhelm **I**, 133
Jakobowski, Edward **I**, 154
James, Louis **I**, 154
Janauschek, Madame **I**, 153, 154
Janis, Elsie **I**, 133
Jarno, Josef **I**, 133
Jarre, Maurice **I**, 23
Jay, Harriet **I**, 133
Jefferson, Joseph **I**, 54, 208; **II**, 47, 48, 49, 50, 51, 52, 54, 55
Jenkins and Armat **I**, 27
Jensen, Thit **I**, 133
Jeoferin, _____ **I**, 133
Jermon, John G. **I**, 133
Jerome, Jerome K. **I**, 114, 133
Jesse, F. Tennyson **I**, 133
Jessen (J. C.) Collection **I**, 19
Jewett, Henry **I**, 50
Jewison, Norman **I**, 70
Joe Jefferson Players **I**, 108
Johan, Ulfstejerna **I**, 133
John Street Theatre (New York) **I**, 9, 210 *See also:* Theatre Royal (N.Y.)
Johnson, Albert **I**, 69
Johnson (George P.) Negro Film Collection **I**, 19, 149
Johnson, Nunnally **I**, 26, 81
Johnston, May **I**, 132
Johnstone, Alexander **I**, 133
Johnstone, Calder **I**, 133
Johnstone, Howard **I**, 133
Johnstone, William B. **I**, 133
Jones, Clark **I**, 72
Jones, Edward **I**, 133
Jones, Henry Arthur **I**, 133
Jones, Robert Edmond **I**, 9
Jonson, Ben **I**, 208
Jordan, Kate **I**, 133
Juilliard School **I**, 1
Jullien, Jules **I**, 133
Justus, Antonia A. **I**, 133
Juvarra, Filippo **I**, 139
Juvenile plays, literature, etc. **I**, 15, 75, 76

Kadelburg, Gustav **I**, 133
Kahn, Gordon **I**, 70
Kahn, Julius **I**, 133
Kalisch, Burnham **I**, 133
Kaltenborn (H. V.) Collection **I**, 219
Kalvar Corporation **II**, 23-24
Kampf, Leopold **I**, 133
Kanter, Hal **I**, 72

Kardos, Andrew **I**, 133
Kardoss, Andor **I**, 133
Karlweis, C. **I**, 133
Kastner, Leo **I**, 133
Katkov, Norman **I**, 72
Kaufman, George S. **I**, 67, 133
Kaufman, S. Jay **I**, 133
Kaye, Danny **I**, 15
Kean, Charles **I**, 49, 51, 53, 208
Kean, Edmund **I**, 45, 53, 208
Kean, Ellen **I**, 53
Keaton, Buster **I**, 26
Kebler, Richard **I**, 133
Keene, Thomas S. **I**, 154
Keller, Henry **I**, 154
Kellog, Mr. **I**, 10
Kellogg, Gertrude **I**, 10-11
Kelly, Lydia **I**, 208
Kemble, Charles **I**, 53, 208
Kemble Family **I**, 45, 208
Kemble, Fanny **I**, 53
Kemble, Frances **I**, 209
Kemble, John Philip **I**, 49, 53, 209; **II**, 12
Kendall (Messmore) Collection **I**, 44-45
Kennedy, John F. **I**, 25 *See also:* Presidential libraries
Kenny, Robert W. **I**, 70
Kent, Charles **I**, 154
Keroul, Henry **I**, 133
Kerr, Clarence Vincent **I**, 133
Kerr, Jean **I**, 68
Kerr, Walter **I**, 69
Kessler, Richard **I**, 133
Kidder, Edward E. **I**, 133, 154
Kimball, David **I**, 133-134
King, Thomas **I**, 53
King's Theatre (London) **I**, 209
Kinora Company, Ltd. **II**, 86-87
Kinoy, Ernest **I**, 72
Kipling, Rudyard **I**, 134
Kirby, J. Hudson **I**, 209
Kirkland, Muriel **I**, 15
KIRO (Seattle) **I**, 219
Kistemaeckers, Henry **I**, 134
Klaue, Wolfgang **II**, 21-22
Klein, Charles **I**, 134, 154
Klein, Manuel **I**, 103-105, 134
Kleine, George **I**, 89
Kling, Saxon **I**, 134
Knight, Arthur **I**, 81
Knight, Percival **I**, 134
Knoblauch, Edward **I**, 134
Knowles, Edwin **I**, 154
Knox, Donald **I**, 82
Knutson, Robert **I**, 22
Kober, Arthur **I**, 67
Koch, Howard **I**, 70
Kohn, Simon **I**, 134

Kornell, William **I**, 134
Kovacs, Ernie **I**, 20
Kraatz, Curt **I**, 134
Krafsur, Richard P. **I**, 149
Kramer, Stanley **I**, 21
Kreigsman, SaliAnn **I**, 149
Krenn, Leopold **I**, 134
Kubelka, Peter **I**, 2
Kuchler, Kurt **I**, 134
KUIPER, JOHN B. **I**, 149
Kummer, Clare **I**, 134

Labiche, Eugene **I**, 134
Lablache, Luigi **I**, 209
Lachaume, Aime **I**, 134
Lackaye, Wilton **I**, 154
Lackaye, Wilton, Jr. **I**, 134
Lackey, R. B. **I**, 134
Laemmle, Carl **I**, 30, 81
Lailson's Boston Amphitheatre **I**, 207
Lamb, Arthur J. **I**, 134
Lamb, Charles **I**, 209
Lambarde Family (of Kent) **I**, 52
Lambert, Gavin **I**, 82
Lambert-Thiboust, Pierre *See:* Thiboust, Lambert
Lambinus **I**, 43
Lambs Club **I**, 99, 105, 107
Lambs Gambols **I**, 106
Landauer (Bella C.) Collection **I**, 11
Landesberg, Alexander **I**, 134
Landis, Frederick **I**, 134
Langer, Frantisek **I**, 134
Langtry, Lilly **I**, 114
Larcher, Eugene **I**, 134
Lardner, Ring, Jr. **I**, 70
Lascelles, Erinta **I**, 53
Lathrop, William Addison **I**, 134
Laufs, Carl **I**, 134
Lavedan, Henri **I**, 134
Law, Arthur **I**, 134
Lawrence, Gertrude **I**, 96
Leach, Archie *See:* Grant, Cary
Leader, James **I**, 134
Leavitt, Douglas **I**, 134
Le Baron, William **I**, 134
Leblanc, Maurice **I**, 134
Le Clercq, Adolphe **I**, 134
Ledoux, Jacques **II**, 21
Lee, Henry **II**, 49
Lee, Ming Cho **I**, 9
Lee, Rowland V. **I**, 83
Leesugg, Catharine **I**, 209
Le Gallienne, Eva **II**, 52 *See also:* Civic Repertory Theatre
Legouve, E. **I**, 135 (Misspelled Logouve)
Lehmann (Ernest) Collection **I**, 44, 46
Lehmann, Lotte **I**, 12

Leighton, Isabel **I**, 134
Leipziger, Leo **I**, 134
Leisen, Mitchell **I**, 25
Le Maire, George **I**, 134
Lemaitre, Jules **I**, 134
Le Marchant, Peter **I**, 134
Le Moyne, William J. **I**, 154
Lengel, William C. **I**, 134
Lengyel, Melchior **I**, 134-135
Lennard, Gwynne **I**, 135
Lennart, Isobal **I**, 21
Lenotre, G. **I**, 135
Leonard, Harold **I**, 19-20
Leonardo da Vinci **I**, 43-44
Leporello, Signor **I**, 209
Lequel, Louis **I**, 135
Leroux, Gaston **I**, 135
Le Roy, Charles **I**, 135
Lester, J. W. *See:* Wallack, Lester
Lestocq, William **I**, 135
Levee, Mike C. **I**, 26
Levenson, Lew **I**, 135
Levin, Herman **I**, 68
Levy, Jose G. **I**, 135
Levy, Newman **I**, 15
Levy, Parke **I**, 135
Lewin, Albert **I**, 23
Lewis, Alfred Henry **I**, 135
Lewis, Cecil **I**, 135
Lewis, Jerry **I**, 23
Library of Congress **I**, 6, 17, 24, 80, 147, 151, 223-224
Library of Congress, Motion Picture Section **I**, 88-92, 148, 149, 223
Liebling, Leonard **I**, 135
Lighting **I**, 209
Lincoln's Inn Fields Theatre (London) **I**, 53
Lind, Jenny **I**, 10, 13, 209
Lindau, Carl **I**, 135
Lindgren, Ernest **II**, 22
Lindsay, Howard **I**, 67
Liorat **I**, 135
Lippschitz, Arthur **I**, 135
Lipscott, Alan **I**, 135
Lisman, Robert G. **I**, 135
Lissom, Simon **I**, 3, 46
Liston, John **I**, 209
Locke, William J. **I**, 135
Logan, Stanley **I**, 135
Lolli, Alberto Carlo **I**, 135
Lonsdale, Frederick **I**, 135
Lope de Vega (Vega Carpio, Lope Felix de) **I**, 4
Lorde, Andre de **I**, 135
Lortzing, Gustav Albert **I**, 135
Los Angeles County Museum, Industrial Technology Department **I**, 27
Loseley Collection **I**, 51, 52

Lothar, Rudolph **I**, 135
Louys, Pierre **I**, 135
Love, Bessie **I**, 83
Lucas, John Seymour **I**, 51
Ludlow, Kate **I**, 154
Ludlow, Noah **I**, 209
Lumiere Brothers **II**, 85-86
Lunt, Alfred **I**, 10, 15
Lyceum Theatre (London) **I**, 51
Lytton, Edward Bulwer-Lytton, Lord **I**, 39-40, 209

MacArthur, James **I**, 135
McCarey, Leo **I**, 26, 81
McCarthy, Sen. Joseph **I**, 70
McCarthy, Justin Huntley **I**, 135
McCarty, Laurence **I**, 135
McCarty, Lawrence **I**, 135
McCormick, Langdon **I**, 135
MacCulloch, Campbell **I**, 135
MacDonough, Glen **I**, 135-136
McDougald, W. Worth **II**, 31
McDowell, John H. **I**, 33-34
McDowell (John H.) Film Archives (microfilm) **I**, 34-37, 38, 40-41
McGaw, Robert A. **I**, 217
MacGill, Patrick **I**, 136
McGlocklin, Mr. **I**, 209
MacGowan, Kenneth **I**, 19
Mack, Willard **I**, 136
Mackall, Lawton **I**, 136
Mackay, F. F. **I**, 154
Mackay, W. Gayer **I**, 136
McKee, Thomas **I**, 44
McKenna, Stephen **I**, 136
McLellan, C. M. S. **I**, 136
McLeod, J. R. **I**, 136
McNally, John J. **I**, 136
McNeile, Herman Cyril **I**, 136
Macready, William Charles **I**, 40, 49, 53, 153, 209; **II**, 11-12
Macro manuscript **I**, 52
Maeder, Clara Fisher *See:* Fisher, Clara
Mager's Concert Hall (New York) **I**, 210
Magic collections **I**, 14, 60
Malibran, Maria **I**, 209
Malin, Henri **I**, 136
Malkin, Audree **I**, 23
Maltby, H. F. **I**, 136
Maltheser Maschinenbau **II**, 94-95
Maltz, Albert **I**, 70
Mandel, Frank **I**, 136
Mandel, Loring **I**, 72
Mander, Raymond *See:* Mander and Mitchenson Theatre Collection
Mander (Raymond) and Mitchenson (Joe) Theatre Collection **II**, 9-13

Manhattan School of Music I, 1
Manners, John Hartley I, 136
Mannes College of Music I, 1
Mansfield, Richard I, 54
Mantell, Robert B. I, 15
Mapes, Victor I, 136
Marble, Dan I, 209
March, Frederick I, 15
Marchand, Leopold I, 136
Maretzek, Max I, 209
Marey, E. J. II, 95-96
Margaret Herrick Library I, 18-19 (also 21-22)
Margolis, Ben I, 70
Markbreit, Bertha I, 136
Markham, Pauline I, 154
Markopoulos, Gregory I, 2
Marlowe, Charles I, 136
Marlowe, Christopher I, 209
Marlowe, Julia I, 9, 50, 154
Mars, Antony I, 136
Marsele, Jean I, 136
Marsh, Richard I, 136
Marshall, N. M. I, 136
Marshall, Robert I, 136
Marsolleau, Louis I, 136
Martin, G. I, 136
Martin, Mary I, 10
Martinetti, Pearl I, 136
Martinez, Sierra I, 136
Martin-Harvey, Sir John II, 12
Martos, Franz I, 136
Maryland Board of Censors I, 148
Masetto, Novelli I, 209
Mason, A. E. W. I, 136
Mason, Mrs. Emma (Wheatley) I, 209
Mass Communications History Center (University of Wisconsin) I, 72, 219
Masseras, Mr. I, 209
Master of the Revels I, 49, 51-52
Mathews, Cornelius I, 209
Matthews, Brander I, 54
Matthews, Charles I, 45
Matthews, William I, 99, 107-108
Maturin, Charles R. I, 209
Maugham, Somerset I, 110, 112, 136
Maupassant, Guy de I, 12, 136
Maxwell, Elsa I, 94
Mayer, Edwin Justus I, 136
Mayer, Gaston I, 136
Mayer, Louis B. I, 87
Mayer (Louis B.) Foundation I, 26, 80-81
Mayo, Frank I, 154
Mayrargue, Lucien I, 136-137
Mazuel, H. Dupuy I, 137
Meany, John II, 74-75
Mears, Stannard I, 137
Medcraft, Russell I, 137

Megrue, Roi Cooper I, 137
Meilhac, Henri I, 137
Mekas, Jonas I, 2
Melies, Georges I, 2
Meltzer, Charles Henry I, 137
Melville, Herman I, 175, 195
Memphis State University I, 222
Menken, Helen I, 95
Menotti, Gian Carlo I, 3
Mercer, Johnny I, 137
Merrelle, Edna I, 137
Merrick, David I, 68
Merrick, Leonard I, 137
Merry-Mount I, 209
Meschianza, La (fete champetre) I, 209
Metro Studio I, 31
Metro-Goldwyn-Mayer (MGM) I, 19, 23, 26, 82
Metropolitan Museum of Art, Costume Institute I, 1
Miami University-WLW Collection I, 220-221
Michigan State University I, 221
Milch, Robert I, 137
Miles, Grace C. I, 137
Milhaud, A. I, 137
Miller, Arthur I, 46
Miller, Winston I, 72
Millocker, Carl I, 137
Milne, A. A. I, 110, 137
Milwaukee Repertory Theatre I, 69
Minshull, John I, 209
Mirande, Y. I, 137
Mitchell, Dodson L. I, 137
Mitchell, George I, 137
Mitchell, Langdon Elwyn I, 137
Mitchell, Norma I, 137
Mitchenson, Joe *See:* Mander and Mitchenson Theatre Collection
Modjeska, Helena I, 14, 54, 154
Moeller, Philip I, 137
Moliere I, 39
Moller, Alfred I, 137
Molnar, Franz I, 137
Monnier, Jacques I, 137
Monogram Pictures I, 69, 89
Montesanti, Fausto II, 21
Montgomery, James I, 137
Moore, James I, 149
Moore, John I, 50
Moore, Tom I, 209
Mordaunt, Frank I, 154
More, Hannah I, 53
More, Sir William I, 51
Morehouse, Ward I, 96
Morel, Ernest I, 137
Morgan, Charles I, 137
Morgan State College I, 149, 151
Morosco, Oliver I, 137

Morris, Clara **I,** 154
Morris, Grant **I,** 137
Morris, Ramsay **I,** 137
Morris, Robert S. **I,** 70
Morrison, Lewis **I,** 154
Morrow, John C. **I,** 41
Morse, Wollson **I,** 137
Morton, Charles **I,** 137
Morton, Howard E. **I,** 137
Morton, Hugh **I,** 137
Morton, Martha **I,** 137
Morton, Michael **I,** 137
Morton, Thomas **I,** 209
Mosconi, Charles **I,** 137
Moser, Gustav von **I,** 137
Motion Picture Association of America **I,** 1, 147
Mouezy-Eon, Andre **I,** 137
Mulholland (John) Magic Collection **I,** 14
Munden, Kenneth **I,** 149
Munich Marionettes **II,** 72
Munich University **II,** 72
Munoz Seca, Pedro **I,** 138
Murger, Henri **I,** 138
Murphy, Joseph **I,** 154
Murray, Alfred **I,** 138
Murray, Douglas **I,** 138
Murray, William B. **I,** 138
Museum of Modern Art **I,** 149; **II,** 74
Museum of Modern Art, Film Archives **I,** 7-8, 17
Museum of The City of New York, Theatre and Music Collection **I,** 8-10
Music collections **I,** 1, 4-5, 9, 11, 12, 14, 16, 29, 45, 46, 56-65, 68, 76-77, 109, 220, 223; **II,** 12
Music Study Center (University of Florida) **I,** 64, 65
Musical comedy **I,** 5-6, 9-10, 64, 68
Myerberg, Michael **I,** 68
Myers, Fred J. **I,** 99, 107
Myers, Paul **I,** 93-94
Myers, Richard **I,** 68

Naden, Thomas **I,** 138
Najac, Emile comte **I,** 138
Nancey, _____ **I,** 138
Nancey, Nic **I,** 138
Nash, N. Richard **I,** 68
Nassau Street Theatre (New York) **I,** 210
National Academy of Television Arts and Sciences (NATAS)—UCLA, Television Library **I,** 19, 20-21 (*also* 24-25), 220
National Archives **I,** 222-223
National Archives, Audio-Visual Section **I,** 149, 223

National Archives and Records Service **II,** 27
National Association of Broadcasters **I,** 225 *See also:* Television Information Office
National Broadcasting Company (NBC) **I,** 13, 24, 72, 219, 224
National Building Record (England) **II,** 72
National Design Center **I,** 1-2
National Educational Television (NET) **I,** 72 *See also:* Corporation for Public Broadcasting; Public Broadcasting Service
National Endowment for the Arts **I,** 147; **II,** 15, 28, 29
National Endowment for the Humanities **I,** 147
National Film Archive (London) **II,** 22
National Film Board of Canada **II,** 17
National Gallery (London) **II,** 72
National Theatre (London) **II,** 10
National Theatre (New York) **I,** 210; **II,** 45
National Theatre Museum (London) **II,** 10
National Voice Library (Michigan State University) **I,** 221
Nationala Filmoteka (Bulgaria) **II,** 17
Neal, M. **I,** 138
Neal, Max **I,** 138
Nederlands Filmmuseum **II,** 21
Negro in films **I,** 19, 149, 151
Neighborhood Playhouse School of the Theatre **I,** 1
Neill, James F. **I,** 41
Neilson, Francis **I,** 138
Neilson, Marie **I,** 138
Nestors Studio **I,** 31
Nethersole, Olga **I,** 154
Neuman, E. Jack **I,** 72
*New York Dramatic Mirror,* Interviews **I,** 153-155
New York Historical Society **I,** 10-11
The New York Public Library, Manuscript Division **I,** 109, 116
The New York Public Library, Theatre Collection **I,** 1, 6, 17, 33, 34, 57, 93, 94, 99, 108, 109, 114, 116, 118 *See also:* Brown (C. and L.) Theatrical Agency Collection; Burnside (R. H.) Collection
New York State Board of Regents **I,** 148
New York State Council on the Arts **I,** 7
New York State Motion Picture Commission **I,** 148
New York University **I,** 149

Newhall, Beaumont II, 73
Newman, Greatrex I, 138
Newman, Rehba I, 138
News programs (radio and television) II, 37
Niblo's Garden (New York) I, 210
Niccodemi, Dario I, 138
Nichols, Dudley I, 19
Nichols, Harry I, 138
Niepce, Nicephone II, 73-74
Nixon, Richard I, 71, 214-215 *See also:* Presidential libraries
Noah, Mordecai M. I, 210
Noble (Edward John) Foundation I, 94
Nordlinger, Charles Frederick I, 138
Norini, Amiel I, 138
Northern Arizona State University, Art Museum I, 170
Northwestern University, Radio Archive Project I, 221
Novelty Hall (New York) I, 210
Nozieres, Fernand de I, 138

O'Dea, James I, 138
Oden, Clarence Doubleday I, 138
Oenslager, Donald I, 3, 9, 33, 36
Oesterheld, Erich I, 138
Oesterreicher, Rudolph I, 138
Offenbach, Jacques *See:* Farnie, H. B.; Halevy, Ludovic
Office of Censorship (U.S.) I, 222
Office of War Information I, 223
Ogilby, John I, 49
Ogilby's Theatre (Dublin) *See:* Smock Alley Theatre
Ohio State University, Print and Document File I, 34, 37-38, 40
Ohio State University, Institute for Education by Radio and Television I, 221-222
Ohio State University, Theatre Museum I, 34, 37, 38, 40
Ohio State University, Theatre Research Institute I, 33-42
Ohnet, Georges I, 138
O'Keefe, Lester I, 138
Okonkowski, George I, 138
Olympic Theatre (New York) I, 210
Olympic Theatre (Philadelphia) I, 211
O'Neill, Eugene I, 9
O'Neill, James I, 153, 154
Ongley, Byron I, 138
Opera I, 175, 210
Opera House in the Rue Francaise (New Orleans) I, 210
Oral History Association I, 84
Oral history programs and collections I, 20, 23, 26, 77, 80-87, 222, 223, 225
Ord, Robert I, 138

Ordonneau, Maurice I, 138
Ornitz, Samuel I, 70, 152
Osborn, Paul I, 68
Otis, James F. I, 210
Ottoboni, Cardinal Pietro I, 39
Owens, John E. II, 49
Oxenford, John I, 138

Pacific Broadcast Pioneers I, 225
Pacifica stations I, 225
Palace Theatre (New York) I, 9
Palmer, A. M. I, 54
Palmo's Opera House (New York) I, 210
Pantheon (London) I, 3
Paradels, Octave I, 138
Paramount Pictures I, 20, 21, 23, 26, 89, 114
Paris, J. A. II, 77
Park Theatre (New York) I, 210; II, 43
Parker, Louis N. I, 138
Parsons (E. A.) Collection I, 43, 46
Parsons, Louella I, 23
Parsons School of Design I, 2
Passeu, Steve I, 138
Pasta, Giuditta I, 210
Pastor, Tony I, 154
Pasztor, Aeped I, 139
Paull, H. M. I, 139
Patents and catalogs
 Film equipment I, 27
 Radio equipment I, 27
Pathe Freres II, 92, 96
Patti, Amalia I, 210
Payne, B. Iden I, 139
Payne, John Howard I, 211
Peabody, George Foster II, 32
Peabody (George Foster) Awards II, 31-40
Peabody (George Foster) Collection II, 31-40
Peake, Richard B. I, 211
Peck, Jabez I, 10
Peep shows I, 3
Peile, F. Kinsey I, 139
Pelby, William I, 211
Pemberton, Max I, 139
Pendrell, Ernest I, 72
Percival, T. Wigney I, 139
Percy, Edward I, 139
Perelmuter, Sholem I, 16
Perper, Leo I, 46
Pertwee, Roland I, 139
Pessard, Emile Louis Fortune I, 139
Peterkin, Julia I, 139
Peters, Mason I, 139
Pettitt, Henry I, 139
Peyssonnie, Paul I, 139
Phelps, Samuel I, 49; II, 43-45

Philadelphia-Baltimore Company **I**, 206
Philadelphia Sesquicentennial (1926) **I**, 103
Philippi, Felix **I**, 139
Philips, F. C. **I**, 139
Phillips, Stephen **I**, 139
Phillpotts, Eden **I**, 139
Photography, History of **II**, 69-129
Picard, Andre **I**, 139
Pierpont Morgan Library **I**, 11-12
Pigott, J. S. **I**, 139
Pigott, Mostyn **I**, 139
PILKINGTON, JAMES P. **I**, 217
Pinero, Arthur Wing **I**, 54, 110, 139
Pirandello, Luigi **I**, 139
Piranesi, Giovanni **I**, 44
Pitou, Augustus **I**, 154
Placide, Eliza **II**, 43
Placide Family **I**, 211
Placide, Henry **I**, 211
Placide, Thomas **I**, 211
Planche, J. R. **I**, 139
Planquette, Robert **I**, 139
Plateau, Joseph **II**, 71, 78
Plautus **I**, 43
*The Play of Herod* **I**, 40
The Players **I**, 14; **II**, 12, 52 *See also:* Walter Hampden Memorial Library
Players Pipe Nights **I**, 14-15
Playfair, Nigel **I**, 139
Playwrights' Company **I**, 68
Plukas, Victor R. **I**, 31
Pogson, Bertha **I**, 139
Poland: Union of Jewish Actors **I**, 16
Pollock, Channing **I**, 139
Pollonais, Gaston **I**, 139
Polonsky, Abraham **I**, 70
Ponisi, Madame **I**, 153, 154
Poole, John **I**, 211
Pope, Mrs. **I**, 53
Popular Culture Library and Audio Center (Bowling Green State University) **I**, 74-78, 222
Porter, Cole **I**, 139
Potter, Paul **I**, 154
Potter, Paul M. 139
Povey, John **I**, 211
Power, Tyrone **I**, 211; **II**, 49
POWERS, JAMES **I**, 81
Powys, Stephen **I**, 139
Poynter, Beulah **I**, 139
Prada, Malcolm la **I**, 139
Pratt, George **I**, 149
Pratz, Claire de **I**, 139
Praxy, Raoul **I**, 139
Presbrey, Eugene W. **I**, 139
Preservation and storage **I**, 58, 61-65; **II**, 35

of film **I**, 5-6, 8, 30, 90; **II**, 15-29, 95-96
of graphics **I**, 156-171
of videotape **II**, 16, 26-28, 35
Preservation via microfilm **I**, 34-37, 61, 62
Presidential Libraries **I**, 223
Preval, _____ **I**, 139
Price, Thomas **II**, 48
Proctor, Bryan W. **I**, 211
Proszynski, K. **II**, 94
Prudden, Theodore M. **I**, 139
Pryce, Richard **I**, 139
Public Broadcasting Service **I**, 221 *See also:* Corporation for Public Broadcasting; National Educational Television
Public service programs (radio and television) **II**, 37, 39-40
Punch and Judy **I**, 3; **II**, 83
Puppetry **I**, 3, 60; **II**, 12, 72

Queen's Theatre (Dublin) **I**, 50
Quigley, Martin **II**, 71

Raboteau, Leon **I**, 139
Raceward, Thomas **I**, 140
Radio and television networks **II**, 32-33, 36-37 *See also:* Names of individual networks
Radio and television stations (local) **II**, 32-33, 34, 36-37
Radio Archive Project (Northwestern University) **I**, 221
Radio Corporation of America (RCA) **II**, 20
Radio equipment **I**, 27, 224
*Radio Flash* (RKO house organ) **I**, 26
Radio periodicals (early technical journals) **I**, 27, 224
Radio research resources **I**, 18, 20, 21, 24, 27, 60, 63, 65, 67, 71-72, 76-77, 218-231; **II**, 31-40 *See also:* Scripts, radio
Radio research resources, commercial dealers **I**, 225-226
Radio series **I**, 20, 21, 72, 77, 222; **II**, 37-40
Raleigh, Cecil **I**, 140
Ralph, B. Carpenter **I**, 140
Randle, Bill **I**, 74
Ranken, Frederick **I**, 140
Rankin, Mrs. M'Kee **I**, 154
Ransom, Harry H. **I**, 45
Raphael, John N. **I**, 140
Ravold, John **I**, 140
Rawlinson, A. R. **I**, 140
Reed, Daniel **I**, 140
Reed, Rochelle **I**, 81
Reeves, Arnold **I**, 140
Rehan, Ada **I**, 54

Rehfisch, Hans J. I, 140
Reilly, James I, 114
Rembrandt I, 12
Rennie, James I, 140
Rey, Etienne I, 140
Renoir, Jean I, 70
Revels, Court *See:* Master of the Revels
Rex, Richard I, 140
Rhea, Hortense I, 154
Rhodes, Harrison I, 140
Rice, Elmer I, 46, 140
Richards (E. V.) Collection I, 44
Richardson, Abbey Sage I, 140
Richepin, Jean I, 140
Richings, Peter I, 211
Richman, Arthur I, 140
Richmond Theatre (Richmond, Va.) I, 211
Rickett's Circus (New York) I, 210
Riddle, Richard Gray I, 10
Ridley, Arnold I, 140
Riesner, Lawrence I, 140
Ringling Museum Theatre Collection I, 63-64
Riskin, Robert I, 26
Ritchie, Anna Cora (Ogden) Mowatt I, 175, 211
RKO Pictures I, 26, 69, 89
Roach, Hal I, 23 *See also:* Hal Roach Studios
Road companies I, 112
Robertson, Ian I, 140
Robertson, T. W. I, 140
Robey, Sir George II, 12
Robins, Denise I, 140
Robinson, Casey I, 81
Robson, E. M. I, 140
Robson, Stuart I, 155; II, 50-51
Robyn, Alfred George I, 140
Rodman, Howard I, 72
Rogosin, Lionel I, 70
Rohr, Louis I, 140
Rollitt, George I, 140
Rose, Edward E. I, 140
Rose, Reginald I, 71
Rosen, Julius I, 140
Rosenfeld, Sydney I, 140
Rosenfield, Sydney I, 155
Rosenthal, Jean I, 69
Rosmer, Milton I, 140
Ross, Adrian I, 140
Ross, Fred G. II, 50
Ross, Jerome I, 72
Ross, Thomas II, 90
Rostand, Edmond I, 140
Rostand, Maurice I, 141
Roth, Wolfgang I, 69
Rousseau, Jean-Jacques I, 12

Roux, Xavier I, 141
Rowson, Susanna I, 211
*Royal American Gazette* (periodical) I, 11
Royal Photographic Society of Great Britain II, 72
Royle, Edwin Milton I, 141
Rubens, Paul A. I, 141
Rubini, Giovanni I, 211
Russell, Annie I, 155
Russell, Lillian I, 100
Russell, Sol Smith I, 155; II, 50
Ruth, Burnell F. I, 45
Ryan, Milo I, 219
Ryan (Milo) Phonoarchive (University of Washington) I, 219
Ryley, Lucette I, 141
Ryskind, Morrie I, 67, 141

Sabatini, Rafael I, 141
Sadler's Wells Theatre (London) I, 41; II, 43-45, 48
St. Cyr, Dirce I, 141
Salem Theatre (Massachusetts) I, 10
Salten, Felix von I, 141
Salvini, Alexander I, 155
Samuels, Maurice V. I, 141
Sanders, Louise I, 141
San Francisco Mime Troupe I, 69
San Francisco Opera House I, 60
Sanger, Frank W. I, 155
Sanger, Joan I, 141
Santley, Joseph I, 141
Sardou, Victorien I, 54, 141
Sargent, Frank I, 155
Sargent, John Singer I, 9
Sargent, Ralph II, 15-16, 28-29
Sarony, Napolean I, 153, 155
Sarris, Andrew I, 81
Savior, Alfred I, 141
Savoy Theatre (London) I, 100
La Scala Opera House (Milan) I, 156-157
Scamozzi, Vincenzo I, 3
Schanzer, Rudolf I, 141
Schary, Dore I, 69, 141
Scheff, Fritzie I, 95
Schiffer, Marcellus I, 141
Schildkraut, Elise (Mrs. Joseph) I, 96
Schildkraut, Joseph I, 96
Schiller, Friedrich von I, 141
Schisgal, Murray I, 68
Schlack, Emil I, 141
SCHLOSSER, ANNE G. I, 25
Schmidt, Lothar I, 141
Schneider, Alan I, 68
Schnitzer, J. I, 141
Schnitzler, Arthur I, 141

Schoenbaum, S. **I**, 52
Scholar Access Modules (SCAM) **II**, 33-35
Schonthan, Franz von **I**, 141
SCHURK, WILLIAM L. **I**, 78
Schwartz, Maurice **I**, 16
Schwartz, Ruth **I**, 20
Schweefert, Fritz **I**, 141
Schweid, Mark **I**, 16
Scott, Clement **I**, 141
Scouten, A. H. **I**, 52
Screen Guild **I**, 26
Scribe, Eugene **I**, 141
Scripts: collections
  Burlesque **I**, 14
  Film **I**, 2, 8, 18, 19, 21, 23, 25-26, 27, 28, 29, 30, 46, 60, 69-70, 141
  Plays **I**, 4, 5, 7, 9, 10, 14, 16, 33, 35, 36, 39, 41-42, 44, 45, 46, 49-50, 52, 53, 55, 60, 63-64, 67, 103, 109-110, 115-146; **II**, 11
  Puppet plays **I**, 3
  Radio **I**, 20, 21, 23, 60, 72; **II**, 33
  Television **I**, 19, 20, 23, 26, 29, 60, 71-72; **II**, 33
  Vaudeville **I**, 14
Scudamore, F. A. **I**, 141
Searelle, Luscombe **I**, 141
Seaton, George **I**, 70
Sebesi, Erno **I**, 141
Security Pacific National Bank, Los Angeles (photograph collection) **I**, 31
Seguin Troupe **I**, 211
Seigneur, M. de **I**, 141
Selby, Charles **I**, 141
Selig, Col. **I**, 21
Selwyn, Edgar **I**, 141
Selznick, Daniel **I**, 81
Seneca **I**, 43
Sennett, Mack **I**, 21
Serard, Eugene **I**, 141
Serling, Rod **I**, 72
Seymour, William **I**, 141; **II**, 52
Shadwell, Thomas **I**, 48
Shakespeare, William **I**, 43, 45, 48-52, 60, 64, 175, 211; **II**, 9, 12
  *Hamlet* **I**, 3, 9, 51, 211; **II**, 12
  *King Henry IV* **I**, 52, 211
  *King Henry VIII* **I**, 51
  *King Lear* **I**, 51, 211
  *King Richard III* **I**, 63, 211
  *Macbeth* **I**, 51, 211
  *Much Ado About Nothing* **I**, 141
  *Othello* **I**, 211
  *Romeo and Juliet* **I**, 153, 211
Shannon, Effie **I**, 155
Sharpe, Mrs. **I**, 211
Shattuck, Charles H. **I**, 50; **II**, 42

Shaw, George Bernard **I**, 44, 46, 110, 112, 114, 141
Shaw, Mary **I**, 155
Sheldon, Edward **I**, 141
Sheridan, Frank **I**, 141
Sheridan, Richard Brinsley **I**, 53, 211; **II**, 44
  *The Rivals* **II**, 41-55
Sheriff, Miss **I**, 211
Sherwood, Robert Emmet **I**, 142
Shipman, Samuel **I**, 142
Shirley, Arthur **I**, 142
Shirreff, Jane **I**, 211
Shuberts, the **I**, 100-101, 102, 115
Shubert Theatre (New York) **II**, 52
Shumlin, Herman **I**, 68
Siddons, Sarah **I**, 53, 211
Sidney, F. W. **I**, 142
Sidney, Frederick **I**, 142
Silliphant, Stirling **I**, 20
Simon, Charles **I**, 142
Simpson, Mildred **I**, 18, 149
Simpson, Paul C. **I**, 214, 217
Sims, George R. **I**, 142
Sinclair, John **I**, 211
Sirk, Douglas **I**, 82
Skinner, Ralph McHay **I**, 142
Smith, Albert E. **I**, 19
Smith, David **I**, 28
Smith, Edgar McPhail **I**, 142
Smith, Harry B. **I**, 9, 142, 155
Smith, Irwin **I**, 52
Smith, J. C. **I**, 142
Smith, Oliver **I**, 9
Smith, Richard Penn **I**, 211
Smith, Robert B. **I**, 142
Smith, Sol **I**, 212
Smith, William **I**, 53
Smith, William Henry **I**, 212
Smith, Winchell **I**, 142
Smithers Collection (photographs) **II**, 75
Smithsonian Institution **I**, 224 *See also:* Cooper-Hewitt Museum of Design
Smock Alley Theatre (Dublin) **I**, 49
Sneddon, Robert W. **I**, 142
Soffe, W. **II**, 78
Sondheim, Stephen **I**, 68
Sophocles **I**, 212
Sothern, E. A. **I**, 9
Sothern, Edward H. **I**, 50, 54, 142, 155
Southern, Harry **I**, 142
Soulaine, Pierre **I**, 142
Soulie, Maurice **I**, 142
Sousa, John Philip **I**, 153, 155
Southern Illinois Theatrical Designs Competitions **I**, 170

Southwark Theatre (Philadelphia) **I**, 211
Spier, William **I**, 72
Spoleto (Italy) Arts Festival **I**, 45
Staatliches Film Archive der D.D.R. **II**, 21
Stage equipment **I**, 37, 102
Stage models **I**, 3, 9, 37, 40
Stage properties: collections **II**, 12
Stanford University **I**, 220, 221
Stange, Hugh Stanislaus **I**, 142
Stark Collection **I**, 43, 46
State Historical Society of Wisconsin **I**, 66, 67
Steell, Willis **I**, 142
Stein, Grant **I**, 142
Stein, Joseph **I**, 68
Stein, Leo **I**, 142
Stein, Miriam H. **I**, 142
Stein-Landesmann, Alice **I**, 142
Stephany, Victor **I**, 142
Stephens, Robert Neilson **I**, 142
Stephenson, B. C. **I**, 142
Stevens, George, Jr. **I**, 148, 149
Stewart, Donald Ogden **I**, 81
Stewart, Grant **I**, 142
Stewart, Michael **I**, 68
Stewart, William G. **I**, 142
Stieber, Ferdinand **I**, 143
Stoblitzer, Heinrich **I**, 143
Stock companies **I**, 41, 95
Stoddard, George E. **I**, 143
STODDARD, RICHARD **I**, 212
Stoddart, James Henry **I**, 153, 155
Stokes, Mrs. Walter **I**, 53
Stolz, Robert **I**, 143
Stone, Fred **I**, 143
Story, Ralph **I**, 24
Strange, Michael **I**, 143
Strobridge Collection of Lithograph Posters of Theatre and Circus **I**, 11
Strolling companies **I**, 212
Strong, Austin **I**, 143
Stuart, Aimee **I**, 143
Stuart, Philip **I**, 143
Sturges, Arthur **I**, 143
Sturges, Preston **I**, 21, 143
Sturm, Hans **I**, 143
Styne, Jule **I**, 46
Suber, Howard **I**, 20
Sullivan, Sir Arthur **I**, 54 *See also:* Gilbert and Sullivan
Sullivan, Ed **I**, 72
Suppe, Franz von **I**, 143
Susskind, David **I**, 68
Sutherland, E. G. **I**, 143
Sutro, Alfred **I**, 143
Swan, Mark E. **I**, 143
Swayne, Martin **I**, 143

Swanwide, Anne **I**, 143
Swete, E. Lyall **I**, 143
Sylvane, Andre **I**, 143
Syndicate, the **I**, 111, 115
Szebenyei, Joseph **I**, 143
Szigeti, Joseph **I**, 12
Szulc, Jozef Zygmunt **I**, 143

Tableaux vivants **I**, 212
Taglioni, Maria **I**, 212
Talbot, Fox **II**, 73
Tallien, A. **I**, 143
Talma, F. J. **I**, 212
Tamburini, Antonio **I**, 212
Tanner, James T. **I**, 143
Tarbe des Sablons, Edmond Joseph Louis **I**, 143
Tarkington, Booth **I**, 143
Tate, Nahum **I**, 48
Taubes, Frederic **I**, 166
Tavary, Marie **I**, 155
Taylor, Charles **I**, 143
Taylor, Tom **I**, 143
Teague, Norwood **I**, 27
Television *See also:* Radio and television; Scripts
Television Information Office (TIO) **I**, 13, 17
Television networks **I**, 214-215, 224 *See also:* Names of individual networks
*Television News Index and Abstracts* **I**, 215, 216
Television Print Collections (Tape, film, kinescope) **I**, 24-25, 29, 71, 72, 88-89, 213-217, 222, 224-225; **II**, 33-34
Television research resources **I**, 13, 17-32, 60, 63, 65, 67, 71-72, 76, 88-89, 213-217, 218-231; **II**, 31-40 *See also:* Scripts, television
Television research resources, commercial dealers **I**, 31-32, 226-227
Television series **I**, 19, 20, 26, 71-72, 222; **II**, 37-40
Temple University **I**, 149, 221
Tennyson, Alfred, Lord **I**, 54
Teramond, Guy de **I**, 143
Terriss, William **I**, 54
Terry, Edward **I**, 100
Terry, Ellen **I**, 53, 54
Terry Family **II**, 12
Terry, J. E. Harold **I**, 143
Terwilliger, George **I**, 143
Thackeray, William **I**, 12, 143
Theatre
15th-16th century **I**, 11, 36, 48, 49, 51, 52
17th century **I**, 3, 4, 36, 48, 49, 50, 52; **II**, 11
18th century **I**, 3, 9, 10-11, 12, 15, 36,

48, 49, 50-51, 53-54; **II,** 11
19th century **I,** 3, 5, 9, 10-11, 12, 14-16, 35, 36, 44, 48, 49, 50, 51, 53, 54, 56, 63, 64, 173-212; **II,** 11
20th century **I,** 3, 4, 5-7, 9-10, 11, 12, 14-16, 44, 50, 51, 53, 55, 56, 63, 64, 93-98; **II,** 11
Theatre de l'Oeuvre (Paris) **I,** 3
Theatre d'Orleans (New Orleans) **I,** 210
Theatre: Geographical breakdown
 American (U.S.) **I,** 8, 14, 44, 46, 49-50, 54-55, 56, 63-64, 93-98
 Australian **I,** 46
 British **I,** 3, 12, 35-36, 44, 46, 48, 50, 53-54, 63-64, 96, 198, 222; **II,** 11
 Canadian **I,** 56, 222
 Dutch **I,** 35-36
 European **I,** 15-16, 48-49, 56
 French **I,** 3, 12, 35-36, 97, 208
 German and Austrian **I,** 35
 Hungarian **I,** 35
 International **I,** 6-7
 Italian **I,** 3, 35-36, 39, 49
 Latin American **I,** 56, 65
 Polish **I,** 16
 Russian **I,** 15-16
 Scandinavian **I,** 36
 Spanish **I,** 4-5
Theatre Guild **II,** 52
Theatre Library Association **I,** 94
Theatre Royal (Bath) **I,** 50
Theatre Royal (Birmingham) **I,** 50
Theatre Royal (Edinburgh) **I,** 50
Theatre Royal (Manchester) **I,** 50
Theatre Royal (New York) **I,** 10 *See also:* John Street Theatre
Theatre Royal (York) **I,** 50
Theatres **I,** 9, 35, 49, 111, 174, 212 *See also:* Names of individual theatres
Theatrical figurines **II,** 11, 12-13
Theschton, Herbert **I,** 143
"Thespis" *See:* Brownell, John
Thexton, Herbert **I,** 143
Theyre-Smith, Spenser **I,** 143
Thiboust, Delacour **I,** 143
Thiboust, Lambert **I,** 143
Thimpson, A. M. **I,** 143-144
Thomas, Albert Ellsworth **I,** 144
Thomas, Augustus **I,** 144
Thomas, Marlo **I,** 222
Thomas, Oliver **I,** 144
Thompson, A. M. **I,** 144
Thompson, Charlotte **I,** 144
Thompson, Denman **I,** 155
Thorndike, Sybil **II,** 12
Throne, Kathyrne **I,** 144
Thumb, Tom **I,** 212
Thumb, Mrs. Tom **I,** 10
Thurner, Georges **I,** 144

Thursby, Emma **I,** 11
Thurston, E. Temple **I,** 144
Tiffany-Stahl Studio **I,** 31
Tivoli Theatre (Philadelphia) **I,** 211
Tobin (Edgar G.) Foundation **I,** 45
Tobin, Robert L. B. **I,** 45
Toland, Gregg **I,** 19
Toledo-Lucas County Public Library **I,** 76
Tomashevski, Boris **I,** 16
Torrence, Bruce T. **I,** 30
Townsend, Ralph Milbourne **I,** 144
Traphagan School of Fashion **I,** 2
Trarieux, Gabriel **I,** 144
Trevor, Leo **I,** 144
Tremont Theatre (Boston) **I,** 207
Tressel, George **II,** 24
Trobriand, P. R. D. de K., Comte de **I,** 212
Trotha, Thilo von **I,** 144
Truffi, Teresa **I,** 212
Truffier, Jules **I,** 144
Trumbo, Dalton **I,** 70
Trussel, Vance **II,** 40
Tulsa Little Theatre **I,** 60
Turner, Paul **I,** 144
Turney, Arthur **I,** 144
Twain, Mark **I,** 54
Twentieth Century-Fox Collection **I,** 19, 21, 23, 26

Unger, Gladys **I,** 144
Urban, Erich **I,** 144
Uris Theatre (New York) **I,** 9
*Uncle Tom's Cabin* **I,** 37
UNESCO **I,** 6
Union Square Theatre (N.Y.) **I,** 15
United Artists Corporation **I,** 69-70, 71, 89
Universal Pictures **I,** 23, 81
University of California, Los Angeles (UCLA) **I,** 19, 22, 26, 80, 149, 220; **II,** 28-29 *See also:* National Academy of Television Arts and Sciences— UCLA Television Library
UCLA Film Archive **I,** 20-21
UCLA Theater Arts Library **I,** 23-24 (*also* 19-20)
University of California Regents **I,** 24
University of Florida *See:* Balknap Collection of Performing Arts
University of Georgia *See:* Peabody Collection; Scholar Access Modules
University of Illinois **I,** 222
University of Iowa **II,** 57
University of North Carolina **I,** 222
University of Southern California (USC) **I,** 19, 22, 26, 222 *See also:* Doheny Library

University of Texas at Austin **I**, 43-47, 222 *See also:* Gernsheim Collection
University of Washington, Milo Ryan Phonoarchive **I**, 219
University of Wisconsin *See:* Wisconsin Center for Theatre Research
Urvantzov, Leo **I**, 144

Vachell, Horace Annesley **I**, 144
Vajda, Ernest **I**, 144
Valabreque, Albin **I**, 144
Valentino, Rudolph **I**, 94
Vanbrugh, Sir John **I**, 212
Vance, Katherine **I**, 144
Vandenhoff, George **II**, 45
Vanderbilt (University) Television News Archives **I**, 213-217, 220
Van Dyke, Willard **I**, 149
Vanlov, Albert **I**, 144
Varney, Louis **I**, 144
Vaudeville collections **I**, 14, 77
Vauxhall Gardens (New York) **I**, 210
Veberx, Pierre **I**, 144-145 *See also:* Webber, Pierre
Veiller, Bayard **I**, 145
Verneuil, Louis **I**, 145
Vestris, Mme. **I**, 212
Vestris, Mme. Ronzi **I**, 212
Victor, David **I**, 72
Vidal, Gore **I**, 68
Vidor, King **I**, 19
Viereck, George Sylvester **I**, 145
Villanyi, Andor **I**, 145
Vilna YIVO Collection **I**, 16
Vitagraph Company **I**, 19
Volk, Gustav **I**, 145
Vollmer, Lula **I**, 145
Voltaire **I**, 11
Von Sternberg, Josef **I**, 152

Wagner, Franz **I**, 145
Wall, Harry **I**, 145
Wallace, Edgar **I**, 145
Wallace, G. Carlton **I**, 145
Wallace, Irwin **I**, 76
Wallack family **I**, 212
Wallack, Henry **I**, 212
Wallack, J. L. **I**, 54
Wallack, James **I**, 212
Wallack, Lester **II**, 47-48
Wallack's Lyceum (New York) **II**, 47-48, 54
Wallack's National Theatre (New York) **II**, 54
Walnut Street Theatre (Philadelphia) **I**, 211
Walsh, Austin **I**, 145
Walt Disney Productions Archives **I**, 28-30

Walter, Eugene **I**, 145
Walter Hampden Memorial Library **I**, 13-15
Wanger, Walter **I**, 69
Warburg Institute (London University) **II**, 72
Ward, Mrs. Humphrey **I**, 145
Warhol, Andy **I**, 2
Warner, Anne **I**, 145
Warner Brothers **I**, 20, 23, 69, 89
Warner, Frederick E. **I**, 41
Warren, William **I**, 212; **II**, 54
Warwick, J. H. **I**, 155
Washington Gardens (Boston) **I**, 207
Wasserman, Dale **I**, 70
Watanna, Onota **I**, 145
Watson, Henry C. **I**, 212
Watson, Malcolm **I**, 145
Wayang Golek puppets **I**, 3
Webber, Pierre **I**, 145 *See also:* Veberx, Pierre
Webster, Alfred A. **I**, 145
Weinberg, Herman **I**, 152
Weiss, Raoul Ernest **I**, 145
Weld, Arthur **I**, 145, 221
Welisch, Ernst **I**, 145
Welles, Orson **I**, 70
Wellman, William **I**, 26, 70
West, Clarence **I**, 145
Westcott, Edward Noyes **I**, 145
Westervelt, Leonidas **I**, 145
Wexley, John **I**, 70
Weyman, Stanley **I**, 145
Whale, Master (the Infant Vestris) **I**, 212
Wharton, Edith **I**, 145
Wheatcroft, Adeline Stanhope **I**, 155
Wheatcroft, Nelson **I**, 155
Wheatley, Mrs. **I**, 212
Wheeler, Andrew Carpenter **I**, 11
Wheelock, Joseph **I**, 155
White, Richard Grant **I**, 212
Whitfield, Frank **I**, 145
Wicheler, Fernand **I**, 145
Whitlatch, Michael **I**, 155
Whitney, James **I**, 2
Whitney, John **I**, 2, 114
Wiggin, Kate Douglas **I**, 145
Wignell, Thomas **I**, 212
Wilcox, Ella Wheeler **I**, 145
Wilde, Oscar **I**, 44, 110, 112, 118, 145
Wilkes, Thomas Egerton **I**, 145
Wilks, Robert **I**, 53
WILL (Illinois radio station) **I**, 222
Willemetz, A. **I**, 145
Willers, Alfred C. **II**, 53
Williams, E. Harcourt **I**, 145
Williams, Tennessee **I**, 46
Willis, Nathaniel P. **I**, 212

Willner, Alfred Maria **I**, 145
Wills, Freeman **I**, 146
Wills, W. G. **I**, 146
Wilson, Francis **I**, 146, 155; **II**, 52
Wilson, George W. **II**, 49
Wilson, Harry Leon **I**, 146
Wilson, John P. **I**, 146
Wiman, Dwight Deere **I**, 68
Wimperis, Arthur **I**, 146
Winston, James **I**, 54
Winston, Jemmie **I**, 146
Winter, William **I**, 44, 54-55
The Wisconsin Center for Theatre Research **I**, 17, 57, 66-73, 219-220
Wisconsin State Historical Society *See:* Mass Communications History Center
Wise, Robert **I**, 23
Wise, Thomas A. **I**, 146
Witham, Charles W. **I**, 9
Wittman, Carl Friedrich **I**, 146
WLW (Cincinnati) **I**, 220-221
Wodehouse, P. G. **I**, 146
Wolf, Pierre **I**, 146
Wolper, David **I**, 20, 24-25
Wood, A. C. Fraser **I**, 146
Wood, Peggy **I**, 96
Woodhull, Jacob **I**, 212
Woodward, Frank **I**, 45
Woodworth, Samuel **I**, 212
Woollcott, Alexander **I**, 146
Works Progress Administration (WPA) **I**, 20

Worrall, Lechmere **I**, 146
Wrenn Collection **I**, 43, 46
Wright, J. B. **II**, 46
Wright, Lyle H. **I**, 174, 176, 212
Wright, Margaret **I**, 146
Wyatt, Benjamin **I**, 53
Wycherley, William **I**, 146, 212

Yale University **I**, 2, 222 *See also:* Crawford Collection
Yeamans, Annie **I**, 155
Yeats, William Butler **I**, 44
Yiddish theatre **I**, 10, 15-16
YIVO Institute for Jewish Research **I**, 15-16
Young, Charles M. **I**, 212
Young, Nedrick **I**, 70
Young, Rida Johnson **I**, 146
Young, William C. **I**, 37, 42

Zamacois, Miquel **I**, 146
Zamescnik, John **I**, 146
Zamrof, _____ **I**, 146
Zangwill, Israel **I**, 146
Zglinicki, Friedrich **II**, 71
Ziegenfelder, Jane **I**, 146
Ziegfeld, Florenz **I**, 10
Zilahy, Ludwig **I**, 146
Zito, Steven **I**, 149
Ziv Television Programs, Inc. **I**, 71, 219
Zobel, Konrad **I**, 41
Zucchero, William H. **I**, 41